Marriage and the Catholic Church

Disputed Questions

Michael G. Lawler

A Michael Glazier Book

THE LITURGICAL PRESS
Collegeville, Minnesota

www.litpress.org

Cover design by Greg Becker. Photo: Getty Images.

All translations from languages other than English are the author's.

All documents of the Second Vatican Council are taken from Walter M. Abbott, *The Documents of Vatican II* (New York: America Press, 1966).

1   2   3   4   5   6   7

Library of Congress Cataloging-in-Publication Data

Lawler, Michael G.
    Marriage and the Catholic Church : disputed questions / Michael G.
Lawler.
       p.   cm.
    Includes bibliographical references and index.
    ISBN 0-8146-5116-X (alk. paper)
    1. Marriage—Religious aspects—Catholic Church.   2. Catholic Church—
Doctrines.   I. Title.

BX2250.L3695   2002
234'.165—dc21   2002069548

For Sean and Kate,
who have abundantly demonstrated
that remarriage can be a sacrament

Contents

Abbreviations

AA   *Apostolicam Actuositatem* (Decree on the Apostolate of the Laity)
AAS   *Acta Apostolicae Sedis* (Rome: Typis Polyglottis Vaticanis)
CL   *Christifideles Laici* (On the Lay Faithful)
DH   *Dignitatis Humanae* (Declaration on Religious Freedom)
DS   *Enchiridion Symbolorum Definitionum et Declarationum de Rebus Fidei et Morum,* ed. H. Denzinger and A. Schoenmetzer (Fribourg: Herder, 1965).
DV   *Dei Verbum* (Dogmatic Constitution on Divine Revelation)
FC   *Familiaris Consortio* (On the Family)
GE   *Gravissimum Educationis* (Declaration on Christian Education)
GS   *Gaudium et Spes* (Pastoral Constitution on the Church in the Modern World)
LG   *Lumen Gentium* (Dogmatic Constitution on the Church)
PG   *Patrologiae Cursus Completus: Series Graeca,* ed. J. P. Migne
PL   *Patrologiae Cursus Completus: Series Latina,* ed. J. P. Migne
SC   *Sacrosanctum Concilium* (Constitution on the Sacred Liturgy)
ST   *Summa Theologiae Sancti Thomae de Aquino*
TS   *Theological Studies* (Georgetown University)
UR   *Unitatis Redintegratio*

Prologue

In the Western world, marriage is in crisis. There are those who bemoan the passing of what is called, incorrectly, traditional marriage and family, with its clearly demarcated structures of authority and role assignments.[1] There are those who denigrate the marital structures of permanence and exclusivity which continue to exist, to be valued,[2] and to be achieved by some 60 percent of the married population. Both sides claim, for different reasons, that marriage is in crisis, and a mounting body of social-scientific evidence supports their claim.

The profile of the crisis shows that, compared to 1970, marriage rate and marital fertility are down, and age at first marriage, the divorce rate, non-marital childbearing, and non-marital cohabitation are all up. The profile also shows the increasingly common social phenomena of single motherhood and father absence, and the resultant feminization and childrenization of poverty. It shows that approximately half of all children under the age of eighteen will spend at least part of their childhood in a single-parent family, some 90 percent of those families headed by single mothers.[3] The profile further documents the consequences for children being raised by only one parent and suggests that the erosion of the cultural norm that mothers and fathers live with, support, and nurture their children into adulthood has serious negative implications for the whole of society.[4] Later marriage has not translated into stronger and happier marriages. The percentage in intact and happy first marriages "has declined substantially in recent years, the proportion now being about one-third," but the proportion of children living with unhappily married parents has not declined,[5] despite the high rate of divorce.

Marriage and family scholars in the United States continue to be concerned about the long-term negative impact of expressive individualism on marriages, families, churches, and the nation. Their analysis of the situation leads to a call for the restoration of a marriage culture in which the roles of husband and wife are mutual and complementary,[6] and the parenting of children a cooperative partnership.[7] They argue for strategies, marital, familial, educational, economic, political, and religious, that highlight the value of and, therefore, reinvigorate the institution of marriage. They assert that committed, competent, and generative motherhood and fatherhood, which produce a functioning adult, not merely biological maternity and paternity, which produce a child, are critical needs that humans continue to ignore at their peril.

An ancient definition of marriage, found in the *Instituta* of the Emperor Justinian (1.9.1), has exercised tight control over discussions of the nature of marriage in the Western world. "Marriage is a union of a man and a woman embracing an undivided communion of life." That definition recurs in the definition of marriage offered by the Second Vatican Council, "an intimate partnership of marital life and love,"[8] and it was reaffirmed also by the Congress of the United States in the Defense of Marriage Act in 1996. Definitions, however, no matter how clear they appear to be, are always in need of interpretations, and this one is no different. In the classical days of Western and Catholic marriage theory, when Western and Catholic were not entirely separable, the marital communion of life was interpreted as an unequal partnership, the husband being the senior and authoritative partner, and the wife a minor, frequently merely biological, partner. It is in this interpretive process, and specifically in its outcomes, that there has been a change in current marriage theory in both the Western and the Catholic worlds, and this change has contributed to the crisis marriage faces.

Up to the 1930s, the Catholic Church looked upon marriage as a *procreative institution,* in which the ends were firmly established. The *primary* end was procreation, which included not only biological generation but also nurture; the mutual help the spouses provided to one another was very much a *secondary* end. It could not be otherwise in a procreative institution. In the 1930s, fueled by Pius XI's *Casti Connubii,*[9] there was an important development from marriage as a procreative institution to marriage as a *procreative union.* Procreation continued to be the primary end of marriage but, under the influence of the personalist philosophy that flourished in Europe after the devastations of World War I, the union of the spouses and its importance in both marriage and family moved more into focus. That development, which acknowledged the union of the spouses as an important element of marriage, reached its high-point in the Second Vatican Council, which defined marriage as an *interpersonal union,* an "intimate partnership of married life and love . . . rooted in the conjugal covenant of irrevocable personal consent." From that personal consent, "whereby spouses mutually bestow and accept each other, a relationship arises."[10] The emphasis is no longer exclusively on procreation but squarely on the marital union of the spouses.[11] Though marriage and conjugal love "are by their very nature ordained to the generation and education of children," that "does not make the other ends of marriage of less account." Marriage "is not instituted solely for procreation."[12] That this significant change was not the result of some oversight was confirmed when this theological approach was enshrined in the revised Code of Canon Law (Can 1055.1) in 1983.

This change of perspective on marriage is not without consequences. The consequences of the analogue model, procreative institution, which are mainly biological and act-focused, are different from the consequences of the analogue model, interpersonal union, which are mainly interpersonal and union-focused. So far, though there have been contemporary adjustments in the Catholic theology and law of marriage, there has been little official systematic reflection on those different consequences. This has caused some serious pastoral problems for the Catholic Church. Catholics divorce at about the same rate as other Americans, and many of those divorced Catholics remarry while their first spouse is alive and without seeking an annulment of their first marriage. This leads their Church, because of their "objective situation,"[13] to declare their situation irregular and to exclude them from sharing eucharistic communion.

Three recent studies demonstrate what Catholics think about this situation. A large majority of American Catholics (68 percent) believe they can be good Catholics without having their marriage approved by the Church, and an equally large majority (65 percent) believe they can be good Catholics without obeying the Church's teaching on divorce and remarriage. When asked who has the final moral authority about the right and wrong of divorced Catholics remarrying without annulment, 45 percent respond the individuals concerned and only 20 percent respond Church leaders.[14] These results are part of a trend toward seeing the individual as having the final say on moral issues and toward indifference to Church leadership. Following a five-year study of divorced and remarried Catholics in England, Buckley reports that the consensus of bishops, priests, and people is that "something is seriously wrong with the present teaching and that more than that is a scandal."[15] These findings must be of some pastoral concern to the whole Church, and it is to that pastoral concern that this book seeks to respond.

In the introduction to a recent collection of articles about divorced and remarried Catholics, Cardinal Ratzinger writes that "only what is true can be pastoral."[16] No Catholic theologian could withhold applause from that principle. Neither could he, however, refrain from the addition of an ancient caveat: What is truth? Specifically, what is the current Catholic truth about marriage, sacrament, divorce, remarriage, and family? The goal of this book is to clarify, highlight, and make that truth accessible to all, hierarchy and laity alike.

I inquire, therefore, what it means to say that marriage is a sacrament (Chapter 1), and what models of marriage function in the contemporary Catholic Church (Chapter 2). I ask what it takes, beyond mechanical physical baptism, to transform the social reality of marriage into the Catholic sacrament, and I answer that it takes personal faith (Chapter 3). I look into the bonds or relationships in marriage, specifically into the root bond, the bond of love between the spouses that makes every other legal and religious bond possible (Chapter 4). I offer an extended consideration of divorce and remarriage in the Catholic Church, seeking to highlight theological truth to provide a foundation for truthful and healing pastoral practice (Chapter 5). Since at least one-third of all Catholics who marry now marry a Christian from a Protestant Christian denomination, I offer theological and pastoral reflections on such interchurch marriage (Chapter 6). In response to the new personalist context of marriage, I analyze the Christian reality and value of friendship and reflect on its contribution to the stability of marriage (Chapter 7). Acknowledging the social-scientific fact that more than half of all those who marry today, including more than half of all Catholics, cohabit with their spouse prior to marriage, I inquire whether cohabitation could, again as in the past, be counted as a step in the process of becoming married in the Catholic tradition (Chapter 8). Finally, I seek to construct a theology of Christian family and reflect on what that theology, and the families rooted in it, can contribute to American families in their present crisis (Chapter 9).

Because marriage is not only an ecclesial but also a societal reality, all of this reflection takes place, as it must, within what Adrian Thatcher calls "two dialogues." There is an internal dialogue in the Catholic, and more extended Christian, Church about what the Bible and the two-thousand-year theological tradition say about marriage and divorce, and how that is to be interpreted and appropriated. There is also an external dialogue between Christians and their neighbors in the world, many of whom are as deeply troubled as Christians about the crisis of marriage but think that Christians have little of importance to say to them about marriage and family.[17] My conviction is that both sides of this dialogue are essential and that both sides have something important to say to overcome the crises that confront them both. Both, therefore, are represented in what follows.

Two facts should be noted about the dialogue. First, the theological or Catholic part of the dialogue is situated in the category of the *quaestio disputata,* the disputed question, beloved of the Scholastics. The Scholastic Master had three tasks: *lectio,* or commentary on the Bible; *disputatio,* or teaching by objection and response to a theme; *praedicatio,* or theology and pastoral application.[18] Peter Cantor speaks for all the Scholastics when he argues that "it is after the *lectio* of scripture and after the examination of the doubtful points thanks to the *disputatio, and not before,* that we must preach."[19] It is important to be aware that this book is a series of *disputationes* to uncover the Catholic truth that precedes any theology or pastoral *praedicatio.* Second, since all the disputations are connected directly to the same theme, marriage and Christian marriage or sacrament, all are indirectly connected to one another. There is, therefore, a certain amount of unavoidable repetition from one disputation to another. This repetition has been kept to a minimum. Facets of the question are analyzed at length only in one place and are, then, summarized in other places where they are part of the argument.

I confess again what I have confessed several times before. No author writes a book in isolation; he is subject to many influences. I am no exception to that rule, and I freely express my gratitude to all those teachers, colleagues, students, and friends with whom I have disputed over the years and from whom I have learned what marriage truly means in the Catholic tradition. Since I cannot name all of them, it always seems to me churlish to name any of them. In this case, however, it would be more than churlish not to name specifically all those married, divorced, and sometimes remarried Catholic friends who have instructed me over the years about the honest social and theological truth embedded in their canonically "regular" and "irregular" situations. The dedication of this book to Kate and Sean is a grateful dedication to all of them.

Michael G. Lawler
Creighton University
Feast of the Epiphany, 2001

Notes

¹ See Stephanie Coontz, *The Way We Never Were: American Families and the Nostalgia Trap* (New York: Basic Books, 1992).

² Theodora Ooms, *Toward More Perfect Unions: Putting Marriage on the Public Agenda* (Washington, D.C.: Family Impact Seminar, 1998); National Marriage Project, *The State of Our Unions: 1999* (New Brunswick, N.J.: Rutgers University, 1999) 6.

³ Dennis A. Ahlburg and Carol J. DeVita, "New Realities of the American Family," *Population Bulletin* 47 (1992) 2–38; Larry L. Bumpass, "What's Happening to the Family? Interactions between Demographic and Institutional Change," *Demography* 27 (1990) 483–95; David Eggebeen and Peter Uhlenberg, "Changes in the Organization of Men's Lives: 1960–1980," *Family Relations* 34 (1985) 251–7.

⁴ Sara McLanahan and Gary Sandefur, *Growing Up with a Single Parent: What Hurts, What Helps* (Cambridge, Mass.: Harvard University Press, 1994); David Popenoe, *Life Without Father* (New York: Free Press, 1996).

⁵ Norval Glenn, "Values, Attitudes, and the State of American Marriage," *Promises to Keep: Decline and Renewal of Marriage in America*, ed. David Popenoe, Jean Bethke Elshtain, and David Blankenhorn (Lanham, Md.: Rowman and Littlefield, 1996) 15–33.

⁶ David Blankenhorn, *Fatherlessness in America: Confronting Our Most Urgent Social Problem* (New York: Basic Books, 1995); Maggie Gallagher, *The Abolition of Marriage: How We Destroy Lasting Love* (Washington, D.C.: Regnery, 1996); Barbara Dafoe Whitehead, "Dan Quayle Was Right," *Atlantic Monthly* 271 (1993) 47–84.

⁷ Henry Biller, *Fathers and Families: Paternal Factors in Child Development* (Westport, Conn.: Auburn House, 1993); McLanahan and Sandefur, *Growing Up with a Single Parent;* Don Browning and Ian Evison, "The Family Debate: A Middle Way," *Christian Century* 110 (1993) 712–6.

⁸ GS 48.

⁹ See Michael G. Lawler, *Marriage and Sacrament: A Theology of Christian Marriage* (Collegeville: The Liturgical Press, 1993) 67–71.

¹⁰ GS 48.

¹¹ An extended explanation of this short summary is presented in Chapter 2.

¹² GS 50.

¹³ Joseph Cardinal Ratzinger, "A propos de la pastorale des divorcés remariés," *La Documentation Catholique* (April 4, 1999) 319–20.

¹⁴ William V. D'Antonio, "The American Catholic Laity in 1999," *National Catholic Reporter* (October 29, 1999) 12.

¹⁵ Timothy J. Buckley, *What Binds Marriage? Roman Catholic Theology in Practice* (London: Chapman, 1997) 178.

¹⁶ Ratzinger, "A propos de la pastorale des divorcés remariés," 325.

[17] Adrian Thatcher, *Marriage after Modernity: Christian Marriage in Post-modern Times* (Sheffield: Sheffield Academic Press, 1999) 31.

[18] See Jean-Pierre Torrell, *Saint Thomas Aquinas,* vol. 1, trans. Robert Royal (Washington, D.C.: Catholic University of America Press, 1996) 54–74.

[19] Peter Cantor, *Verbum Abbreviatum* 1, PL 205.25, my emphasis.

1

Marriage and the Sacrament of Marriage

Every Catholic approaching marriage knows that the Catholic Church teaches that marriage is a sacrament. They do not, however, always understand what this means. This opening chapter, therefore, considers the two realities involved in marriage as sacrament, namely, marriage and the sacrament of marriage. To fully understand these two realities, however, we must consider also another common human reality closely related to them: love. This chapter, therefore, considers three things: the sacrament of marriage, marriage, and marital love. Each is dealt with in turn.

The Sacrament of Marriage

Marriage has not always been listed among the sacraments of the Catholic Church. The early Scholastics defined sacrament as both a sign and a cause of grace and, since they looked upon marriage as a sign but not a cause of grace, they did not list it among the sacraments. Marriage could not be a cause of grace, ran their argument, because it involved sexual intercourse which Augustine had taught was always sinful, even between a husband and a wife, except in the case when it was for the procreation of a child. "Conjugal intercourse for the sake of offspring," he taught, "is not sinful. But sexual intercourse, even with one's spouse, to satisfy concupiscence is a venial sin."[1] It should be, and is not always, noted that, for Augustine, it is not sexual intercourse itself that is sinful

1

but concupiscence, the sexual appetite out of control. No matter, his opinion was sufficient to present sexual intercourse as negative and to prevent marriage from being listed among the sacraments of the Church throughout the first millennium of its existence. In the twelfth century, Peter Lombard, for instance, defined sacrament in the categories of both sign and cause. "A sacrament, properly speaking, is a sign of the grace of God and the form of invisible grace in such a way that it is its image and its cause." He then goes on to distinguish marriage, which is a sign of grace, from the sacraments of the new law, which are both signs and causes of grace.[2]

It was the thirteenth-century Dominicans, Albert the Great and his most famous pupil, Thomas Aquinas, who securely established marriage among the sacraments of the Church. In his obligatory commentary on Lombard's *Sententiae,* Albert lists the various opinions about the sacramentality of marriage and judges "very probable" the opinion that holds that "it confers grace for doing good, not just any good but that specific good that a married person should do."[3] In his Commentary on the *Sententiae,* Aquinas goes further, judging "most probable" the opinion that "marriage, in so far as it is contracted in faith in Christ, confers grace to do those things which are required in marriage."[4] In his *Contra Gentiles* he is even more positive, stating bluntly that "it is to be believed that through this sacrament [marriage] grace is given to the married."[5] By the time he wrote his mature theology in the *Summa Theologiae,* he lists marriage as one of seven sacraments with no demur whatever. Aquinas' theological authority, albeit late in Catholic history, thus ensured for marriage a place among the sacraments of the Church.

The first Church document to list marriage as a sacrament was aimed against the Cathari by the Council of Verona (1184). The Cathari preached that sexuality and marriage were sinful and the council countered them by listing marriage as a sacrament in the company of baptism, Eucharist, and confession.[6] The Council of Lyons (1274), to which Aquinas was traveling when he died, first listed marriage among seven sacraments as part of the formula for healing the great schism between East and West,[7] a listing repeated by the Council of Florence (1439) with the notation that these seven sacraments "both contain grace and confer it on those who receive them worthily."[8]

The concluding section of the Florentine decree deals explicitly with marriage and is an excellent summary of everything taught about it up to that point.

> The seventh sacrament is marriage, which is a sign of the union between Christ and his church. . . . A triple good is designated for marriage. The first is offspring accepted and raised to worship God; the second is fidelity, in which each spouse ought to serve the other; the third is the indivisibility of marriage because it signifies the indivisible union of Christ and the church. And, although separation is permissible in the case of fornication, remarriage is not, for the bond of legitimately contracted marriage is perpetual.[9]

That marriage is a sacrament, that it contains and confers grace, that it is indissoluble, all these are now established doctrines of the Catholic Church. When the Church asserts them against the Reformers at the Council of Trent in the sixteenth century, it is merely reasserting the doctrine and the faith of the Church. There remains to ask only what does it mean that marriage is a sacrament.

Hebrew prophets were fond of symbolic actions which came to be called prophetic symbols. Jeremiah, for instance, buys a potter's flask, dashes it to the ground before a startled crowd, and proclaims the meaning of his action. "Thus says the LORD of hosts: so will I break this people and this city, as one breaks a potter's vessel" (Jer 19:11). Ezekiel takes a brick, draws a city on it, builds siegeworks around the city, and lays siege to it. This city, he explains, is "even Jerusalem" (Ezek 4:1) and his action "a sign for the house of Israel" (4:3). He takes a sword, shaves his hair with it, and divides the hair into three bundles. One bundle he burns, another he scatters to the wind, a third he carries in procession around Jerusalem, explaining his action in the proclamation: "This is Jerusalem" (5:5). The prophet Agabus binds his hands and feet with Paul's belt and proclaims the meaning of his action: "This is the way the Jews in Jerusalem will bind the man who owns this belt and will hand him over to the Gentiles" (Acts 21:11).

The prophetic explanations clarify for us the meaning of a prophetic symbol. It is a human action which reveals and celebrates in representation the action of God. Jeremiah's shattering of the pot is, in symbol, God's shattering of Jerusalem. Ezekiel's action is not the besieging of a brick but, again in symbol, God's overthrowing of Jerusalem. The prophetic symbol is a representative action, an action which reveals and proclaims in representation another more crucial action. It is a representative symbol.

Prophetic, symbolic action is not limited to prophets. Israel, a prophetic people, performed prophetic, symbolic actions. In the solemn seder meal, for instance, established as the memorial of the Exodus (Exod 12:14), the head of the gathered family took, and takes, unleavened bread and proclaims "This is the bread of affliction our fathers ate in Egypt." It was at such a meal, Mark, Matthew, and Luke report, that Jesus took bread and, when he had prayed in thanksgiving, broke it and proclaimed "This is my body, which is given for you. Do this in remembrance of me" (Luke 22:19). It is difficult not to notice the semantic correspondence between "this is Jerusalem," "this is the bread of affliction," and "this is my body." It is difficult to avoid the conclusion that each action is equally a prophetic, symbolic action.

Self-understanding in Israel was rooted in the covenant between the God Yhwh and the people Israel. It is easy to predict that Israelites, prone to prophetic action, would search for such an action to symbolize their covenant relationship with Yhwh. It is just as easy, perhaps, to predict that the symbol they would choose is the covenant of marriage between a man and a woman. The prophet Hosea was the first to speak of marriage as prophetic symbol of the covenant. On one level, the marriage of Hosea and his wife, Gomer, is like any other marriage. But on another level, Hosea interpreted it as a prophetic symbol, revealing and celebrating in representation the covenant communion between Yhwh and Israel. As Gomer left Hosea for other lovers, so Israel left Yhwh for other gods. As Hosea waited in faithfulness for Gomer's return, as he received her back without recrimination, so too does Yhwh wait for and take back Israel. Hosea's human action and reaction is prophetic symbol of Yhwh's divine action and reaction. In both covenants, the human and the divine, the covenant relationship has been violated, and Hosea's actions reflect Yhwh's. In symbolic representation, they reveal and proclaim not only Hosea's faithfulness to Gomer but also Yhwh's faithfulness to Israel.

Contemporary feminist theologians rightly object to the allegorization of the story of the marriage of Hosea and Gomer which establishes Hosea, and all husbands, in the place of the faithful God and Gomer, and all wives, in the place of faithless Israel. The story is not an allegory, but a rich parable whose meanings remain to be discovered anew in each changing circumstance. One constant meaning is clear, if mysterious, not so much about Gomer and Hosea as about their marriage. Not only is marriage a universal human institution; it is also a religious, prophetic symbol, revealing and proclaiming in the human world the union between God and God's people. Not only is it law, it is also grace and redemption. Lived into in this context of grace, lived into in faith in Christ, as Aquinas says, marriage appears as a two-storied reality. In and on one story, the human, it bespeaks the mutually covenanted love of this man and this woman, of every Hosea and Gomer; in and on another story, the religious, it prophetically symbolizes the mutually covenanted love of God and God's people. This two-storied view of marriage became the Christian view, found for instance in the Letter to the Ephesians. Jewish prophetic symbol became Christian sacrament.

In the New Testament, there is a change of *dramatis personae* in the prophetic symbol of marriage, from YHWH-Israel to Christ-Church. Rather than presenting marriage in the then-classical Jewish way as a symbol of the covenant union between YHWH and Israel, the writer of the Letter to the Ephesians presents it as an image of the relationship between Christ and his Church. This presentation is of such central importance to the development of a Christian view of marriage, and unfortunately has been used to sustain such a diminished Christian view, that we have to consider it here in some detail.

The passage in which the writer offers his view of marriage (Eph 5:21-33) is situated within a larger context (5:21–6:9), which sets forth a list of household duties that exist within a family in his first-century Mediterranean culture. This list is addressed to wives (5:22), husbands (5:25), children (6:1), fathers (6:4), slaves (6:5), and masters (6:9). All that concerns us here is what is said to wives and husbands. There are two similar lists in the New Testament, one in the Letter to the Colossians (3:18–4:1), the other in the first letter of Peter (2:13–3:7). But the Ephesians' list is the only one to open with a strange injunction. "Because you fear Christ subordinate yourselves to one another," or "give way to one another," or "be subject to one another." This injunction, commentators agree, is an essential element of what follows.

The writer takes over the household list from traditional material, but critiques it in Eph 5:21. His critique challenges the absolute authority of any one Christian group over any other, of husbands, for instance, over wives, of fathers over children, of masters over slaves. It establishes a basic attitude required of all Christians, an attitude of mutual giving way, an attitude which covers all he has to say not only to wives, children, and slaves, but also to husbands, fathers, and masters. Giving way is an attitude demanded of all Christians, because their fundamental attitude is that they "fear Christ." That phrase will ring strangely in pious ears, clashing with the deeply rooted claim that the basic attitude toward the Lord of the New Testament is not one of fear but of love. It is probably for this reason that the Revised Standard Version rounds off the rough edge of the Greek *phobos* and renders it as *reverence*. *Phobos,* however, does not mean reverence. It means fear; as in the Old Testament aphorism, the fear of the Lord is the beginning of wisdom (Prov 1:5; 9:10; 15:33; Ps 111:10).

The apostle Paul is quite comfortable with this Old Testament perspective, twice using the phrase "fear of God" in his second Letter to the Corinthians (5:11 and 7:1). The latter would seem to be a better parallel for the passage in Ephesians. Second Corinthians 6:14-18 recalls the initiatives of God in the covenant with Israel and applies them to Christians, who are invited to respond with holiness "in the fear of God" (2 Cor 7:1). The fear of God that is the beginning of wisdom is a radical awe and reverence that grasps the mighty acts of God and responds to them in faith. In 2 Corinthians 6:14-17 the response is specified as avoiding marriage with unbelievers; in Ephesians 5:21 it is specified as giving way to one another. That mutual giving way is required of all Christians, even of husbands and wives as they seek holiness together in marriage, and in spite of traditional relationships which permitted husbands to lord it patriarchally over their wives.

As Christians have all been admonished to give way to one another, it comes as no surprise that a Christian wife is to give way to her husband, "as . . . to the Lord" (Eph 5:22). What does come as a surprise, at least to that ingrained male attitude that sees the husband as supreme lord and master of his wife and appeals to Ephesians 5:22-23 to ground and sustain that un-Christian attitude, is that a husband is to give way to his wife. That follows from the general instruction that Christians are to give way to one another. It follows also from the specific instruction given to husbands. That instruction is not that "the husband is the head of the wife," the way in which some males prefer to read and cite it, but rather that "the husband is head of the wife just as Christ is the head of the church" (Eph 5:23).

A Christian husband's headship over his wife is in image of, and totally exemplified by, Christ's headship over the Church. When a Christian husband understands this, he will understand the Christian responsibility he assumes toward the woman-gift he receives in marriage as his wife. In a marriage between Christians, faith-full Christians, as Chapter 3 will explain, spouses are required to give way mutually, not because of any inequality between them, not because of any subordination of one to the other, not because of human fear, but only because they seek to live in service of one another as Christ lives in service of the Church. Spousal giving way is no more than the total availability and responsiveness to one another required of best friends and lovers to become two in one body (Gen 2:24).

The way Christ exercises authority is set forth unequivocally in Mark 10:45: "The Son of Man came not to be served but to serve, and to give his life as a ransom [redemption] for many." *Diakonia,* service, is the

Christ-way of exercising authority; it was as a servant that "Christ loved the church and gave himself up for her" (Eph 5:25). A Christian husband, therefore, is instructed to be head over his wife by serving, giving way to, and giving himself up for her. Authority modeled on that of Christ does not mean control, giving orders, making unreasonable demands, reducing another person to the status of servant or, worse, of slave to one's every whim. It means service. The Christian husband-head, as Markus Barth puts it so beautifully, becomes "the first servant of his wife."[10] It is of such a husband, and only of such a one, that a wife is to stand in awe (v. 33b) as all Christians stand in awe of Christ (v. 21b).

The reversal of verses 22 and 25 in verse 33 is interesting and significant. Verse 22 enjoins wives to give way to their husbands and verse 25 enjoins husbands to love their wives. Verse 33 reverses that order, first commanding that husbands love their wives and then warmly wishing that wives fear or stand in awe of their husbands. This fear is not fear of a master. Rather, it is awe and reverence for loving service, and response to that service with one's own love-as-giving-way. Such love cannot be commanded by a tyrant. It is won only by a servant-lover, as the Church's love and giving way to Christ is won by a lover who gave, and continues to give, himself for her (v. 25). This is the author's recipe for becoming one body, for the fusion of two individual beings into one coupled being, joyous giving way in response to, and for the sake of, loving service. It is a recipe echoed unwittingly by many a modern marriage counselor, though we need to recall that the love the Bible urges upon spouses is not exclusively interpersonal affection but more willed loyalty, service, and giving way.[11] That such love is to be mutual is clear from verse 21, "Be subject to one another," though it is not stated that a wife is to love her husband. The reasons that the writer adduces for husbands to love their wives apply to all Christians, even to those called wives.

Three reasons are offered to husbands for loving their wives, all of them virtually the same. First of all, "husbands should love their wives as they do [for they are] their own bodies" (Eph 5:28a); second, the husband "who loves his wife loves himself" (v. 28b); third, "the two will become one flesh" (v. 31b). There is abundant evidence in the Jewish tradition for equating a man's wife to his body. But even if there was no such evidence, the sustained comparison throughout Ephesians 5:21-33 between Christ-Church and husband-wife, coupled with the frequent equation of Church and Body of Christ (1:22-23; 2:14-16; 3:6; 4:4-16; 5:22-30), clarifies both the meaning of the term "body" and the fact that it is a title of honor rather than of humiliation.

Love is always essentially creative. The love of Christ brought into existence the Church and made its believers "members of his body" (Eph 5:30). In the same way, the mutual love of a husband and a wife creates such a union between them that, in image of Christ and Church, she may be called his body and his love for her, therefore, may be called love for his body or for himself. But it is only within the creative and committed love of marriage that "the two shall become one body." Prior to marriage, a man did not have this body, nor did a woman have this head. Each receives a gift in marriage, a complement neither had before, which so fulfills each of them that they are no longer two persons but effectively a coupled one person, a coupled-We. For each to love the other, therefore, is for each to love also herself or himself.

The second reason offered to a husband for loving his wife is that "he who loves his wife loves himself" (v. 28b; cf. v. 33a). Viewed within the perspective we have just elaborated, such reasoning makes sense. It makes even more Christian sense when we realize that it is a paraphrase of the great commandment cited by Jesus: "You shall love your neighbor as yourself" (Lev 19:18; Mark 12:21). Ephesians, of course, does not say that a husband should so love his wife. Where, then, is the link to the great commandment? It is provided through that most beautiful and most sexual of Jewish love songs, the Song of Songs, where in the Septuagint version the one lover addresses the other nine separate times as *plesion*, neighbor (1:9, 15; 2:2, 10, 13; 4:1, 7; 5:2; 6:4). "The context of the occurrence of *plesion* in the Song of Songs confirms that *plesion* is used as a term of endearment for the bride."[12] Other Jewish usage further confirms that conclusion, leaving no doubt that the author of Ephesians had Leviticus 19:18 in mind when instructing a husband to love his wife as himself.

The great Torah and Gospel injunction applies also in marriage: "You shall love your neighbor as yourself." As all Christians are to give way to one another, so also each is to love the other as himself or herself, including husband and wife in marriage. The paraphrase of Leviticus 19:18 repeats in another form what had already been said before in the own-body and the one-body images. What the writer concludes about the Genesis one-body image, namely, "This is a great mystery, and I am applying it to Christ and the church" (Eph 5:32), will conclude our analysis of this central teaching of the New Testament on marriage.

"This is a great mystery," namely, as most scholars agree, the Genesis 2:24 text just cited. The mystery, as the Anchor Bible translation seeks to show, is that "this [passage] has an eminent secret meaning," which is that it refers to Christ and the Church. All that has gone before about Christ and the Church comes to the forefront here: that Christ chose the Church to be united to him, as body to head; that he loved the Church and gave himself up for her; that the Church responds to this love of Christ in awe and giving way. Christ who loves the Church, and the Church who responds in love, thus constitute one body, the Body of Christ (Eph 1:22-23; 2:14-16; 3:6; 4:4-16; 5:22-30), as Genesis 2:24 said they would. The writer is well aware that this meaning is not the meaning traditionally given to the text in Judaism, and he states this forthrightly. Just as in the great antitheses of the Sermon on the Mount Jesus puts forward his interpretations of biblical texts in opposition to traditional interpretations ("You have heard that it was said to the men of old . . . but *I* say to you"), so also here the writer asserts clearly that it is his own reading of the text ("*I* am applying it to Christ and the church," v. 32b).

Genesis 2:24 was an excellent text for the purpose the writer had in mind, for it was a central Old Testament text traditionally employed to ordain and legitimate marriage. He acknowledges the meaning that husband and wife become one body in marriage; indeed, in verse 33 he returns to and demands that husband and wife live up to this very meaning. But he chooses to go beyond this meaning and insinuate another. Not only does the text refer to the union of husband and wife in marriage, but it refers also to that union of Christ and his Church which he has underscored throughout Ephesians 5:1-33. On one level, Genesis 2:24 refers to human marriage; on another level, it refers to the covenant union between Christ and his Church. It is a small step to see human marriage as prophetic symbol of the covenant between Christ and his Church, and to see the communion between Christ and his Church as providing a model for human marriage and for the mutual conduct of the spouses within it.

The classical Roman Catholic definition of sacrament, "an outward sign of inward grace instituted by Christ," which took a thousand years to become established,[13] can now be more fully explicated. A sacrament is a prophetic symbol in and through which the Church, the Body of Christ, reveals and celebrates in representation that presence of God which is called grace. To say that a marriage between Christians is a sacrament is to say, then, that it is a prophetic symbol, a two-storied reality. In and on one story, it reveals and celebrates the intimate communion of life and love between a man and a woman. In and on another story, it reveals and celebrates the intimate communion of life and love and grace between God and God's people and between Christ and Christ's people, the Church.

A couple entering any marriage say to one another, before the witnesses of the society in which they live, "I love you and I give myself to and for you." A Christian couple entering, in faith, a specifically sacramental marriage say that, too, but they also say more. They say "I love you as Christ loves his church, steadfastly and faithfully." From the first, therefore, a Christian marriage is intentionally more than just the communion for the whole of life of this man and this woman. It is more than just human covenant; it is also religious covenant. It is more than law and mutual rights; it is also undeserved grace. From the first, God and God's Christ are present and active in it, modeling it, gracing it, and guaranteeing its stability. This presence of grace in its most ancient Christian sense, namely, the presence of the loving God, is not something extrinsic to Christian marriage. It is something essential to it, something without which it would not be *Christian* marriage at all. Christian sacramental marriage certainly reveals and proclaims the mutual love of the spouses for one another. It also reveals and proclaims their love for, and their faith in, the Christ they confess as Lord. It is in this sense that it is a sacrament, a prophetic symbol, both a sign and a cause, of the gracious presence of Christ and of the God he reveals.

In every symbol there are, to repeat, two levels of meaning. There is a foundational level and, built on this foundation, a symbolic level. The foundational level in a sacramental marriage is the marriage, "the intimate partnership of life and love" (GS 48), the loving communion for the whole of life between a man and a woman who are disciples of Christ and members of his Church. The symbolic or sacramental level is the representation in their communion of the communion of life and love between Christ and his Church. This connected meaningfulness is what is meant by the claim that marriage between Christians is a sacrament. In a truly Christian marriage, a marriage between two *believing* Christians, the mutual love of the spouses serves as symbol of the love of God and Christ for them and for all creation, and the steadfast love of God and of Christ serves as symbol of the steadfast love to which the spouses are constantly called. In and through the mutual love of the spouses, God and God's Christ are present in a Christian marriage, gracing the spouses with their presence and providing for them models of steadfast and abiding love. This is what the Catholic Church intends when it teaches that marriage is a sacrament, simply that loving marriage is a symbol of the presence of God in the world.

There is one final question for this section. When the Catholic Church claims that marriage between the baptized is a sacrament, what precisely is the meaning of the word *marriage*? In ordinary language, the word is ambiguous. Sometimes it refers to the wedding ceremony, in which a couple freely commit to one another "for the purpose of establishing a marriage" (Can 1057.2). Sometimes it means the marriage and the life that flows from the wedding commitment, the communion of life and love that lasts until death. Both these common meanings of the word *marriage* are intended here in the claim that marriage is a sacrament.

Marriage

Every reader of this book has been to a wedding. It may have been a civil wedding presided over by a judge; it may have been a religious wedding presided over by a minister. It has been always a solemn, joyous celebration. For a valid marriage, however, only one moment of the ritual radically counts, the solemn moment of giving consent. At the wedding, those gathered would have hung breathlessly on these, or similar, solemn words: "I, Sean, take you, Kate, for my lawful wife, to have and to hold, from this day forward, for better, for worse, for richer, for poorer, in sickness and in health, until death do us part." When Kate had declared her intention in the same or similar words, you would have heard them pronounced married, "husband and wife." If that moment of free consent is missing or in any way flawed, there may be a wedding ceremony but there is no valid marriage. Without free and full consent, in both civil and Church law, the wedding ceremony yields a marriage which is null from the start and can be declared annulled as soon as its nullity is demonstrated.

That friendship and love die over the years is immortalized in the great love stories of our culture, Tristan and Isolde, Romeo and Juliet, even Titanic. That marriages die is immortalized in the more mundane statistics of our divorce courts, which tell us that some 40 percent of marriages die in the United States. Important though love and marriage may be to any couple, marriage is even more important to society in which they live, because it is still the ordinary way to provide citizens for the society. The societal stake in marriage so outweighs in importance the individual commitment to it that every society has prescribed for marriage the solemn ritualization of commitment. It is this public, ritual, ceremonial commitment that makes married love quite different from unmarried love. This section seeks to understand and to specify that statement.

Not surprisingly, the wedding of Sean and Kate was conducted according to laws not of their making. For our purposes here, we need only note that those laws have a long history in Western civilization, being rooted in the Roman Empire. Already in the sixth century, the Emperor Justinian decreed that the only thing that was required for a valid marriage was the mutual consent of both parties.[14] In Roman law, a marriage is created by mutual consent, not by sexual intercourse, as it was in the Germanic tribes. That difference of opinion about what constituted a marriage eventually created a widespread legal discussion in Europe, the solution of which has major impact on the marriage of Sean and Kate. That question, which would be easily answered by the two lovers but not so easily answered by canon lawyers, is the question of when precisely their marriage is so validly stable that it is also indissoluble.

We already know the ancient Roman answer to the question: mutual consent between the parties makes a marriage. The ancient Germanic answer was different: sexual intercourse between the spouses makes a marriage. Both answers had long histories; both were supported by good reasons; in twelfth-century Europe, both had brilliant proponents. Then, in mid-century, Gratian, the Master of the University of Bologna, proposed a compromise solution which combined both views. Consent *initiates* a marriage; subsequent sexual intercourse completes or *consummates* it. This compromise opinion settled the debate and is today still enshrined in the Code of Canon Law that governs marriages in the Roman Catholic Church (Can 1061). I shall have occasion to ponder the implications of this law in a later chapter. For the moment, I note only this single implication: when Sean and Kate have given exchanged consent, when they have exchanged their vows, and when the wedding ceremony is over, they are not nearly as indissolubly married as they and everyone else might think.

Consent initiates marriage and sexual intercourse then consummates it. But what is the marriage into which Sean and Kate have entered? Two definitions, again Roman in origin, have dominated the Western discussion of this question. The first is found in Justinian's *Digesta* (23.2.1) and is attributed to the third-century jurist Modestinus. "Marriage is a union of a man and a woman, and a communion of the whole of life, a participation in divine and human law." The second is found in the same emperor's *Instituta* (1.9.1), and is attributed to Modestinus' contemporary, Ulpianus. "Marriage is a union of a man and a woman, embracing an undivided communion of life."

Though the two "definitions" are really only generic descriptions of a long-existing social institution in Roman culture, they subsequently controlled every discussion about marriage in Western culture. Both definitions agree on the bedrock: marriage is a union of a man and a woman and, though the words are different in each definition, a union and a communion embracing the whole of life. That phrase, "the whole of life," is ambiguous, open to two different if connected interpretations. The "whole of life" can mean as long as life lasts, and then it implies that marriage is a life-long commitment. It can also mean everything that the spouses have, and then it implies that nothing is left unshared between them. Over the years, both meanings have been so interwoven that marriage is looked upon as the union of a man and a woman embracing the sharing till death of all goods, both material or spiritual. In the freshness of their love, Sean and Kate certainly approach it in that way. Their mutually well-wishing love impels them to promise marital communion in everything "until death do us part." It will be instructive to reflect more precisely on that "everything."

To consent or to covenant in marriage is to commit oneself radically, totally, and solemnly. When they covenant in a marriage that is also a sacrament, Sean and Kate commit themselves to create a life of equal and intimate partnership in steadfast and faithful love. When God created the heavens and the earth, when no plant had yet sprung up from the earth because God had not yet brought rain, a mist rose up and watered the earth. The mist turned the dry earth to mud, in Hebrew 'adamah, and from that 'adamah God formed 'adam and breathed into her and his nostrils the breath of life. And 'adam became a living being (Gen 2:4-7). "When God created 'adam, he made 'adam in the likeness of God. Male and female he created them, and he blessed them and he named them 'adam" (Gen 5:1-2).

This myth, for it is indeed a myth and not historical description, responds to the perennial human question: From where did we come? We, in Hebrew 'adam, in English *humankind*, came from God. Male and female as we are, we are from God, and together we make up humankind. This fact alone, that God names woman and man together 'adam, establishes the equality of men and women as human beings. The further myth which speaks of the creation of woman from man's rib intends in the Hebrew metaphor to emphasize the equality of man and woman, not their separate creation. The Catholic bishops of the United States underscore this fact in their pastoral response to the concerns of women in the Church. Since "in the image of God . . . male and female [God] created them" (Gen 1:27), woman and man are equal in human dignity and favor in God's eyes. They are equal in everything that is human; they are "bone of my bones and flesh of my flesh" (Gen 2:23). It is only because they are so equal, says the myth, that they may marry and "become one flesh" (Gen 2:24).

In the Hebrew myth, *body* does not refer only to the external, physical part of the human being, as it does in English. It refers also to the whole person. In marriage, therefore, a man and a woman covenant to unite not only their bodies but also their whole persons, "the whole of life." Marriage is for the good of persons, not for the good of bodies. In the Hebrew culture of Jesus' time, in contrast with contemporary Western culture where individuals consent to a marriage which society guarantees as a legal reality, families consented to a marriage which society guaranteed as a blood relationship. That blood relationship makes the spouses one body, one person, in a way that escapes the understanding of those who think only in physical and legal terms. They become, as God intended in the beginning, equal man and woman complementing one another to re-create together *'adam* and the image of God. Rabbis have long taught that, according to God's design, neither man nor woman is wholly human until each receives the complement of the other in marriage. The equal partnership of marriage is demanded by the founding myth in which both Judaism and Christianity are rooted.

Christian marital covenant demands not only the creation of a life of equal partnership but also the sustaining of that life. As the God of Jesus is not a deist God who creates and then abandons creation, as Jesus is not a Christ who gives himself up for the Church (Eph 5:25) and then abandons her, so no Christian believer creates a marriage and a sacrament and then leaves them to survive by themselves. When Sean and Kate marry, they commit themselves mutually to create rules of behavior which will nurture and sustain their marriage. As believing Christians, they will come to those rules by paying careful attention to their tradition.

There is an effort, sound and correct, across the Christian traditions to move away from what may be called a "biblical rules" approach to morality. "Realizing the impossibility of transposing rules from biblical times to our own, interpreters look for larger themes, values, or ideals which can inform moral reflection without determining specific practices in advance."[15] Sean and Kate, and all the married, will find the ideals to inform their covenant marriage succinctly summarized in a careful reading of the Letter to the Ephesians. There, as we have seen, the author critiques the list of traditional household duties in first-century Palestine, together with the inequality embedded in it, and challenges all Christians, including husbands and wives, to "Be subject to one another out of [awe] of Christ" (5:21).

The Christian way to exercise authority is to serve. Christ-like authority is not absolute control over another human being; it is not making unilateral decisions and transmitting them to another to carry out; it is not reducing another to the status of a slave. To be head as Christ is head is to serve. The Christian husband, to recall Barth, is called to be "the first servant of his wife,"[16] and she is equally called to be his first servant. One rule of behavior by which Sean and Kate may nurture both their marriage and their sacrament is the Christian rule of service, of God, of one another, and of others around them. Another Christian rule for behavior, both in and out of marriage, is the great commandment: "You shall love your neighbor as yourself" (Lev 19:18; Mark 12:31). Husbands, the Letter to the Ephesians instructs, are to "love their wives as their own bodies," for the husband "who loves his wife loves himself" (5:28). We can rightfully assume that the same instruction is intended also for wives. The great Torah and Gospel commandment to love one's neighbor as oneself applies in marriage to one's spouse who, in that most beautiful and most sexual of Jewish love songs, the Song of Songs, is addressed nine times as *plesion*-neighbor (1:9, 15; 2:2, 10, 13; 4:1, 7; 5:2; 6:4). A paraphrase of Paul clinches the rule of love for Christian spouses: those who love their spouses have fulfilled all the rules for nurturing and sustaining a Christian marriage (Rom 13:8).

A sacramental marriage is not just a wedding to be celebrated; it is also, and more critically, an equal and loving partnership to be lived for the whole of life. A marriage that is also a sacrament is an equal partnership to discover together the very depths of life. When Sean and Kate covenant to one another in the sacrament of marriage, they commit themselves to explore together the religious depth of their life together and to respond to that depth in the light of their mutual covenant to Christ and to the Church in which he abides.

One way to describe Christian life is to describe it as discipleship. *Disciple* is a gospel word, implying both a call from Jesus and a response from a believer. Disciples are students, and the disciples of Jesus are students of a triple mystery. They ponder the mystery of the Spirit-God who calls them to love and to serve, the mystery of the Christ in whom this God is embodied and revealed, the mystery of the Church, which is the Body of Christ (Eph 1:22-23; Col 1:18, 24), and which calls them to communion and to service. Sean and Kate, members of the Church, disciples of the Christ and believers in the God he reveals, consent in covenant to ponder together these mysteries and to uncover their implications for life. Marriage does not isolate the spouses from life. It immerses them in life, and confronts them with the ultimate questions of life and death that are the stuff of religion. Sometimes the questions are easy, concerning things like happiness, friends, success, the birth of children; sometimes they are difficult, concerning pain, suffering and alienation, fear, grief and death. Life demands that sense be made of the questions; marriage demands that the spouses make sense of them together; Christian marriage demands that they make sense of them in the light of their shared Christian faith.

As Sean and Kate find adequate Christian responses to the questions that life and marriage impose on them, they mutually nurture one another in Christian discipleship. They learn and grow together in Christian maturity. The more they mature in their marriage, their partnership of love and life, the more they come to grasp the ongoing nature of their marriage as sacrament. They come to realize that, though their marriage is already a sacramental sign of the covenant between Christ and his Church, it is not yet the best sign it can be. As relationship takes time to mature, as marriage takes time to mature, so also does sacrament take time to mature. In Christian marriage, even more than in any other marriage, the answer to the age-old question of when are two people married is simple: a lifetime after they exchanged consent.

In our age, the disciples of Christ have to study the signs of the times and then decide what sign they want their marriage to offer to a world divided and broken by racism, sexism, and classism. Since they are believing Christians, that sign will depend, at least in part, on Jesus' assertion, already considered, that he came "not to be served but to serve" (Mark 10:45). No Christian, individual, couple, or church can be anything less than that for others. No Christian family can be anything less than a "domestic church"[17] for others, reaching out to heal the brokenness in the communities in which it exists. Service to the society in which they live is the responsibility of all Christians, married or unmarried. Sacramental marriage adds only the specification that the spouses exercise their service as part of their marital life.

I conclude this section, as I began it, with a characterization of marriage, only now a more fully elaborated characterization of *Christian* marriage. Christian marriage is an intimate and equal partnership of life and love. Its origin is, ultimately, in God's act of creating 'adam male and female, proximately, in the covenant of the spouses' free consent; its goal is the continuation of Christ's mission to establish the reign of God in the lives of the spouses and their children, and in the world in which they live. Sean and Kate are instructed about such marriage in the prayers of their wedding service. "Father, keep them always true to your commandments. Let them be living examples of Christian life. Give them the strength which comes from the gospels so that they may be witnesses of Christ to others."[18] If ritual prayers are always the best indicators of ritual meaning, and they are, there can be no doubt about the meaning of Christian covenant and sacramental marriage.

Marriage is in serious decline in the United States. Fewer people are marrying, those who do marry are postponing it to later in life, as many children are born outside as inside marriage, and some 40 percent of all marriages end in divorce.[19] It has, therefore, become fashionable to be cynical about the marital promise "until death do us part," not only because divorce statistics appear to make a mockery of it but also because, so it is argued, unconditional promises covering a period of forty or fifty years just are not possible. To promise I will do something next week is one thing; to promise I will do it fifty years from now, when so much will have changed, is quite an impossible other. Only conditional marital promises, only those promises made on the condition that there be no change in either spouse, so the argument runs, can be made with any moral weight. I must disagree.

The claim that the marriage vow "until death do us part" is somehow impossible is false. It is perfectly possible for Sean and Kate to commit themselves unconditionally, for commitment is a statement of present intention, not an act of future clairvoyance. Love is not only an airy sentiment, not only a warm feeling about another human being. Sentiment and warm feeling may be part of love, but they are not all there is to love. At the roots, love is a steely decision, a free act which wills the good of another self. It is not true that either Sean or Kate is helpless when and if one or the other waivers in marital commitment, even if one or the other or both have moved beyond their present standpoint. It is entirely possible that principles, freely chosen and willingly embraced now, can continue to be freely chosen and willingly embraced fifty years hence in substantially changed circumstances. History is full of examples. I cite three.

I offer as a first, widespread example the prisoner of conscience. Contemporary history has made heroes of many of them, the German Pastor Dietrich Bonhoeffer, the Jewish convert to Catholicism Edith Stein, the anti-apartheid South African Nelson Mandela, the Russian physicist Andre Sacharov. For my purposes here, however, I choose a literary hero, Addison's Cato. When offered life, freedom, and the friendship of Caesar, and asked to name his terms, he replied thus: "Bid him disband his legions, restore the commonwealth to liberty. . . . And stand the judgment of a Roman Senate. Bid him do this and Cato is his friend."[20] Like any other human, Cato valued life, liberty, and friendship. He valued, however, not just any life. He had opted for the life of honor and, from that moment of freely chosen and freely embraced commitment, life without honor was no longer a real option for him. The principles of the life he had chosen, and to which he willed to be faithful, did not permit it.

The second, equally widespread example is the soldier going off to war. Like Cato, and us too, the soldier values life and liberty and peaceful living with his family and friends, but like Cato he does not value them at any cost. He also has committed himself to the principle of honor and, at any cost, he will be faithful to that principle. He even enunciates his principle to his distraught lover as he marches off to war. "I could not love thee, dear, so much, Lov'd I not honor more."[21] That same declaration has been made for centuries by a third group, married women and men who have freely chosen and freely embraced love and honor and who have willed to be faithful to them "for better, for worse, for richer, for poorer, in sickness and in health, until death do us part." If the statistics are correct, that group comprises 60 percent, an almost two-thirds majority, of all those who marry in the United States. Sean and Kate properly embrace those same principles on their wedding day.

Love and marriage are like a flower garden. It is never enough to plant seeds in the garden and then to sit back and wait for flowers to grow. The seeds must be lovingly watered and fed, the garden must be assiduously weeded, if flowers are to grow. So it is, every study shows, with love and marriage. If love and marriage are to flower into things of lifelong beauty, they must be watered and nurtured and weeded by lovers and spouses. Lovers must work unceasingly at friendship and love, they must care for them, nurture them jealously, and sustain them, for they will not sustain themselves. Sean and Kate must work unceasingly to nurture and sustain their marriage, for old, unnurtured marriages are a lot like old, unnurtured soldiers, they simply fade away, promise and love and honor notwithstanding.

One final consideration completes this section. We must ask, not now what marriage *is*, but what is it *for*. As we shall deal with that question in some detail in a later chapter, we shall answer it here only summarily. In both the Western and the Catholic traditions, a pair which is not completely separable, marriage is held to have two purposes or ends. These ends are consistently articulated, from Augustine to the twentieth century, as they are in the 1917 Code of Canon Law. "The primary end of marriage is the procreation and nurture of children; its secondary end is mutual help and the remedying of concupiscence" (Can 1013.1). The Code did not invent this hierarchy of ends;[22] it merely repeated them from a long history. This hierarchy of ends, which implicitly establishes also a subordination of ends, gave rise to a moral principle. When there is conflict between the fulfillment of the primary end of procreation and the secondary end of marital love, the secondary end must always yield to the primary. Sean and Kate should be aware that, in the twenty-first century, it has become a common experience that sustaining the primary end is frequently in conflict with and destructive of the secondary end, and sometimes even of the marriage itself. They should know also that, at least in the Catholic Church, the second half of the twentieth century brought a significant change.

The Second Vatican Council met each fall from 1962 to 1965 to consider the teachings of the Catholic Church. Among the many questions raised and answered was the one that concerns us presently: the ends of marriage. In The Church in the Modern World, the council teaches that both the institution of marriage and the marital love of the spouses "are ordained for the procreation and education of children, and find in them their ultimate crown" (GS 48). Given Western intellectual history, there is nothing surprising there. There is something surprising, however, in the council's approach to the question of the primary and secondary ends.

Despite insistent demands to reaffirm the traditional, hierarchical terminology, the council refused to do so. Indeed, the Commission that prepared the final formulation of the Pastoral Constitution was careful to explain explicitly that the text cited above was not to be read as suggesting a hierarchy of ends in any way.[23] The council taught explicitly that procreation "does not make the other ends of marriage of less account" and that marriage "is not instituted solely for procreation" (GS 50). The intense debates that took place in the Preparatory Commission and in the executive sessions of the council itself make it impossible to claim that the refusal to speak of a hierarchy of ends in marriage was the result of some geriatric lapse of memory. There is not the slightest doubt that it was the result of deliberate choice.

Any possible doubt was definitively removed in 1983 with the publication of the revised Code of Canon Law. The Church in the Modern World had described marriage, in language whose Justinian parentage is obvious, in this way. It is an "intimate partnership of married life and love . . . established by the Creator and qualified by his laws. It is rooted in the conjugal covenant of irrevocable personal consent. Hence, by that human act whereby spouses mutually bestow and accept each other, a relationship arises which by divine will and in the eyes of society too is a lasting one" (GS 48). The Code picked up this description and repeated it, declaring that "the marriage covenant, by which a man and a woman establish between themselves a partnership of their whole life, and which of its very nature is ordered to the well-being of the spouses and to the procreation and upbringing of children, has, between the baptized, been raised by Christ the Lord to the dignity of a sacrament" (Can 1055.1). These two documents sum up for now the essence of marriage. It is an equal partnership of love for the whole of life, ordered equally to the well-being of the spouses and to the generation and nurture of children. That equal and loving partnership, the Catholic Church teaches, is also a sacrament, a sign and a cause of both their love for one another and of God's love for them.

Love

The word *love* has appeared consistently throughout the preceding two sections, and demands explanation. I have needs, and so do others: needs for trust, for respect, for safety, for understanding, for encouragement, for honesty, for acceptance as I am. Some people commit themselves to respond to my needs and I commit myself to respond to theirs. We are, we say, friends. We companion one another on life's journey; we reveal ourselves mutually to one another; we assist one another and sustain one another when one or the other is weak; we provoke one another to realize our highest potential, to be the best we can be; we rejoice together when the best is achieved. In short, we will good to one another; in an ancient word, we love one another.[24] It is love that is willing good to one another that I seek to clarify in this section.

In contemporary American usage, love almost always means romantic love, usually a passionate feeling of affection for another person of the opposite sex. That is not entirely what love means. Feeling is frequently part of love, but it is not always part of it, and it is certainly not all there is to love. If it were, love would end when the transient things that fuel romantic love end. Marriages based on feeling-love would also end, as many of them indeed do. If love were merely feeling, the love of neighbors and enemies commanded by Jesus would be impossible, for few of us can *feel* love for some of our neighbors and even fewer for all of our enemies (Matt 22:39; 5:44). The love that is steadfast and lasting and that gives stability to marriages is more than feeling, it is also *will-*

ing or *intending*. It wills the good of the beloved. This is the love I am talking about in this section.

That love is willing or intending the good of another human being raises the question: Is love, then, free? The answer is yes, it is, and no, it is not. An ancient maxim illustrates the no: *nihil amatum nisi praecognitum*, nothing is loved that is not first known. The first movement of love is a response, a response to knowledge of the other's being, the other's goodness, beauty, and lovableness. To the extent that it is spontaneous response to what is judged to be good and lovable, to the extent that I am "swept off my feet," as we say, love is not entirely free. That I am not, however, totally overwhelmed by this response of love illustrates the yes. I remain free to choose to attend to my response or not, to nurture it or not, to be persuaded by it or not. "I can take responsibility for my love—not just be carried away by it or victimized by it."[25] To the extent that I am responsible for it, love is free. It is something I do as well as something that happens to me; it is action as well as passion.

As a freely willed act, love is a species of promise or commitment, the giving of my word to do something, namely, to will the good of another. The action in which my commitment is expressed is the symbol of my love and the symbol of my intention to love for the whole of life. This symbol relates me and bonds me to the one I love so that she or he can legitimately object ever after: "but you promised." The symbol not only expresses to the one I love my intention to love her for the whole of life, it also confirms me in that intention. We mutually commit to one another as lovers to make our love permanent and to communicate it as permanent.

In reality, of course, because of how our human lives are structured, though we can *intend* our love to be indissoluble, we cannot actually *make* it indissoluble at any given moment of our lives, for love stretches out into the unknown future along with life. What we can do, in Margaret Farley's words, is "initiate in the present a new form of relationship that will endure in the form of fidelity or betrayal." Commitment, she continues, "is love's way of being whole while it still grows into wholeness."[26] The point discussed earlier recurs here. The commitment to love is also a commitment to the principle of honor and to fidelity to that honor. As the poet says, "I could not love thee, dear, so much, Lov'd I not honor more." As already noted, the mutual commitment of love between lovers creates between them an interpersonal relationship and a bond which is morally binding. That interpersonal bond can be further bound by further ritual. In civil marriage, it can be bound by civil law; in Christian marriage, it can be bound by sacrament and the grace of God. In Christian marriage, therefore, as we shall see in detail in Chapter 4, there are three bonds binding the spouses: the bond of love, the bond of legal marriage, and the bond of sacrament. None of these bonds occurs in any physical reality, they occur only, but really and ontologically, in the interpersonal sphere of the human spirit.

The Greeks distinguished between four kinds of love: *storge,* the love we call affection; *eros,* the love we call desire; *philia,* the mutual love we call friendship; *agape,* the love we call unconditional or self-sacrificing love. Though all four are legitimately called love, the good that is striven for in each is distinct. *Eros* is love of another person for my good; *agape* is love of another person for the other's good; *philia* is mutual love of the mutual good of both persons. Because *philia* is mutual love, seeking the good of both persons, I suggest it is the best foundation for a stable marriage. That is what Wallerstein found in her study of the "good marriage." "My marriage depends on friendship," one man told her. "Sex you can have with anyone, I got married for companionship and respect and most of all for friendship."[27] A woman agreed. "Let me describe what makes our marriage work. We like each other. We have mutual respect. We trust each other." Love is important, she explained, but what gives love stability is "a basic sense of real trust, of really knowing where that other person is at and knowing that whatever they are going to do is going to be in your best interest as well as theirs."[28] In marriage, when the mutuality of *philia* prepares the foundation on which the one-sidedness of both *eros* and *agape* are raised, spouses achieve mutual well-being through a love that is always mutual *(philia),* always unconditional *(agape),* and always embodied *(eros).* When friendship is the foundation of a relationship, each person recognizes that the other's good is the only way to their common good and to each individual's good.

We continue our search for the meaning of love in a way that will appear strange but that will lead us surely to an important conclusion. Aquinas makes a distinction between knowing and loving. "Knowledge is of things as they exist in the knower; the will [love] is related to things as they exist in themselves."[29] To know means to receive into oneself; to love or to will good means to transcend oneself, to go out of oneself to another. Love, as every lover knows, is essentially *ec-static;* I go out of myself to another. To know someone is to know her within me; to love her is to love her as she is in her own uniqueness apart from me. In love, I go out of myself to another self like me. The importance of this discovery about love is already hinted at in Cicero's description of a friend as "a second self."[30] If there is ever to be a second self, however, there must be a first self. For me, that first self is me; for you, it is you. If I am ever to grasp and value and cherish you as a second self, I must first consciously grasp, value, and cherish me as a first self. This self is a richness, a powerful center of action, always present but mysterious, always experienced as capable of new revelations, never exhaustively understood. It is this first self I love when I love myself; it is a similar, but distinctively unique, self I love when I love you.

This realization of the self-based character of love leads us forward to a further discovery. "You shall love your neighbor as yourself," the gospel says (Matt 22:39). Just what we have been talking about, I hear you say. Not quite, I respond, at least not until the full story is told. Both Aristotle and Aquinas insist that love happens, not when I love another as myself but only when my love is reciprocated. "Friendship requires mutual love, because a friend is a friend to a friend."[31] Anyone who has ever loved another "from afar" knows that. Real love is never one-sided; there is no real love, until love is reciprocated by the beloved. This mutual love between two equal selves, between a distinct I and a distinct Thou, creates between them the intimate communion that is the distinguishing characteristic of lovers. A commentary on that communion will conclude this section.

Webster derives *communion* from the Latin *communis,* common, and defines it as common sharing, common possession, common ownership. We could add common responsibility and, in the matter that concerns us here, the communion between lovers, common creation and maintenance by love. A frequent problem comes into focus here. In the loving communion between an I and a Thou, in which each loves the other self, communion cannot mean fusion of the two selves, it cannot mean absorption of one of the lovers by the other. An element of otherness is central to the communion that arises from and is maintained by love. I love, not my self, though self-love is and has to be involved, but another self, "a unique and free initiative who in his uniqueness is turned towards me and . . . reveals somehow that hidden treasure which is himself."[32]

The communion between lovers has no obvious models in our world other than itself. It is certainly not a monarchy, which emphasizes unequal individuals. It is not even a democracy, which emphasizes equal but separate individuals. Without models, all I can say is that it is a communion, in which a unique I and a unique Thou become an organic, coupled-We, lovingly sharing in common their thoughts, their feelings, their dreams, their possessions, their bodies, their total selves. The well-known biblical aphorism about a husband and a wife becoming "one body" (Gen 2:24) creates a paradoxical problem here, because it is better known than understood. It is never to be interpreted as meaning that the persons in the communion that is love merge their selves into one or the other. Such submergence and loss of self-identity sometimes happens in relationships, but it happens always with the loss, not only of identity, but also of love and communion. Togetherness is to be created in a marriage; the spouses have to become one coupled-We. Admired, valued, and cherished otherness, however, is also integral to true love and marriage. It is that very coupled otherness, the marriage that is the communion between a distinct I and a distinct Thou, with all its negative, conflicted, and sad moments as well as its positive, peaceful, and happy moments, that is also the sacrament of the presence and love of God in Christ, under conditions which I will specify in Chapter 3.

Questions for Reflection

1. In general, what do you understand to be the meaning of the word "sacrament"? In particular, what do you understand to be the meaning of the Catholic teaching that the marriage between two Christian believers is a sacrament of the union between Christ and his Church?

2. How do you understand the relationship between marriage and the sacrament of marriage? What are the differences, if any, between the two?

3. How do you understand the definition of marriage as "the union of a man and a woman, and a communion of the whole of life"? Is such a definition, in your opinion, still valid in our world?

4. Do you believe it is possible today for love and marriage to last "till death do us part"? Under what conditions is it possible?

5. How do you define love? Does your definition agree in any way with the claim that love is a matter of the will, reaching out to the good in others and wishing them well?

Notes

[1] Augustine, *De bono conjugali (Bon. conj.)* 6.6, PL 40.377–8; *Bon. conj.* 10.11, PL 40.381; *De Conjugiis Adulterinis* 2.12, PL 40.479; *Contra Julianum (C. Jul.)* 2.7, PL 44.687.

[2] Peter Lombard, *Sententiae,* 4, d. 1, c. 4; 4, d. 2, c. 1.

[3] Albert the Great, *Commentarium in Libros Sententiarum,* d. 26, a. 14, q. 2 ad 1.

[4] Thomas Aquinas, *Commentarium in Quartum Librum Sententiarum,* d. 26, q. 2, a. 3.

[5] Thomas Aquinas, *Contra Gentiles* 4.78.

[6] DS 761.

[7] DS 860.

[8] DS 1310.

[9] DS 1327.

[10] Markus Barth, *Ephesians: Translation and Commentary on Chapters Four to Six,* The Anchor Bible (New York: Doubleday, 1974) 618.

[11] See William Moran, "The Ancient Near Eastern Background of the Love of God in Deuteronomy," *Catholic Biblical Quarterly* 25 (1963) 82.

[12] J. Paul Sampley, *"And the Two Shall Become One Flesh": A Study of Traditions in Ephesians 5:21–33* (Cambridge: Cambridge University Press, 1971) 30.

[13] See Michael G. Lawler, *Symbol and Sacrament: A Contemporary Sacramental Theology* (New York: Paulist Press, 1987) 29–34.

[14] *Justiniani Digesta* 35.1.15.

[15] Lisa S. Cahill, "Is Catholic Ethics Biblical?" Warren Lecture Series in Catholic Studies, No. 20 (University of Tulsa) 5–6.

[16] Barth, *Ephesians,* 618.

[17] LG 11. Se also Joann Heaney-Hunter, "Domestic Church: Guiding Beliefs and Daily Practice," *Christian Marriage and Family: Contemporary Theological and Pastoral Perspectives,* ed. Michael G. Lawler and William P. Roberts (Collegeville: The Liturgical Press, 1993) 59–78; William P. Roberts, "The Family as Domestic Church: Contemporary Implications," *Christian Marriage and Family: Contemporary Theological and Pastoral Perspectives,* ed. Michael G. Lawler and William P. Roberts (Collegeville: The Liturgical Press, 1993) 79–92.

[18] *The Rites* (New York: Pueblo, 1976) 544.

[19] See Michael G. Lawler and Gail S. Risch, "Covenant Generativity: Toward a Theology of Christian Family," *Horizons* 26 (1999) 7–11.

[20] Cited in J. Casey, "Actions and Consequences," *Morality and Moral Reasoning* (London: Methuen, 1971) 201.

[21] Richard Lovelace, "Song to Lucasta: Going to the Wars," *Seventeenth-Century Prose and Poetry,* ed. Robert P. Coffin (New York: Harcourt Brace, 1946) 193.

[22] See, however, Urban Navarrette, "Structura Juridica Matrimonii Secundum Concilium Vaticanum II," *Periodica* 56 (1967) 366. Navarrete argues that the Code of Canon Law is the first official document of the Roman Catholic

Church to so order hierarchically the ends of marriage. Whether that claim is true or not, it is clearly not the first hierarchical ordering of the ends in Western theological and legal history.

²³ See Bernhard Haring, *Commentary on the Documents of Vatican II* (New York: Herder, 1969) 5:234.

²⁴ ST I, q. 20, a. 1 ad 3.

²⁵ Margaret Farley, *Personal Commitments: Beginning, Keeping, Changing* (San Francisco: Harper & Row, 1986) 33.

²⁶ Ibid., 34.

²⁷ Judith S. Wallerstein and Sandra Blakeslee, *The Good Marriage: How and Why Love Lasts* (Boston: Houghton Mifflin, 1995) 156.

²⁸ Ibid., 169–70.

²⁹ ST I, q. 19, a. 3 ad 6. In his "Le désir du bonheur et l'existence de Dieu," *Revue des Sciences Philosophiques et Theologiques* XIII (1924) 163, M. Roland-Gosselin cites fifty similar citations spanning Aquinas' entire career.

³⁰ Cicero, *De amicitia (Amic.)* 6.22: "quid dulcius, quam habere, quicum omnia audias sic loqui, ut tecum?" and 7.23: "verum etiam amicum qui intuetur, tamquam exemplar aliquod intuetur sui."

³¹ Aristotle, *Nichomachean Ethics* 8.2; ST II-II, q. 23, a. 1 corp.

³² Robert O. Johann, *The Meaning of Love* (Westminster: Newman Press, 1955) 36.

2

Catholic Models of Marriage[1]

College textbooks today describe marriage as a trap, especially for women. It puts women at risk for violence, they say, and it is bad for their mental health.[2] One could be forgiven for concluding that marriage is going out of style and is being replaced by more attractive alternatives, but that would be a serious mistake. Every reputable study of the attitudes of young Americans demonstrates they expect to be married, and still have high hopes for a happy marriage. Unfortunately, given all they see around them, they also have a debilitating fear of their ability to achieve a stable marriage.[3]

Many things have changed in the contemporary world with respect to marriage. The cultural climate has changed: the feminist movement has led a majority of educated women to reject patriarchal marriage in which they are made legally dependent on a man. The economic climate has changed: women's entry into the career market has led to their economic independence and has changed their attitudes toward and their will to endure unhappy marriages. The legal climate has changed: no-fault divorce law has made it possible for the unsubstantiated whim of one partner to bring a marriage to an end. The religious and theological climate has changed: Catholics, who use divorce to escape from unhappy marriages as much as other Americans, are confused about the nature of marriage and what it might mean that marriage is a sacrament. In a recent study of the impact of marriage preparation, young Catholics complained that marriage preparation programs educated them relatively well in the psychological dimensions of marriage but less well in the religious and theological dimensions.[4] To make a real contribution to the resolution of the crisis in marriage the Catholic Church, indeed all the Christian churches, will have to better fulfill their specifically religious task of clarifying sacrament and covenant. Before anyone can prepare a couple for marriage, however, she or he must be clear on the theory of marriage they will promote. This is where a consideration of models of marriage becomes mandatory.

Models

The acceptance of the theoretical model is widespread, indeed obligatory, in science, which seeks the understanding of physical reality. A theoretical model is an imaginative construct, postulated by analogy with a familiar reality and used to construct a theory to correlate a set of observations.[5] Models are analogical, that is, they represent and enable us to understand selected aspects of reality and close us off to other, equally important aspects. The astronomer Arthur Eddington explains the analogical character of scientific models in a powerful parable. A scientist was studying deep-sea life using a net with a three-inch mesh. After bringing up repeated samples from the deep, he concluded there were no deep-sea fish less than three inches in length.[6] What this parable suggests may be put plainly like this: the method of fishing determines what we catch. The scientific method of asking the questions determines the answers it gets. Its picture of reality, therefore, is not complete. The common scientific way of stating this point is *all data are theory laden;* there is no theory-free, neutrally-objective observation. In fact, the process of observation itself may actually alter the perception of the object being observed. Since this is so, models and theories can never be taken as literal descriptions of reality, as naive realism assumes.

If models do not describe reality literally, what then is their use? They are heuristic devices, aids to discovery and learning. Though a model should never be taken literally, it should always be taken seriously as representing, however inadequately and selectively, particular aspects of reality for specific purposes. A model is realistic, but only up to a point. Beyond that point it is open-ended, a fluid source of insight, application, and even modification of existing theory. Models are neither literal pictures nor pure fictions; they are limited and inadequate ways of humanly, and creatively, imagining what is not observable. The validity of a model is established not by its longevity or accepted intelligibility, but by its ability to explain all the observations it seeks to explain. This latter point is very important in the discussion of models of marriage.

Models may be categorized as either scale models, which are explanatory, or analogue models, which are exploratory. Scale models, like the model airplane I have hanging in my office, synthesize what we already know or believe. Analogue models, like scientific models of the atom or religious models of God or marriage, lead us heuristically to new insights into what we do not yet fully understand. As already stated, models are always to be taken seriously as heuristic, educational tools, but they are never to be taken literally. I could never have a literal airplane hanging in my study, it is simply too big; nor could I ever have a definitive insight into God, for God is too big for the human intellect and its language to grasp definitively.

Models are as widely used in theology as in science. It could not be otherwise when human beings seek to understand the transcendent God and the things of God in this world.[7] Remember that models are neither literal pictures nor pure fictions; they are limited and inadequate ways of humanly imagining what is not observable, and that God is not observable has been, and continues to be, a central affirmation of the Catholic tradition. The Jewish tradition, from which Christianity springs, affirms the incomprehensible mystery of God in a pregnant conversation between God and Moses. "You cannot see my face," God tells Moses, "for no one shall see me and live" (Exod 33:20). The evangelist John, good Jew that he was, reaffirms God's transcendence: "No one has ever seen God" (John 1:18). The great Augustine, perhaps the most influential of all Catholic theologians, continues that tradition of unfathomable mystery. "If you have understood," he asserts, "then this is not God. If you were able to understand, then you understood something else instead of God. If you were able to understand even partially, then you have deceived yourself with your own thoughts."[8]

Thomas Aquinas stands firmly in that tradition of God's absolute transcendence and brings us to analogical models. For Aquinas all language about God is analogy. On the one hand, words used about God are not *univocal,* that is, they do not have the same meaning as when they are said of humans, for that would ignore the difference between God and God's creatures. On the other hand, neither are they *equivocal,* having no relation to their human meanings. Rather they are *analogical,* taking their human meanings as a starting point and at the same time insisting that, since these human meanings could never literally apply to God, these human meanings are only analogical images or metaphors of God and the things of God. Analogies, like all models, are to be taken seriously as creating rich images of God but never literally as picturing what God is.[9] If God is unfathomable mystery, known only in limited and inadequate analogical models, then God incarnate in sacrament, including in the sacrament of marriage, is known only in models. We can now turn to the models of marriage employed in the Catholic tradition.

Models of Marriage

Procreative Institution

One model of marriage dominated the Catholic tradition from the second to the twentieth century. That model imaged marriage as a *procreative institution,* a socioreligious, thoroughly stable structure of meaning in which a man and a woman become husband and wife in order to become mother and father; in order, that is, to procreate children. That model has its origin in the Genesis command to "be fruitful and multiply" (Gen 1:22), but it was greatly strengthened in the Christian churches' struggle to legitimate marriage as something good. At the opening of the second century, echoing the biblical "God saw everything that he had made, and indeed, it was very good" (Gen 1:31), Clement of Alexandria combated the Gnostics, who argued that sexuality and marriage were evil, by asserting that they were good because they were created by the good God. They are good, however, only when used for procreation and for no other purpose.[10] Lactantius agrees: "We have received the genital part of the body for no other purpose than the begetting of offspring, as the very name itself teaches."[11]

In his fourth-century debate with the Manichees, Augustine also presented marriage and sexuality as good because they were created by a good God.[12] Procreation is the primary purpose of both sexuality and marriage because "from this derives the propagation of the human race in which a living community is a great good."[13] Earlier in the same book, however, he had suggested another good of marriage, which

> does not seem to me to be good *only* because of the procreation of children, but also because of the natural companionship of the sexes. Otherwise, we could not speak of marriage in the case of old people, especially if they had either lost their children or had begotten none at all.[14]

This is a clear linking of marriage and sexual intercourse, not to procreation but to the relationship of the spouses. Consideration of this relationship in the twentieth century will yield a quite different model of marriage.

In the thirteenth century, Aquinas gave this priority of procreation its most reasoned theoretical argument. "Marriage has its principal end in the procreation and education of offspring." It has also "a secondary end in man alone, the sharing of tasks which are necessary in life, and from this point of view husband and wife owe each other faithfulness." There is a third end in believers, "the meaning of Christ and Church, and so a good of marriage is called sacrament." For Aquinas, then, marriage has three ends: a primary end, procreation; a secondary end, faithful love; and a tertiary end, sacrament. "The first end is found in marriage in so far as man is animal, the second in so far as he is man, the third in so far as he is believer."[15] This is a very tightly reasoned argument, as is customary in Aquinas, and its primary end–secondary end terminology dominated Catholic marriage manuals for the next seven hundred years. Remember, however, that the validity of a model is determined not by its intelligibility, the authority of its author, or its age, but by the fact that it explains all the observations it seeks to explain. Aquinas' authority cannot obscure the fact that his argument is a curious one, since the primary end of specifically *human* marriage is dictated by the human's generically *animal* nature. It was on that basis that his argument was challenged in the twentieth century. Before that challenge, however, it had been enshrined for the first time in an official Catholic document in the Code of Canon Law in 1917.[16] "The primary end of marriage is the procreation and nurture of children; its secondary end is mutual help and the remedying of concupiscence" (Can 1013.1).

The procreative institution is the result of a contract in which, according to the 1917 Code of Canon Law, "each party gives and accepts a perpetual and exclusive right over the body for acts which are of themselves suitable for the generation of children" (Can 1081.2). Notice that the procreative marital contract was about bodies and acts; the procreative institution was not about persons and their mutual love. Couples who hated one another could consent to the procreative institution as long as they exchanged legal rights to each other's bodies for the purpose of the procreation of children. The model of marriage as procreative institution was thrust into center stage in the 1960s in the great debate over artificial contraception. I cannot provide in this essay a detailed analysis of that debate, but neither can I pass over it in silence, for it is inextricably connected to my discussion of Catholic models of marriage.[17]

Norbert Rigali offers a useful category in which to consider that debate. He asks not what was the *outcome* of the debate in Pope Paul VI's controverted *Humanae Vitae,* that is well-known, but what was the *process* by which that outcome was reached.[18] That process can be quickly summarized. At the instigation of Cardinal Suenens, Archbishop of Malines, Belgium, whose ultimate intent was that an adequate document on Christian marriage be brought before the Second Vatican Council for debate, Pope John XXIII established a commission to study the issue of birth control. The commission was confirmed and enlarged by Pope Paul VI until it ultimately had seventy-one members, not all of whom attended its meetings or voted.[19] The final voting took place in two separate groups: the theologians on the commission voted 15-4 in favor of a change in the Catholic teaching on artificial contraception; the Bishops and Cardinals on the commission voted 9-2 in favor of a change. Both a majority report and a minority report were then submitted to Paul VI who, professing himself unconvinced by the arguments of the majority, and probably also sharing the concern of the minority report that the Church could not repudiate its long-standing teaching on contraception without undergoing a serious blow to its overall moral authority, approved the minority report in his encyclical letter *Humanae Vitae.*[20] The differential between the two groups is easily categorized.

The minority report, which became the controverted part of the encyclical, argued that "each and every marriage act *[quilibet matrimonii actus]* must remain open to the transmission of life."[21] The majority report argued that it is marriage itself *(matrimonium ipsum),* not "each and every marriage act," that is to be open to the transmission of life. It asserted that "human intervention in the process of the marriage act for reasons drawn from the end of marriage itself should not always be excluded, provided that the criteria of morality are always safeguarded."[22] The differential in the two positions was precisely the differential created by adherence to two different models of marriage, the minority report being based on the traditional procreative institution model, the majority report being based on the new interpersonal union model that emerged, as we shall see, from the council. The question of contraception had been preempted from council debate and reserved to the Pope and the commission he had set up to study it. It was exempted, therefore, from the discussion of the meaning and ends of marriage from which the interpersonal model of marriage emerged as an established Catholic model. Richard McCormick commented in 1968 that "the documents of the Papal Commission represent a rather full summary of two points of view. . . . The majority report, particularly the analysis of its rebuttal, strikes this reader as much the more satisfactory statement."[23] That judgment continues to be the judgment of the majority of Catholic theologians and the vast majority of Catholic couples, because they adhere to the same interpersonal model on which the majority report was based. Thirty-five years later, despite a concerted minority effort to make adherence to *Humanae Vitae* a test case of Catholicity, the debate between the procreative and interpersonal models perdures in the Church and is far from resolved.

Procreative Union

In December 1930, Pope Pius XI published *Casti Connubii*, an important encyclical on marriage, which initiated the expansion of the procreative model into a more personal model of conjugal love and intimacy. This document shows that procreative institution, in which procreation was everything, had begun to give way to procreative union, in which procreation remained an important facet of marriage but did not encompass all that marriage is. Predictably, Pius insisted that procreation was the primary end of marriage. Unpredictably, he insisted also on the importance of the mutual love and marital life of the spouses.

This mutual love, proved as always by loving deeds, has "as its primary purpose that husband and wife help each other day by day in forming and perfecting themselves in the interior life . . . and above all that they may grow in true love toward God and their neighbor." So important is the mutual love and life of the spouses, Pius argued, that "it can, in a very real sense, be said to be the chief reason and purpose of marriage, if marriage be looked at not in the restricted sense as instituted for the proper conception and educating of the child but more widely as the blending of life as a whole and the mutual interchange and sharing thereof."[24] If we do not focus in a limited way on procreation, Pius taught, but broaden the scope of the model to embrace also the marital love and life of the spouses, then that love and life is the primary reason for marriage. With this teaching, Pius provided a transitional procreative union model of marriage which, after thirty-five years of growing pains, blossomed into an entirely new and unheard of model of marriage, a model of interpersonal union.

Interpersonal Union

Pius XI suggested there is more to marriage than the biologically-rooted, act-focused procreative institution model can explain. He suggested a personal procreative-union model, a suggestion which was taken up by European thinkers, most influentially two Germans, Dietrich Von Hildebrand and Heribert Doms. In the opening paragraph of his work *Marriage,* Von Hildebrand highlights the problem with the procreative model. The modern age, he suggests (and remember he is talking of Europe in the 1930s, still reeling from the horrors of World War I), is guilty of anti-personalism, "a progressive blindness toward the nature and dignity of the spiritual person." This anti-personalism expresses itself in various forms of materialism, the most dangerous of which is biological materialism, which considers humans only more highly developed animals. "Human life is considered exclusively from a biological point of view and biological principles are the measure by which all human activities are judged."[25]

The procreative institution model of marriage, with its insistent emphasis on bodies and their biological functions, is wide open to the charge of biological materialism. It ignores the higher, personal, and spiritual characteristics of the human animal. So, too, is the centuries-old Stoic-cum-Christian doctrine that argues from physical structure to human "nature" and "natural" ends. So, too, is Aquinas' position which founds the primary end of human marriage in the physical animality of men and women. To correct this biological, materialistic approach, Von Hildebrand offers a new model of marriage, claiming support from *Casti Connubii* for his central thesis that marriage is for the building up of loving communion between the spouses. Conjugal love, he argues, is the primary meaning and end of marriage.

In marriage, spouses enter an interpersonal relationship in which they confront one another as "I" and "Thou" and initiate a mysterious fusion of their very beings. This fusion of their personal beings, and not merely the physical fusion of their bodies, is what the oft-quoted "one body" of Genesis 2:24 intends.[26] It is this interpersonal fusion which the bodily fusion of sexual intercourse both signifies and causes, and intercourse achieves its primary end when it actually does signify and cause interpersonal union. "Every marriage in which conjugal love is thus realized bears spiritual fruit, becomes *fruitful*—even though there are no children."[27] The parentage of such thought in modern personalist philosophy is as clear as the parentage of the traditional biological-natural thought in Greek Stoic philosophy. More important, however, and more clear, is the resonance of an interpersonal description of marriage and lovemaking with the lived experience of married couples.

Doms agreed with Von Hildebrand that what is natural or unnatural for human animals is not to be decided exclusively on the basis of what is natural or unnatural for nonhuman animals. Humans are specifically spiritual animals, vitalized by a human soul, and their sexuality is not to be judged, as the Stoics and Aquinas judged it, on the exclusive basis of animal biology. Human sexuality is essentially the capacity and the drive to fuse, not only one's body, but also and primarily one's very self with another human being. Sexuality drives a man and a woman to make a gift of himself and herself (not just of his or her body) to another person, to create a communion of persons which complements and fulfills the lives of both. In this perspective marital intercourse, which should never be reduced to only genital intercourse, is an interpersonal activity in which a woman gives herself to a man and a man gives himself to a woman, and in which each accepts the gift of the other, to both signify and create interpersonal communion.

The primary end of sexual intercourse, then, is the marital union between the spouses, and this primary end is achieved in every act of intercourse in and through which the spouses actually enter into intimate communion. Even in childless marriages, which are becoming increasingly common today, marriage and sexual intercourse achieve their primary end in the marital union of the spouses, their two-in-oneness, in Doms' language. "The immediate purpose of marriage is the realization of its meaning, the conjugal two-in-oneness. . . . This two-in-oneness of husband and wife is a living reality, and the immediate object of the marriage ceremony and their legal union." The union and love of the spouses tends naturally to the creation of a new person, their child, who fulfills both parents individually and as a two-in-oneness. "Society is more interested in the child than in the natural fulfillment of the parents, and it is this which gives the child primacy among the natural results of marriage."[28]

The Catholic Church's reaction to these new ideas was, as so often in theological history, a blanket condemnation, which made no effort to sift truth from error. In 1944, the Holy Office (now the Congregation for the Doctrine of the Faith) condemned "the opinion of some more recent authors, who either deny that the primary end of marriage is the generation and nurture of children, or teach that the secondary ends are not essentially subordinate to the primary end, but are equally primary and independent."[29] In 1951, after yet another world war of even greater horror, as the ideas of Von Hildebrand and Doms persisted and gained more adherents, Pius XII felt obliged to intervene again. He taught:

> Marriage, as a natural institution in virtue of the will of the creator, does
> not have as a primary and intimate end the personal perfection of the

spouses, but the procreation and nurture of new life. The other ends, in as much as they are intended by nature, are not on the same level as the primary end, and still less are they superior to it, but they are essentially subordinate to it.[30]

The terms of the question could not have been made more precise. Twenty-three years later, the Second Vatican Council would reject the model in which this papal argument is based.

Though the council did not deal in detail with marriage and the sacrament of marriage, its Constitution on the Church in the Modern World did provide material intimately related to our present discussion. Marriage, it taught, is a "communion of love . . . an intimate partnership of life and love" (nn. 47–8). In spite of insistent demands from a small minority to repeat the centuries-old tradition of marriage as procreative institution, thus consigning spousal love to its traditional secondary place, the council declared the mutual love of the spouses and their passionate desire to be best friends for life to be of the very essence of marriage. It underscored its preference for an interpersonal-union model by making another important change in the received tradition. When faced with demands to describe the consent that initiates marriage in the traditional way as legal contract, the council demurred and chose to describe it as interpersonal covenant. Marriage is founded in "a conjugal covenant of irrevocable personal consent" (n. 48). Though in truth "contract" and "covenant" share many of the same meanings, the biblical word "covenant" is saturated with overtones of mutual personal and steadfast love, characteristics which are now applied to marriage. The description of the object of the marital covenant places the interpersonal character of marriage beyond doubt. The spouses, the council teaches, "mutually *gift and accept one another*" (n. 48);[31] the focus on animal bodies and acts is replaced by a focus on persons. In their marital covenant, spouses create not a procreative institution, but a loving interpersonal union which, since genuine love is steadfast, is to last as long as life lasts.

The council devotes an entire section to the love which founds marriage and sacrament. It interprets the Song of Songs as a canticle to human, genital rather than to divine, mystical love, the reading which had long been prudishly traditional in Jewish and Christian hermeneutics.[32] This marital love is "eminently human," "involves the good of the whole person," and is "steadfastly true." It is singularly expressed and perfected in genital intercourse, which signifies and promotes "that mutual self-giving by which the spouses enrich one another" (n. 49). Marriage and the marital love of the spouses are still said to be "ordained for the procreation of children" (n. 48), but that "does not make the other ends of marriage of less account," and marriage "is not instituted solely for procreation" (n. 50).[33] The intense and well-documented debate which took place in the council makes it impossible to claim that the refusal to sustain the received marital tradition was the result of an oversight. It was the result of deliberate and hotly deliberated choice, a choice replicated and given canonical formulation twenty years later in the revised Code of Canon Law in 1983.

Marriage "is ordered to the well-being of the spouses and to the procreation and upbringing of children" (Can 1055.1), with no suggestion that either end is superior to the other. It is "brought into being by the lawfully manifested consent of persons who are legally capable" (Can 1057.1), and that consent "is an act of the will by which a man and a woman by irrevocable covenant mutually give and accept *one another* for the purpose of establishing a marriage" (Can 1057.2). The Catholic Church revised its laws about marriage in the twentieth century to bring its laws about marriage into line with its developing theology of marriage, moving beyond the model of marriage as exclusively procreative institution to embrace a model of interpersonal union which includes the mutual love and communion of the spouses.

Conclusion

In the contemporary Catholic Church, then, two major models are available for marriage: procreative institution, in which procreation is the exclusive focus, and interpersonal union, in which the mutual love of the spouses and their marital life together are as important as procreation. Compared to the centuries-old model of procreative institution, the model of interpersonal union is still in its infancy and struggling to establish itself in repressive official circles. Remember, however, that the intelligibility or longevity of a model is no guarantee of its validity, which is dependent on its ability to explain all the observations that need explanation. In the contemporary approach to marriage, among the observations to be explained are the relationship of the spouses, the interaction that follows from their relationship, and the birth of a child which sometimes follows from their genital interaction. The contemporary Catholic Church has officially chosen a model of interpersonal union as the best model for explaining all these observations.

Does it make any difference which model of marriage one promotes or follows? Yes, it makes a great difference, especially to one's attitudes and actions, for a major characteristic of models is that they evoke attitudes and actions consonant with the model. It is, perhaps, in its call to new attitudes and new action that a new theological model makes its greatest difference. The attitude and action required by the procreative model is obvious, and abundantly evidenced throughout Catholic history, namely, the procreation of children. The sign of a good Catholic marriage and family in the not too distant past, therefore, was how many children a couple had. The relationship of the spouses/parents was very much secondary. Indeed, as I have pointed out, in the terms of the 1917 Code of Canon Law, a man and a woman who hated one another could marry for the sake of procreation.

The action required by the interpersonal union model is quite different: the procreation and nurturing of the relationship between the spouses, a relationship that is mutually loving, faithful, self-sacrificing, just, compassionate, forgiving, and peaceful. In a marriage, the time to procreate children is when the spousal relationship is sound and the climate, therefore, right for the procreation of children and their positive nurture into functioning adults. The difference the interpersonal union model of marriage makes is that it places the procreation of the relationship of the spouses, their marital life and love, on an equal footing with procreation of children.[34] In the language of the received tradition, the mutual marital life and love of the spouses is an equal end of marriage with procreation, a theological and canonical fact magisterially acknowledged by the Second Vatican Council and the new Code of Canon Law.

The birth of a child is an awesome event in a marriage and also an awesome responsibility, for genuine procreation requires not only biological maternity, paternity, and the generation of a child, but also long-term, nurturing motherhood, fatherhood, and the generation of a functioning adult. The overwhelming evidence provided by social-scientific research today is that two parents, a loving mother and a loving father whose own relationship is loving and stable, are far better for the development of a child than either two parents whose own relationship is unloving and unstable or one parent who, despite heroic efforts, simply cannot by herself or himself provide the benefits two parents can provide.[35]

Though there is no evidence that the theological shift to an interpersonal-union model of marriage was influenced in any way by the social sciences, it is thoroughly congruent with both the contemporary social-scientific evidence and the practical implications of that evidence. Theology, however, brings its own insight to the question of marriage and offers its own solution to the contemporary crisis of marriage. That solution highlights the fact that the happiness and stability of a marriage and family, with all the benefits that a happy and stable household brings to genuine procreation, is a function of the happiness and stability of the relationship between the spouses. There is no doubt that the birth of children may contribute greatly to the happiness and the stability of the relationship between their parents, but research evidence shows that often it does not.[36] Besides, those parents who do successfully progress beyond maternity and paternity to motherhood and fatherhood can look forward to some thirty years together after their children have left them. That empty-nest period will be happy and stable only if the relationship between the spouses has been and is loving and faithful.

In a recent study by the Center for Marriage and Family at Creighton University on the first five years of marriage, the most problematic challenge reported by the newly married in general was finding time to balance marriage and job, and the most problematic challenge listed specifically by parents was finding time to balance spousal and parental relationships.[37] The model of marriage as interpersonal union acknowledges the reality of these problems in a marital life, and asserts that it is good that spouses spend time focusing on their mutual relationship, for the happiness and stability of that relationship determines the happiness and stability of their marriage and, therefore, ultimately, the happiness and stability of their family. The model asserts that the interpersonal union of the spouses, with its mutual love, fidelity, self-sacrifice, justice, compassion, forgiveness, and peace, is far and away the best climate for the procreation of functioning adults. It asserts, finally, that a marriage lived as a steadfastly loving interpersonal union is not a trap for the unwary, male or female, but a grace-full way to God, an opportunity to raise in the contemporary world a model, a light, a veritable sacrament, of the steadfastly loving union between God and God's people and between Christ and Christ's Church.

Questions for Reflection

1. What do you understand by the concepts "model," "scale model," "analogue model"? Can you isolate any theoretical models which control or guide your own life?

2. What real difference does a model make in a person's life? Do you believe it is true that a model controls your attitudes and actions?

3. Reflect on the procreative model of marriage and the attitudes and actions it requires. How do you react to this model?

4. Reflect on the interpersonal union model and the attitudes and actions it requires. How do you react to this model?

5. What advice would you offer to the Church as it seeks a model of marriage for the twenty-first century?

Notes

¹ A précis of this essay was published in *America* (March 19, 2001).

² See Institute for American Values, *Closed Hearts, Closed Minds: The Text-book Story of Marriage* (New York: Institute for American Values, 1997); also Institute for American Values, *The Course of True Love: Marriage in High School Textbooks* (New York: Institute for American Values, 1998).

³ See, for instance, Judith S. Wallerstein, Julia M. Lewis, and Sandra Blakeslee, *The Unexpected Legacy of Divorce: A 25 Year Landmark Study* (New York: Hyperion, 2000).

⁴ Center for Marriage and Family, *Marriage Preparation in the Catholic Church: Getting It Right* (Omaha: Creighton University, 1995).

⁵ Ian G. Barbour, *Myths, Models, and Paradigms: A Comparative Study in Science and Religion* (New York: Harper & Row, 1974), 30; also Ian G. Barbour, *Religion in an Age of Science* (San Francisco: Harper & Row, 1990) 41.

⁶ Arthur Eddington, *The Nature of the Physical World* (Cambridge: Cambridge University Press, 1928) 16.

⁷ Perhaps the most influential discussion of theological models is Avery Dulles, *Models of the Church* (Garden City, N.Y.: Doubleday, 1974). See also Bernard J. F. Lonergan, *Method in Theology* (New York: Herder and Herder, 1972) 281–94; Paul Minear, *Images of the Church in the New Testament* (Philadelphia: Westminster Press, 1960); Kevin Irwin, "Models of the Eucharist," *Origins* (May 31, 2001) 33–44.

⁸ Augustine, *Sermo 52*, PL 38.360.

⁹ See Aquinas, ST I, q. 3. For a comprehensive treatment of analogy see David Tracy, *The Analogical Imagination: Christian Theology and the Culture of Pluralism* (New York: Crossroad, 1981); and William Hill, *Knowing the Unknown God* (New York: Philosophical Library, 1971).

¹⁰ Clement of Alexandra, *Stromata (Strom.)* 2.23, PG 8.1086 and 1090. See also *Paedagogus (Paed.)* 2.10, PG 8.498.

¹¹ *Divinarum institutionum (Inst.)* 6.23, PL 6.718.

¹² Augustine, *De nuptiis et concupiscentia ad Valerium comitem (Nupt.)* 2.32.54, PL 44.468–9; also *De bono conjugali (Bon. conj.), passim.*, PL 40.394.

¹³ *Bon. conj.* 9.9, PL 40.380.

¹⁴ *Bon. conj.* 9.9, PL 40.375, emphasis added.

¹⁵ ST III (Suppl.), q. 65, a. 1, c.

¹⁶ See Urban Navarette, "Structura Juridica Matrimonii Secundum Concilium Vaticanum II," *Periodica* 56 (1967) 366.

¹⁷ Those who are interested in that debate and its arguments can profitably begin in Charles E. Curran and Robert E. Hunt, *Dissent in and for the Church: Theologians and* Humanae Vitae (New York: Sheed and Ward, 1969); and Germain Grisez, John C. Ford, Joseph Boyle, John Finnis, and William E. May, *The Teaching of* Humanae Vitae: *A Defense* (San Francisco: Ignatius Press, 1988).

[18] Norbert J. Rigali, "On the *Humanae Vitae* Process Ethics of Teaching Morality," *Louvain Studies* 23 (1998) 3–21.

[19] Clifford Longley, *The Worlock Archive* (London and New York: Chapman, 2000) 232.

[20] For detail on this, see Janet E. Smith, Humanae Vitae: *A Generation Later* (Washington, D.C.: Catholic University of America Press, 1991) 11–33.

[21] *Humanae Vitae* 11 (Washington, D.C.: National Conference of Catholic Bishops).

[22] Cited in Longley, *The Worlock Archive*, 233, emphasis added.

[23] Richard McCormick, *Notes on Moral Theology 1965–1980* (Lanham, Md.: University Press of America, 1981) 164.

[24] AAS 22 (1930) 548–9.

[25] Dietrich Von Hildebrand, *Marriage* (London: Longmans, 1939) v.

[26] See the explanation of this claim in Chapter 1, p. 14.

[27] Von Hildebrand, *Marriage*, 25, emphasis in original.

[28] Heribert Doms, *The Meaning of Marriage* (London: Sheed and Ward, 1939) 94–5.

[29] AAS 36 (1944) 103.

[30] AAS 43 (1951) 848–9.

[31] Emphasis added.

[32] See Marcia Falk, *Love Lyrics from the Bible: A Translation and Literary Study of the Song of Songs* (Sheffield: Almond Press, 1982); Helmut Gollwitzer, *Song of Love: A Biblical Understanding of Sex* (Philadelphia: Fortress Press, 1979).

[33] Emphasis added.

[34] See my extended analysis of the full meaning of fruitfulness in Christian marriage in Chapter 9, pp. 205–9.

[35] See, for example, Sara S. McLanahan and Gary Sandefur, *Growing Up with a Single Parent: What Hurts, What Helps* (Cambridge, Mass.: Harvard University Press, 1994); Paul R. Amato and Alan Booth, *A Generation at Risk: Growing Up in an Era of Family Upheaval* (Cambridge, Mass.: Harvard University Press, 1997); Wallerstein et al., *The Unexpected Legacy of Divorce;* Linda J. Waite and Maggie Gallagher, *The Case for Marriage: Why Married People Are Happier, Healthier, and Better Off Financially* (New York: Doubleday, 2000).

[36] See, for example, Jay Belsky, "Children and Marriage," *The Psychology of Marriage,* ed. F. D. Fincham and T. N. Bradbury (New York: Guilford Press, 1990) 172–200; Linda J. Waite and Lee A. Lillard, "Children and Marital Disruption," *American Journal of Sociology* 96 (1991) 930–53; Center for Marriage and Family, *Time, Sex, and Money: The First Five Years of Marriage* (Omaha: Creighton University, 2000) 22–23.

[37] Center for Marriage and Family, *Time, Sex, and Money.*

3

Faith and Sacrament in Christian Marriage[1]

The opening chapter argued that the equal and loving marriage between two believing Christians is also a sacrament of the love of God and of Christ. This chapter asks a more specific question: Under what condition(s) is marriage transformed into sacrament? I will develop the answer to that question in four theses to be explicated: (1) Christian faith is a comprehensive "yes" to God revealing Godself as the person's savior in Christ; (2) faith is necessary for salvation and for both the validity and fruitfulness of a sacrament, including the sacrament of Christian marriage; (3) faith is necessary for right sacramental intention, again including the sacrament of Christian marriage; (4) marital contract and marital sacrament are not separable in marriages between baptized believers; they are separable in marriages between baptized nonbelievers who can, therefore, enter into valid civil marriages.

Though these questions have troubled the Roman Catholic Church for the past two centuries, they have not as yet received genuine *theological* solutions. In the nineteenth century, political skirmishing between the Church and emerging European states cast both the questions and their solutions in terms which were political and juridical, but which have posed ever since as theological. In the early twentieth century, though their identity was far from theologically traditional, the 1917 Code of Canon Law decreed identity between marital contract and marital sacrament in *matrimonium inter baptizatos,* marriage between baptized persons. This juridical action put an abrupt end to the theological discussion which was, and continues to be, needed to generate theological solutions to theological questions. Ladislas Orsy concluded an essay in 1982 with this statement: "About the doctrine and law of Christian marriage, we ought to think afresh."[2] Susan Wood, in an essay in 1987, invited "criticism and refinement of the theological principles involved."[3] This chapter accepts both Orsy's challenge to think afresh and Wood's invitation to be positively critical.

I agree with Orsy that theology has a firm answer to the foundational question on which all others in this matter rest, the question of the necessity of personal faith for salvation. That answer, in Trent's solemn declaration, is that without faith "it is impossible to please God and to be counted as his sons."[4] This answer is long traditional in Catholic doctrine, and it applies in sacraments, even in the sacrament of marriage. Law, including canon law, is not theology. Law likes things clear and, if they are not clear, it likes to make them clear in juridical norms. Law, therefore, will have difficulty dealing with the theological fact of Christian faith, or Christian love, the presence or absence of which is impossible to make clear beyond doubt. I disagree, therefore, with Wood when she states that "the fact that the new Code [1983] has been promulgated undoubtedly changes the tenor of the present theological discussion of the issue."[5] The publication of the Code has no decisive bearing on the theological facts, for the theological fact of personal faith is always the result of active faith, never of juridical norm. Orsy's comment is more apposite. When theological and legal facts do not accord, "custom may prove itself again as the best interpreter of the law."[6]

Faith

The reality of faith is central in this study, and therefore I must clarify its meaning from the outset. We may start, as one may frequently start in Catholic theology, with Thomas Aquinas. For Thomas, faith is "an act of the intellect assenting to divine truth at the command of the will moved by the grace of God, so that it is subject to free choice in relation of God."[7] Faith is essentially an act of the intellect "assenting to divine truth," but it is not an act of the intellect alone. The will also is involved, and therefore the act of faith is a free act. Thomas explains that "although elements pertaining to the will can be considered accidental to the acts of the intellect, they are however essential to faith."[8] Since the will is involved in faith, so also is love. "Love is called the form of faith, in so far as the act of faith is perfected and formed by love."[9]

This is the kind of faith that the Council of Trent later taught to be necessary for salvation: "We may be said to be justified through faith, in the sense that 'faith is the beginning of man's salvation'. . . without which it is impossible to please God (Hebrews 11:6) and to be counted as his sons."[10] Faith is not only *fides fiducialis*, trusting in God, as Luther implied, but includes also an assent to some truths[11] and, as James taught, "faith by itself, if it has no works, is dead" (Jas 2:17).[12] Though Trent offers no concise definition of faith, its characteristics are clear. It is a free act, embracing more than just intellectual assent to truths, and it is necessary for salvation. That teaching will be continued in both Vatican Councils I and II.

The First Vatican Council (1870) repeated what had become traditional Catholic doctrine: faith, which is "a supernatural virtue by which, under God's inspiration and grace, we believe to be true what he has revealed," is "the beginning of human salvation."[13] It emphasized more than Trent that faith is more than intellectual assent, it is an act "by which a man gives free obedience to God by cooperating and agreeing with his grace, which can be resisted."[14] The Second Vatican Council (1962–65) moved even further away from an overly intellectualist conception of faith, teaching that the obedience of faith is an act "by which man entrusts his whole self freely to God, offering 'the full submission of intellect and will to God who reveals,' and freely assenting to the truth revealed by him."[15] Faith is not only intellectual but is more especially personal.

A characterization of Christian faith, then, is not difficult to provide. I borrow a summary from Juan Alfaro.

> [Faith] includes knowledge of a saving event, confidence in the word of God, man's humble submission and personal self-surrender to God, fellowship in life with Christ, and a desire for perfect union with him beyond the grave. Faith is man's comprehensive "Yes" to God's revealing himself as man's savior in Christ.[16]

Wood might argue that these are "maximalist terms."[17] I respond, on the contrary, that they are minimalist. The faith that is obedience and self-surrender to God, the traditional *fides qua creditur*, the act of faith by which one believes, is a free, and at least a minimally conscious and explicit, act. It is in this sense that the term "faith" will be used throughout this chapter.

Faith and Sacrament

The answer to the theological and canonical questions dealt with in this chapter depend on the answer to one foundational question: Is the personal faith of the sacramental participant[18] necessary for salvation? The answer to that general question will contribute to the answer to a more specific question: Is the personal faith of a participant necessary not just for the fruitfulness, but also for the validity of the sacrament? It will contribute an answer, therefore, to an even more specific question: Is the personal faith of the participants, that is, the marrying couple, necessary for the validity of the sacrament of marriage? The theological answer to the foundational question is, beyond any doubt, yes. The theological answer to the other two is equally yes. It is not enough, of course, simply to record these answers; they must also be explicated theologically. I shall explicate each in turn.

Faith and Salvation

One cannot read the New Testament without being impressed by its emphasis on the necessity of faith for salvation. The Gospels record that Jesus complained about the absence of faith and as insistently praised its presence (Matt 8:5-13, 23-27; 9:2, 20-22; 17:19-21; 21:18-22; Mark 5:25-34; 6:1-6). Paul vehemently defended the necessity of personal faith for salvation (Rom 1:16-17; 3:26-30; 5:1; Gal 3:6-9). The tradition of the necessity of faith continued in the Church and flowered on both sides of the Reformation controversies.

Martin Luther made his stand on "faith alone" *(sola fides)*. The Council of Trent, though wishing to combat the Lutheran teaching that faith alone was necessary for salvation, still left no doubt about the necessity of personal faith: "We may be said to be justified through faith, in the sense that 'faith is the beginning of man's salvation,' the foundation and source of all justification, 'without which it is impossible to please God' (Hebrews 11:6) and to be counted as his sons."[19] The same teaching is repeated in the important chapter on justification, where baptism is described as "the sacrament of faith, without which no man has ever been justified."[20] The Latin text leaves no doubt that the phrase "without which" *(sine qua)* qualifies faith and not sacrament or baptism, both of which would require *sine quo*.[21] There is not the slightest doubt that the Fathers of Trent wished to affirm the primacy of active, personal faith for salvation.

The firm Tridentine position notwithstanding, the polemical context of the times created an uneasiness in Roman Catholic assertions about faith and its place in the process of salvation. Following Trent's lead of isolating, in order to condemn, the error in the assertions of the Reformers, Counter-Reformation theologians advanced their theologies as counterpoint to those of the Reformation. Nowhere did this theological minimalism cause more detriment than in the understanding of the role of personal faith in the sacraments. That detriment crystallized in a restricted notion of the Scholastic expression *opus operatum*.[22]

Faith of the Participant and Sacrament

In the years immediately preceding the convocations at Trent, nominalism was rampant in the theological disciplines. Nominalist theologians taught that the only thing a person receiving *(sic)* a sacrament need do was to place no obstacle to grace. This meant that one needed only to be free from mortal sin; grace was then conferred by the mere physical doing of the rite, which was called *opus operatum*. It was just such a mechanical understanding of *opus operatum* that provided the basis for the objections of the Reformers about automatic grace and led to their rejection of the very notion of *opus operatum*.

However, since nominalist theologians constituted a majority at Trent, it was the nominalist definition that became "*the* exhaustive definition of the *opus operatum* of the efficacy of any sacrament."[23] The complementary Scholastic concept of *opus operantis*, the disposition of the participant, was developed as something separate. One could first receive sacramental grace by receiving a sacrament free from grave sin and with the right intention. Then, *ex opere operantis*, one could receive other graces. Such a dichotomy of *opus operatum* and *opus operantis* was foreign to the thinking of the great Scholastics, of whom Aquinas can again serve as exemplar. Thomas frequently used the concept *opus operatum* in his early Commentary on the Sentences but never in his final work, the *Summa Theologiae*. This fact may be taken as indication that he did not consider the term necessary to the presentation of a mature sacramental theology. Indeed, "the truth that this terminology was intended to bring out was presented satisfactorily, and even in finer detail, in his Christological appreciation of the sacraments."[24]

The Christological character of a sacrament as the work of God in Christ is the fundamental doctrine underlying Thomas' understanding of *opus operatum*. On this fundamental basis rest all other ways of using the phrase. Baptism, for instance, "justifies *ex opere operato*: this is not man's work but God's." Baptism has effect not because of the merits of the person being baptized, "but because of the merits of Christ." It is efficacious "because of the passion of Christ."[25] *Opus operatum* relates sacramental validity to the passion of Christ. It is not the external rite that effects grace, at least not as principal cause,[26] but the sacred reality that is signified by the external rite, namely, the gracious and salvific action of God in Christ.

Opus operatum contrasts the constitution of a sacrament *qua* external sign in the Church and the subjective disposition of either the minister or the recipient. Because of the action of God in Christ embodied in it, a sacrament is constituted as valid sign without any contribution from the recipient, without any *opus operantis.* It is not, however, constituted as an efficacious sign, that is, as a sign which actually mediates grace, without *opus operantis.* Since a sacrament is not just any sign of grace but specifically an efficacious sign, if it is not constituted as efficacious sign, then it is not constituted as sacrament.[27] For the great Scholastics, *opus operatum* and *opus operantis* were not dichotomized as they were to be in the Counter-Reformation church. They were essentially related. The latter was regarded as the "personal aspect in the justifying process of any sacrament, that aspect by which a free and responsible person accepted God's grace" offered in the efficacy of the former.[28]

It is true that Thomas distinguishes two separate effects of sacraments. There is, first, the *perceptio sacramenti,* the reception of a valid sacrament, which he teaches is quite unrelated to the faith of the participant. There is, second, the *perceptio rei sacramenti,* the fruitful reception of sacramental grace.[29] This doctrine on the validity of a sacrament without any contribution on the part of the participant, however, needs to be understood in its own context and not in that of a later, juridically-controlled theology.

Thomas' distinction between *perceptio sacramenti* and *perceptio rei sacramenti* rests on a view of sacrament as a thing. That thing owes its validity to the fact that it is an *opus Dei et Christi* and, therefore, valid *qua* thing-sign irrespective of any contribution from the recipient. But, though he subscribes to this established view, Thomas also has no doubt about "the abnormal and, in the end, monstrous character of this hypothesis. Every sacrament for him remains a sign and a proclamation of personal faith. Whoever receives it without believing in his heart places himself in a violent state of 'fiction' and deprives himself of sacramental grace."[30] Albert the Great is more explicit, stating baldly that the sacrament of marriage derives its efficacy not only *ex opere operato* but also *ex opere operantis.*[31] Bonaventure echoes this opinion, teaching that the sacrament of marriage can be distinguished only by a modicum of personal faith.[32]

Contemporary sacramental theology approaches a sacrament not as a thing which believers receive, but as a graced interaction in and through which they express both their acceptance of the gift of God and the gift of themselves in return through Christ in the Spirit to the Father. Considered in the abstract, a sacrament may be located only within the category of efficacious sign. If that is all there is to a sacrament, then it is constituted as valid without any contribution on the part of the participant. But that is not all there is.

A sacrament in the concrete, one in which a real human person participates, requires a third category, that of participating subject. There is no concrete possibility of a concrete efficacious sign without a human subject for whom it is a real, efficacious sign. There is, specifically, no concrete possibility of sacramental signification without a human subject who participates in a symbolic action and relates this action with the Church to God in Christ.[33] The sacramental sign in baptism, for instance, is not just physical water. It is water poured on a human subject within a matrix of meanings that includes God in Christ, Christ in the Church, and human subject in the Church and in Christ. A sacrament does not happen when a human subject submits to a physical rite, for a sacrament is not a naked physical rite but a symbolic interaction.

A tradition in the Church, established in the controversy between Augustine and Pelagius and verified regularly ever since, is that men and women are free persons and are graced not against their will, but according to their cooperation *(cooperatio).*[34] If they have no intention of personally participating in a sacrament, then no mere physical submission to a physical rite will submit them to a saving sacrament. In such a case, though I have no doubt that a sacramental *opus operatum* is objectively offered by God in Christ in the Church, I equally have no doubt that a subject fails to participate in it. The sacrament offered still signifies the saving action of God in Christ in the Church, but not as concretely significative, and therefore effective and sacramental, for this subject. The subject's *opus operantis* is required in order to transform the *opus operatum* into an efficacious sign of the action of God in Christ. It is required, in other words, to transform *opus operantis* into valid sacrament.[35]

It is for the validity of sacramental signification that the faith of the participant is required. One "must signify acceptance of what the church offers. Otherwise the sacrament is not a concrete, practical sign of the divine will to save all men."[36] Since the Catholic tradition of the past millennium teaches that sacraments cause by signifying, when they do not signify neither do they cause; and when they do not cause, they are not valid sacraments. It is not just that they are valid but fruitless sacraments.

They are fruitless precisely because, for this individual, they are not efficacious signs and, therefore, not valid sacraments. The participant's *opus operantis* is required to make a sacrament fruitful because it is first of all required to make a sacrament a concrete and valid sign.[37]

Personal faith, therefore, enters into the essence of valid sacramentality as the necessary personal complement in the signification and conferral of grace. Men and women are graced and saved according to the nature the creator gifted to them, in the Catholic tradition a free nature. They cannot be graced coercively or automatically, for that would violate their nature.[38] A sacrament is a sign not only of the gracing action of God in Christ *(opus operatum)*, but also of the free faith of the participant cooperating with grace in this ritual *(opus operantis)*. A valid sacrament requires the conjunction of both the action of God and the faith of the participant, and only in such conjunction is there free, and therefore valid and fruitful, interaction between them. As Aquinas taught long ago, the passion of Christ "achieves its effect in those to whom it is applied through faith and love and the sacraments of faith."[39]

In an analysis of remarkable depth, Louis Villette argues that "rooted in the scriptures and the teaching of the Fathers, systematized in various ways in the Scholastic period, defined . . . by the Council of Trent, defended and explicated by the post-Tridentine theologians,"[40] there is a doctrinal constant in the Roman Catholic position vis-à-vis personal faith and sacrament. That constant is the complementary affirmation of the efficacy of sacraments instituted by Christ and the absolute necessity of personal faith for this efficacy to impact on a concrete subject. Up to the Council of Trent, Catholic theologians affirm unanimously that sacraments are efficacious "by" faith, "in" faith, "in proportion to" faith. After Trent, they insist that "faith alone" did not justify, but faith in and through sacraments. This was not, however, to deny the necessity of faith but to deny only that faith alone was necessary. When the Second Vatican Council taught that sacraments "not only presuppose faith but by words and objects they also nourish, strengthen and express it,"[41] it was merely summarizing a long-established Catholic tradition.

Faith and the Sacrament of Marriage

If the argument of the preceding sections is valid, then the assertion of this section is already demonstrated. The active faith of the participants is an essential prerequisite not just for the fruitfulness of a sacrament but also for its very validity. That the Code of Canon Law's assertion, "a valid marriage contract cannot exist between baptized persons without its being by that very fact a sacrament" (Can 1055.2), is at odds with this theological assertion is of no decisive theological import. As I stated at the outset, law likes clarity and likes to create clarity where there is none. Today, the faith-situation of baptized persons is anything but clear, and the Church and its theologians acknowledge two kinds of baptized: believers and nonbelievers.[42] The two are distinguished theologically on the basis of the presence or absence of active personal faith. They ought never, therefore, to be equated in law as easily as the Code equates them.

In any given case, of course, the active faith or nonfaith of a baptized person will not be easy to ascertain. No amount of legal presumption, however, will supply for the lack of active faith and consequent lack of sacramentality. Convinced of the necessity of faith for valid baptism, Augustine sought to make good the evident lack of faith in infant baptism by arguing that *ecclesia fidem supplet* (the Church makes good the faith required).[43] That argument cannot be applied in the case of marriage, for in marriage we are dealing with adults who are required to have an active faith to participate in any sacrament, baptism as well as marriage, a point made clear by the scrutinies at the baptism of adults. Marriage becomes a sacrament not because of some juridical effect of baptism, but because of the active faith of the couple. Those who marry without active Christian faith, be they ever so baptized, marry also without Christian sacrament. Elaboration and demonstration of that assertion follows from a brief consideration of the adjective "Christian."

An extraordinary statement by Wood may serve as introduction and counterpoint to this consideration. "A marriage entered into with an intention to indissolubility, fidelity, and openness to children comprises a sacramental marriage for the baptized person. . . . The religious marriage is valid when the prevailing will is to marry, even if the couple would wish to exclude the sacrament."[44] Surely not. Surely a valid Christian sacrament, something more than a "religious marriage," must have some explicit reference to that *more*. And surely that *more* embraces explicit reference to Jesus, who is actively confessed as the Christ, and to that community of people called Church, which is actively confessed as the Body of Christ in the world. In 1980 the Synod of Bishops considered the question of the relationship of faith and sacrament in marriage and gave quasi-unanimous support (201 *placet*, 3 *non placet*) to this proposition: "We have to take into account the engaged couple's degree of faith maturity and their awareness of doing what the church does.

This intention is required for sacramental validity. It is absent if there is not at least a minimal intention of believing with the church." The *more* involved in sacramental marriage relates to Church, and therefore to Christ and to God. A sacrament is essentially a Christ-event.

The intention to participate in any sacrament is the intention to participate in a Christ-event. The intention to participate in a Christian marriage is the intention to participate in a sacramental marriage explicitly acknowledged as a Christ-event. In Jean Marie Tillard's judgment, "the request for a sacrament can never be the request for a purely external ritual that has no connection with the mystery of salvation. The request for a sacrament is a request for a 'rite that gives salvation.'"[45] The covenant of Christian marriage becomes sacramental, Martelet argues, "only if the future spouses freely consent to enter into married life by passing through Christ into whom they were incorporated in baptism."[46]

The Second Vatican Council had specific theological statements to make about Christian marriage, statements repeated more or less faithfully in the new Code of Canon Law. "The intimate partnership of married life and love . . . is rooted in the conjugal covenant of irrevocable personal consent." It is "a reflection of the loving covenant uniting Christ with the church," and is "a participation in that covenant."[47] If it does nothing else,[48] the word *covenant* returns the conception of Christian marriage to its roots in the Christian Scriptures.

The Christian tradition reveres three covenants. There is, first, the steadfastly loving covenant of the Old Law, uniting YHWH and YHWH's people. There is, second, the steadfastly loving covenant of the New Law, uniting Christ and Christ's Church. There is, third, the steadfastly loving covenant of Christian marriage, uniting a Christian man and woman in an intimate partnership of life and love. The third covenant is rooted in the other two. It is rooted not only in the love of the spouses for one another but also in their love for Christ and Christ's love for them. It is this rootedness that moves the Catholic traditions to speak of Christian marriage as the symbol or sacrament of the loving union between Christ and the Church.[49]

The key that opens the door to such covenantal and sacramental meanings is not just the intention of the spouses to marry, their intention to "fidelity, indissolubility, and openness to children," but rather their intention informed by their Christian faith to be rooted in, to represent, and to pass their marriage through Christ and his Church. Consent may make marriage as a secular institution, but it is only Christian faith, a comprehensive personal "yes" to Christian and salvific realities, that makes it also a sacrament. Ratzinger puts the theological and magisterial position beyond doubt. "Faith belongs to the essence of sacrament. It remains to clarify the juridical question: what level of non-faith would mean that a sacrament has not been effected?"[50]

It is not the naked intention to marry, even to marry in some religious rite, that makes valid Christian sacrament. It is the Christian faith-informed intention to marry in a ritual that publicly proclaims to the spouses, to the Church, and to the world not only "I love you," but also "I love you in Christ and in his Church." That active and faith-informed proclamation creates not only a marriage but specifically a Christian marriage. It is time to consider the intention that undergirds that proclamation.

Faith and Intention

Great stress is laid in sacramental theology on sacramental intention. Wood articulates the classic principle: "To intend to receive a sacrament, it is sufficient to intend by that action what the church intends by its sacrament."[51] This short but integral section asks about the relationship between the intention traditionally required for the valid reception of sacrament and personal Christian faith. Put simply, the question is this: Can a person have a real intention to participate in a sacrament without at least minimal personal faith?

Aquinas suggests an answer: "Faith directs intention, and without [faith] intention cannot be right" *(fides intentionem dirigit, et sine ea non potest esse . . . intentio recta).*[52] The phrase provokes a question: Is the distinction between real intention and faith as clear-cut as the distinction between theoretical intention and faith? The International Theological Commission offers an answer: though intention and personal faith are not to be confused, they are not to be totally separated either. "The real intention," they teach, "is born from and feeds on living faith."[53] One cannot have a right sacramental intention without a minimum of personal faith.

A reprise of the preceding section will substantiate this judgment. The intention necessary to participate in a sacrament is the intention to participate in a rite that gives salvation, a God-in-Christ and Christ-in-the-Church event. None of this, God-in-Christ or Christ-in-Church, can be intended without being at least minimally known and embraced in personal faith. The right intention to participate in a sacrament, therefore, requires a minimum of personal faith. When personal faith is absent, so too is right sacramental intention; and when right intention is absent, then, as the tradition universally holds, the sacrament is not valid, but null.

Denis O'Callaghan underscores that "addressing the question of the sacramentality of the marriage of the nonbelieving baptized couple along the line of the absence of intention rather than that of the absence of faith keeps us within the parameters of what is a very firmly based *theological* tradition."[54] The theological judgment—no personal faith, no right intention—is a well-founded judgment. The conclusion that flows from it is equally well founded: without faith no one can enter into a valid sacramental marriage. Though the canonical judgment is at variance with this theological conclusion continuing to cling to the claim that "a valid marriage contract cannot exist between baptized persons without its being by that very fact a sacrament" (Can 1055.2), "custom may prove itself again as the best interpreter of the law."[55]

In reality, of course, there is no theological debate about whether faith is necessary or not for sacramental validity. It is taken as a given that it is. The real debate is over what qualifies as faith. Wood, for instance, agrees that faith is necessary both for the validity of a sacrament in general and for the validity of the sacrament of Christian marriage specifically. She judges, however, that faith cannot be reduced to "an explicit and conscious act of faith," and that a person "can possess the habit of faith . . . most especially through baptism."[56] This baptismal habit seals the new Christian evermore as "believer." Wood's judgment, I suggest, and that of Canon 1055 too, rests on a classic Scholastic distinction which opens the word "faith" *(fides)* to serious ambiguity and, therefore, misunderstanding.

In the tradition derived from Scholasticism, faith refers either analogically to the power of faith *(virtus fidei)* or univocally to the explicit act of faith *(actus fidei)*. A virtue is a quality[57] ordered to an act,[58] a power to act. A virtue is a necessary prerequisite to the corresponding act, but it is not the act nor does the act ineluctably follow from the virtue. The Catholic tradition holds that it is the virtue of faith that is bestowed in baptism.[59] For that virtue to become a personal act of faith, it must be activated freely, explicitly, however minimally. In a mature person, Orsy comments, "the infused virtue must blossom out in a personal act."[60] It is that personal act of faith, however minimal, and always under the grace of God,[61] that transforms the human being from one who can be a believer into one who is a believer. It is in that act of faith, and not just in the virtue of faith, that one cooperates with God-in-

Christ and Christ-in-Church to transform secular realities, including marriage, into Christian sacraments. It is that act of faith that is required for right sacramental intention.

Relationship of Contract and Sacrament

If baptized nonbelievers cannot enter into a valid sacramental marriage, can they marry at all? Can they enter, at least, into a valid civil marriage? That question, on the answer to which *dissentiunt doctores,*[62] asks about the relationship between the contract of marriage and the sacrament of marriage. If the two are not separable, as the Code claims, then if baptized nonbelievers cannot enter into a valid sacrament of marriage, neither can they enter into a valid contract of marriage. In plain language, they cannot marry validly at all. If, on the other hand, the two are separable, then baptized nonbelievers who cannot enter into the sacrament of marriage because they lack active faith can, at least, enter into a valid civil marriage. Since that second opinion appears to be excluded by present jurisprudence, our analysis of the question must begin in the Code of Canon Law.

The 1917 Code asserts that "Christ the Lord raised the matrimonial contract between baptized persons to the dignity of a sacrament" (Can 1012.1). The theological accuracy of that statement is doubtful. Though institution by Christ of marriage as a sacrament is retained today in Catholic theology, and explained sacramentally,[63] no Catholic theologian argues that it was specifically the contract of marriage that he established as sacrament. Though the Latin Church committed itself in the twelfth century to the conception of marriage as contract, the Orthodox Church has never considered the canonical contract to be of the essence of marriage, preferring the liturgical and priestly blessing symbolized in the crowning of the bride and groom. It is simply wrong, theologically, in the Catholic traditions, to claim without qualification that Christ raised the contract of marriage to the dignity of a sacrament.

Canon 1012.2, repeated verbatim in new Canon 1055.2, lies at the heart of the present question. "Consequently *(quare),* a valid marriage contract cannot exist between baptized persons without its being by that very fact a sacrament." The particle *quare* is of central interest here. It implies consequence from the previous statement and it is, therefore, translated correctly as "consequently." Here too there is a problem.

Canon 1012.1 proclaims that every sacramental marriage is rooted in a valid marriage contract. But does it proclaim also the reverse? Does it teach that every valid matrimonial contract is thereby a sacrament? I think not. I can sympathize with the canonical codifiers in their hesitation "to introduce sponginess into that firm canonical structure which locked the sacrament on to the solid juridical and readily proven fact of baptism."[64] But does what they assert canonically really assert that all that is required for a valid sacrament of marriage is valid baptism? I think not.

Among the Fontes for Canon 1012.2, the 1917 codifier, Pietro Gasparri, includes the Council of Trent's formal teaching: "If anyone says that *marriage* is not one of the seven sacraments . . . let him be anathema."[65] But note the different language in Trent and in the Code, the former asserting that *marriage* is a sacrament, the latter that the *marriage contract between baptized persons* is a sacrament. The two are vastly different assertions.

In a careful analysis of the notions of contract and sacrament at the Council of Trent, Duval points out what is, in fact, well known. It was by deliberate choice, not by some oversight, that the council chose simply the word *marriage* and not something like the marriage contract between baptized persons. It did so to leave open a theological debate in which, as later, experts held different opinions. "Canon 1 of the Council wishes to affirm the existence in the New Law of *a* sacrament of marriage—but not that marriage in the New Law is always a sacrament."[66] To say "that the Council of Trent declared the inseparability of sacrament and contract seems to weigh the texts with a burden they are incapable of bearing logically or historically."[67] Far from declaring, even implicitly, the inseparability of contract and sacrament, Trent deliberately chose to leave the question open.

So, too, did the Theological Commission for the First Vatican Council, swayed by the Roman theologian Giantommaso Tosa. The commission judged that the inseparability of contract and sacrament was not a doctrine that could be defined because neither was it contained in the sources of revelation nor did it flow inescapably from any truth that was in the sources.[68] It is unfortunate that Garibaldi's invasion of the Papal States prevented that judgment from being debated in the council and from being incorporated into the authentic teaching of Vatican I.

Gasparri's expansion of Trent from *marriage* to *marriage contract between baptized persons* may not be considered an explanation, and even less an authentic explanation, of Trent's doctrine. Indeed, the great codifier himself judged in 1891 that "marriage among Christians is a sign of a sacred thing in Christ and in the church, and to it grace is joined, but it is not proved that force of producing grace is placed in the matrimonial contract itself."[69] If we wonder what caused Gasparri to change his mind between 1891 and 1917, the Fontes may provide a clue.

The Fontes for Canon 1012.2 are well known, and need not be rehearsed again here.[70] There is a hermeneutical need, however, to seek to understand them in their context. I suggest that, when the Fontes refer to the "contract," they refer not so much to the contract between the spouses as to the marriage which results from it. The nineteenth-century Fontes particularly assert the identity of "contract," that is, marriage, and sacrament to assert the legitimate power of the Church over "marriage among Christians" more than to assert the identity of legal contract and sacrament. An 1817 instruction from the Holy Office states this conclusion baldly: "There can be a contract of marriage which may not be a sacrament; nevertheless, there cannot be a sacrament of marriage in which the contract itself is not a sacrament."

In *La Lettera* to Victor Emmanuel II in 1852, Pius IX made the clear assertion that "the conjugal union [i.e., marriage] *among Christians* is not legitimate if it is not in the sacrament of marriage."[71] That same year in *Acerbissimum,* he taught that "there cannot be a marriage *among the faithful* without its being at one and the same time a sacrament."[72] In 1864 in the *Syllabus,* he condemned the following as false: "By the force of merely civil contract [i.e., civil marriage] there can exist *among Christians* a true marriage."[73] Finally, in 1875 *Tuae Litterae* condemned Belgian civil law as repugnant to Catholic doctrine because it taught "that the civil contract [i.e., civil marriage] can be separated from the sacrament *among the faithful.*"[74]

Leo XIII's contribution to the Fontes is his encyclical letter *Arcanum Divinae Sapientiae* (1880), in which he follows the path marked out by Pius. In Christian marriage, as opposed to civil marriage, "the contract [i.e., the marriage] is not able to be dissociated from the sacrament; a true and legitimate contract, therefore, cannot be without being by that very fact a sacrament," and "every legitimate union *among Christians* is in itself and through itself a sacrament."[75] "If any union [i.e., marriage] of a man and a woman *among the faithful of Christ* is contracted outside the sacrament, it lacks the force and the principle of a legitimate marriage."[76] Christian marriage is contrasted with civil marriage, and Leo asserts that in every marriage "among Christians" contract and sacrament are inseparable. No more than Trent does he assert that in every marriage *inter baptizatos* the marital contract and the marital sacrament are identical.

The care in formulation and the clarity of the assertions cannot be reduced to a mere matter of words. In Christian marriage, that is, marriage *inter Christifideles,* marriage between Christians of faith, marriage and sacrament cannot be separated. No statement whatever is made about marriage *inter baptizatos,* and Gasparri's expansion of the papal terms in the Code cannot be considered as an authentic interpretation of their much more meaningful words. The Code's teaching in the matter of *matrimonium inter baptizatos* cannot, therefore, be claimed as traditional. It illegitimately closes the theological debate which was, and continues to be, open.

Theologians do not doubt, even today, that sacrament and marriage *inter Christifideles* are identical. Their doubt focuses on marriage *inter infideles,* including *infideles baptizatos.* They judge that *Christifideles* implies "an attitude of vital, no matter how minimal, congress with the community of believers," and that baptism, therefore, "without any faith-commitment, is inadequate as the basis for the sacramentality of marriage."[77]

I do not find convincing Nowak's claim that "it does not appear that there is present here [in the Fontes] any real distinction between the word 'baptized' and the word 'Christian,'" especially when it is sustained only by a truncated citation of Canon 87 of the 1917 Code.[78] Canon 87 states not only that "through baptism man is constituted a person in the church," as Nowak suggests, but also that man is constituted a person "with all the rights and duties of Christians unless, as far as rights go, there is an obstacle in the way of the bond of ecclesiastical communion." Though the Church is prone to emphasize duties more than rights, a thesis of this essay has been that, in adults, the absence of active faith is a major obstacle to the bond of ecclesial communion and that, therefore, baptized nonbelievers have no right to be equated with Christian believers. Palmer's judgment is much more to the point: "We never refer to apostates, atheists, agnostics, free-thinkers, or non-believers as 'faithful.'"[79]

I am, however, in full agreement with Nowak when he judges that, if there is any difference "in faith-content of the two words, it would seem to enter into the question of intentionality."[80] I have already specified in the preceding section how faith enters into right intention, and how the absence of faith is an obstacle to right intention. Where there is no active faith, there is no Christian *fidelis* and no right sacramental intention, and where there is no sacramental intention, there is no sacrament, no matter how physically baptized a person may appear to be. Baptism and the life it initiates are not juridical realities to be passively mandated; they are theological and sacramental realities to be actively celebrated.

If, then, in the marriage of baptized nonbelievers, there is no sacramental marriage, is there any marriage at all? Is it possible for baptized persons to enter into a valid marriage which is nonsacramental? I agree with Orsy: "There is no other answer than 'Yes, it is.'" But I would reverse the reasons he gives for the answer: "(1) baptism does not take away the human capacity and right to marry, and (2) if there is no faith, there cannot be a sacrament."[81]

Conclusion

A first, obvious set of conclusions from this study parallels the questions which initiated it. Active Christian faith, "man's comprehensive 'Yes' to God revealing himself as man's savior in Christ," is necessary, in general, for salvation and, in particular, for the validity of sacraments, including specifically the sacrament of Christian marriage. Without active faith, a man and a woman, no matter how physically baptized, cannot cooperatively participate with God in Christ to co-create a valid sacramental marriage.

A second conclusion relates to and sustains the first. It is that new Canon 1055.2, "a valid marriage contract cannot exist between baptized persons without its being by that very fact a sacrament," is traditional only since the 1917 Code of Canon Law. In 1563, the Council of Trent taught clearly that marriage is one of the seven sacraments, but it left open the question on which *doctores dissentiunt.* It affirmed "the existence in the New Law of a sacrament of marriage—but not that marriage in the New Law is always a sacrament."[82] In 1817, the Holy Office taught explicitly that "there can be a contract of marriage which may not be a sacrament." In 1870, the Theological Commission for the First Vatican Council judged that the inseparability of marital contract and marital sacrament could not be defined. In 1880, in *Arcanum Divinae Sapientiae,* Leo XIII continued along the line laid down by Trent and the Holy Office. In the sacrament of Christian marriage, the marriage *inter Christifideles,* "the contract is not able to be dissociated from the sacrament," and therefore "every legitimate union among Christians is in itself and through itself a sacrament."[83]

The point here is *theological,* and it is this. Prior to the 1917 Code, the relationship of marital contract and marital sacrament was an open theological question. No ecclesiastical document, including the Fontes cited by Gasparri for 1012.2, had ever sought to close it. But canon 1012 effectively closed it by promulgating a juridical norm. That closure stunted the ongoing theological discussion which, at the very least, would have yielded more mature theological data with which to untie the Gordian knot of theological questions. Part of the argument of this essay has been that the juridical closure of the discussion was premature and illegitimate in 1917, continues to be illegitimate in 2002, and that therefore the discussion should be regarded as still theologically open so that the theological facts involved can be examined and fully resolved.

I adduce two signs that the discussion is still open. The first is a proposition from the 1980 Synod of Bishops, which was approved 195 to 6, with 5 abstaining:

> We must investigate further if this statement applies to those who have lost the faith: "A valid marriage between baptized persons is always a sacrament" . . . . We must investigate the pastoral criteria for discerning the couple's faith and the relationship between the intention of doing what the church does and the minimal intention of believing with the church.

The second sign is in *Familiaris Consortio,* Pope John Paul II's response to the synod. In the section in which he deals with "the moral and spiritual dispositions of those being married," he acknowledges that "the faith of the person asking the church for marriage can exist in different degrees." He decrees, nevertheless, that when "engaged couples show that they reject explicitly and formally what the church intends to do when the marriage of baptized persons is celebrated," they are not to be admitted to the sacrament.[84] Most interestingly, though the way was then open to him both to ask whether the civil marriage of these baptized nonbelievers was a valid marriage and to reply that it was not, because "a valid marriage contract cannot exist between baptized persons without its being by that very fact a sacrament," he did not do so.

I acknowledge the force of the axiom *ex silentio nihil probatur.* I find it difficult to accept, however, that the Pope's passing over in silence the new Canon 1505.2, approved if not yet promulgated, was simply an oversight. Rather, I find it an unexpected sign that the marriage of baptized nonbelievers is regarded as possibly valid and that the theological discussion peremptorily ended by the Code in 1917 is, in response to the demand of the Synod, quietly reopened. This essay has sought to be a theological contribution to that discussion at a critical time for marriages between the baptized.

A third and final conclusion relates to the vexed question of the indissolubility of marriage. Anyone familiar with the jurisprudential practice of the Catholic Church knows that the only marriage that it holds to be absolutely indissoluble is the sacramental, consummated marriage (Can 1141). The nonconsummated marriage may be, and frequently is, dissolved "for a just reason" (Can 1142), and the nonsacramental marriage may be, and frequently is, dissolved "in favor of the faith" (Can 1143). If the marriages of nonbelievers, including baptized nonbelievers, are nonsacramental, as I have argued, then they are also dissoluble according to the norms of Canon 1143. That conclusion is evident and needs no further elaboration. It justifies my opening claim that the questions considered here have practical pastoral consequences.

Questions for Reflection

1. What do you understand by the word *faith*? Do you think it is different from the common phrase *the faith*? If it is, how is it different?

2. What do the Christian churches mean when they teach that faith is necessary for salvation? And what do they mean when they teach that the faith of the participant is necessary to make a sacrament fruitful?

3. If faith is necessary for salvation, what dispositions of the couple are necessary to transform the social reality of marriage into the religious reality of sacramental marriage? Have you any suggestions about how to judge levels of faith or non-faith?

4. What do you understand by the term *baptized nonbeliever*? In your opinion, can a baptized nonbeliever ever receive a sacrament? If yes, why? If no, why not?

5. If two baptized, nonbelieving Catholics cannot be sacramentally married, can they still be validly married. If yes, why? If no, why not?

Notes

[1] This essay was originally published in TS 52 (1991) 712–31. It is reprinted here with permission.

[2] Ladislas Orsy, "Faith, Sacrament, Contract, and Christian Marriage: Disputed Questions," TS 43 (1982) 398.

[3] Susan Wood, "The Marriage of Baptized Non-Believers: Faith, Contract and Sacrament," TS 48 (1987) 280. The essays of Orsy and Wood do not exhaust the writing on the subject(s) of this essay. I shall mention here only collections in which the reader will be exposed to both sides of the question: *Foi et sacrement de mariage* (Paris: Chalet, 1974); Walter Cuenin, *The Marriage of Baptized Non-Believers* (Rome: Gregorian University, 1977); Thomas P. Doyle, ed., *Marriage Studies: Reflections on Canon Law and Society,* vols. 2–3 (Washington, D.C.: Canon Law Society of America, 1982 and 1985); Richard Malone and John R. Connery, eds., *Contemporary Perspectives on Christian Marriage* (Chicago: Loyola University Press, 1984); John B. Sequeira, *Tout mariage entre baptisés est-il nécessairement sacramentel?* (Paris: Cerf, 1985); Theodore Mackin, *The Marital Sacrament* (Mahwah, N.J.: Paulist Press, 1989).

[4] DS, see 1529.

[5] Wood, "The Marriage," 283.

[6] Orsy, "Faith, Sacrament," 387.

[7] ST II-II, q. 2, a. 9, c.

[8] Thomas Aquinas, *De Veritate,* q. 14, a. 3, ad 10.

[9] ST II-II, q. 4, a. 3, c.

[10] DS 1532.

[11] DS 1534.

[12] DS 1531 and 1569.

[13] DS 3008.

[14] DS 3010.

[15] DV 5.

[16] "Faith," *Sacramentum Mundi: An Encyclopedia of Theology* (New York: Herder, 1968) 2.315.

[17] Wood, "The Marriage," 282.

[18] Since, in modern sacramental theology, a sacrament is not a thing which one can receive, but a symbolic interaction between God and humans in which one can participate, I choose the personal word *participant* and refuse the objective *recipient.* See Michael G. Lawler, *Symbol and Sacrament: A Contemporary Sacramental Theology* (New York: Paulist Press, 1987).

[19] DS 1532.

[20] DS 1529.

[21] "Huius iustificationis causae sunt . . . instrumentalis item sacramentum baptismi, quod est 'sacramentum fidei' sine qua nulli umquam contigit iustificatio."

[22] It is not without significance that, when Leo XIII enthroned Scholasticism as the official Roman Catholic way to do theology, it was not the Scholasticism of the sixteenth century that he selected but that of the thirteenth.

[23] Piet Fransen, "Sacraments, Signs of Faith," *Readings in Sacramental Theology,* ed. C. Stephen Sullivan (Englewood Cliffs, N.J.: Prentice Hall, 1964) 62, emphasis in original.

[24] Edward Schillebeeckx, *Christ the Sacrament of Encounter with God* (New York: Sheed and Ward, 1966) 83.

[25] Thomas Aquinas, *In IV Sent.,* d. 15, q. 1, a. 3, sol. 3 ad 2; ibid., d. 6, q. 1, a. 3, sol. 2; ibid., d. 4, q. 3, a. 3, qc. 4, obj. 1.

[26] Cf. ST III, q. 62, a. 1.

[27] See Lawler, *Symbol and Sacrament,* 29–36.

[28] Fransen, "Sacraments, Signs of Faith," 63.

[29] *In IV Sent.,* d. 6, q. 1, a. 3, sol. 1; cp. ST III, q. 68, a. 8.

[30] Louis Villette, *Foi et sacrement: De Saint Thomas a Karl Barth* (Paris: Bloud et Gay, 1964) 40.

[31] ". . . in illo est actus personalis et moralis et civilis . . . et non trahit vim ab opere operato tantum sed etiam ab opere operantis," *In IV Sent.,* d. 26, a. 14, q. 1.

[32] "Sunt et alia [sacramenta], quae quodam modo ab instinctu naturae sunt, ut matrimonium in quo est maris et feminae coniunctio . . . partim etiam sunt a fide, scilicet quod illa coniunctio significet coniunctionem dei cum anima," *In IV Sent.,* d. 26, a. 2, q. 1, conclusio.

[33] See Lawler, *Symbol and Sacrament,* 5–28.

[34] Cf. DS 373–97.

[35] Cf. Colman O'Neill, "The Role of the Recipient and Sacramental Signification," *The Thomist* 21 (1958) 257–301, 508–40.

[36] Ibid., 275–6, emphasis in original.

[37] Obvious difficulties with such an approach arise in the baptism of infants. But the baptism of adults, not the baptism of infants, is the paradigm for sacramental baptism. For one solution to such difficulties see ibid., 276–96.

[38] See ST I-II, q. 113, a. 3 and 4.

[39] ST III, q. 49, a. 3 ad 1.

[40] Villette, *Foi et sacrement,* 2.367.

[41] SC 59.

[42] See the paper of the International Theological Commission, "Propositions on the Doctrine of Christian Marriage," 2.3, *Contemporary Perspectives on Christian Marriage,* ed. Richard Malone and John R. Connery (Chicago: Loyola University Press, 1984) 15, 19–21.

[43] See Augustine, *Epistola 98,* 5, PL 33.362. See also ST III, q. 68, a. 9; International Commission for English in the Liturgy, "Baptism for Children," *The Rites of the Catholic Church* (New York: Pueblo, 1976) 188; Jean Charles Didier, *Faut-il baptiser les enfants?* (Paris: Cerf, 1967) *passim.*

[44] Wood, "The Marriage," 300.

[45] "Sacramental Questions: The Intentions of Minister and Recipient," *Concilium* 31 (1967) 130.

[46] G. Martelet, "Sixteen Christological Theses on the Sacrament of Marriage," *Contemporary Perspectives on Christian Marriage,* ed. Malone and Connery, 279.

[47] GS 48.

[48] See Ladislas Orsy, "Christian Marriage: Doctrine and Law," *Jurist* 40 (1980) 282–348; also Orsy, "Faith, Sacrament," 387, n. 9.

[49] See Michael G. Lawler, *Secular Marriage, Christian Sacrament* (Mystic, Conn.: Twenty-Third Publications, 1985) 5–21, 61–72.

[50] Joseph Cardinal Ratzinger, "A propos de la pastorale des divorcés remariés," *La Documentation Catholique* (April 4, 1999) 325.

[51] Wood, "The Marriage," 292.

[52] *In IV Sent.,* d. 6, q. 1, a. 3 ad 5.

[53] "Propositions on the Doctrine of Christian Marriage," 2.3, *Contemporary Perspectives on Christian Marriage,* ed. Malone and Connery, 15.

[54] Denis O'Callaghan, "Faith and the Sacrament of Marriage," *Irish Theological Quarterly* 52 (1986) 172–3, emphasis added.

[55] Orsy, "Faith, Sacrament," 387.

[56] Wood, "The Marriage," 294.

[57] ST I-II, q. 49, a. 1.

[58] ST I-II, q. 49, a. 3.

[59] ST III, q. 69, a. 4.

[60] Orsy, "Faith, Sacrament," 383, n. 7.

[61] Cf. DS 373–97.

[62] Giuseppe Ferrante, *Elementa Juris Canonici* (Rome: Olivieri, 1880) 86.

[63] See, e.g., Lawler, *Symbol and Sacrament,* 48–51.

[64] O'Callaghan, "Faith and the Sacrament of Marriage," 165.

[65] DS 1801, emphasis added.

[66] A. Duval, "Contrat et sacrement de mariage au Concile de Trente," *La Maison Dieu* 127 (1976) 50, emphasis in original. See also Edward Schillebeeckx: "It is therefore historically incorrect to link the later theory [of the inseparability of contract and sacrament] . . . in any way with the Council of Trent" (*Marriage: Human Reality and Saving Mystery* [New York: Sheed and Ward, 1965] 362–3). See also Sequeira, *Tout mariage entre baptisés est-il nécessairement sacramentel?*

[67] James A. Nowak, "Inseparability of Sacrament and Contract in Marriages of the Baptized," *Studia Canonica* 12 (1978) 329.

[68] Eugenio Corecco, "Il sacerdote ministro del matrimonio," *La Scuola Cattolica* 98 (1970) 450.

[69] Pietro Gasparri, *Tractatus Canonicus de Matrimonio* 1 (Paris: Institut Catholique, 1891) 130, n. 2.

[70] See, for instance, Nowak, "Inseparability of Sacrament and Contract," 315–63.

71 *Acta Pii IX* (Rome: Bonarum Artium, n.d.), 2.1.296, emphasis added.

72 *Acta Pii IX,* 1.1.393, emphasis added.

73 DS 2973, emphasis added.

74 *Acta Pii IX,* 7.145, emphasis added.

75 *Acta Leonis XIII* (Rome: Typographia Vaticana, 1882) 2.25–6, emphasis added.

76 Ibid., 37, emphasis added.

77 Raymond C. Finn, "Faith and the Sacrament of Marriage: General Conclusions from an Historical Survey," *Marriage Studies: Reflections in Canon Law and Theology,* vol. 3, ed. Thomas P. Doyle (Washington, D.C.: Canon Law Society of America, 1985) 104–5.

78 Nowak, "Inseparability of Sacrament and Contract," 360.

79 Paul F. Palmer, "Christian Marriage: Contract or Covenant," TS 33 (1972) 642.

80 Nowak, "Inseparability of Sacrament and Contract," 360.

81 Orsy, "Faith and Sacrament," 390.

82 Duval, "Contrat et sacrement de mariage," 50.

83 *Acta Leonis XIII,* 2.25–6.

84 FC 68.

4

On the Bonds in Marriage[1]

I am a married Roman Catholic theologian. When I was married many years ago in the Catholic tradition, I accepted without demur several things as part of the ecclesial world taken for granted. I accepted that marriage is, first, a contract (Can 1012.1); second, a sacrament (Can 1012.2); third, indissoluble (Can 1013.2). In the preceding chapter I sought to clarify the relationship between contract and sacrament in marriage. In this chapter, I seek to clarify the bonds arising from them.

My analysis can be summarized in six theses to be explicated: (1) the bond arising from marriage is a relationship and an obligation between the spouses; (2) the bond arising from marriage relates and obligates the spouses to an intimate consortium for the whole of life; (3) the root bond between spouses is the bond, relationship, and obligation arising from their mutual love; (4) in a marriage between baptized believers, besides the bond arising from love, there are also bonds arising from marriage and sacrament; (5) the Catholic Church regularly dissolves the bonds arising from marriage and sacrament, but never when the marriage has been consummated; (6) the consummation or perfection of a marriage is achieved not in a first act of sexual intercourse, but only when the mutual love of the spouses is consummated or perfected in marital *consortium.*

I continue to accept, with the Church, the definition of marriage found in Justinian's *Digesta* (23.2.1): "marriage is a union of a man and a woman and a communion of the whole of life." I accept that because love, of its very nature, seeks to relate a man and a woman for the whole of life and because covenant, by its very nature, creates a relationship and obligation in which I am honor bound for the whole of life to keep my word.

The doctrine of the Church concerning the indissolubility of marriage, traditional as I will show only since the twelfth century, is that "a ratified and consummated marriage cannot be dissolved by any human power nor by any cause other than death" (Can 1141). That doctrine is problematic theologically, for it makes something outside sacrament, namely, physical consummation, the cause of a sacramental marriage's indissolubility. The problem has been exacerbated, as I again will show, by the revised Code's requiring that consummation be *humano modo* (Can 1061.1). My analysis and suggestions, therefore, will be *theological* before they are canonical. I agree with Orsy. "Because the Church has now firmly placed the law into a theological context, the governing principles for the interpretation of the canons must be taken from appropriate theological sources."[2]

Bond as Relationship

I begin my analysis of the bond arising from marriage in the revised Code of Canon Law. "From a valid marriage there arises between the spouses a bond which of its own nature is permanent and exclusive. Moreover, in Christian marriage the spouses are by a special sacrament strengthened and, as it were, consecrated for the duties and the dignity of their state" (Can 1134). For the purposes of this paper, two things are to be noted in this canon. The first is a distinction which will recur throughout, between marriage as a world-reality, which has always existed in human history in one form or another, and marriage as a religious reality, a mystery, a sacrament, a sign and a cause of the presence of the gracious God in human history, which the Catholic Church has acknowledged for the past thousand years. The second is that from a valid secular marriage a bond arises, a bond which is somehow strengthened in a sacramental marriage. The first fact may simply be noted; the analysis of the second is central to the argument in this chapter.

The Catholic Church did not institute marriage as a world-reality. Rather, it found marriage in the societies in which it originated and accepted local laws governing marriage's institutional requirements. The early and anonymous *Epistle to Diognetus* describes the situation. "Neither in region nor in tongue nor in the social institutions of life do Christians differ from other men."[3] Civil jurisdiction over marriage as a world-reality continued into the mid-ninth century. Then, under the impetus of the forged Isidorian Decretals, fraudulently attributed to the early Popes Evaristus and Callixtus and prescribing that marriages be celebrated in church and solemnized by a priest,[4] jurisdiction over the marriages of Christians[5] passed to the Church. Final transfer of jurisdiction over marriage from state to Church, however, was not fully complete until the twelfth century. This history, which is well known and not in debate, relativizes any absolute claim for the present system of ecclesiastical jurisdiction over marriage.

Though the Church did not institute marriage, it did institute the *sacrament* of marriage and its institutional forms. It taught, with Augustine, that "in the City of God [or Church]"[6] secular marriage is transformed into a kingdom-sacrament, and that this sacrament falls under its jurisdiction.[7] This *theological* change, which had its root in Jerome and Augustine, opened the way to a *juridic* change, which had its root in the medieval canonists, especially after the Church assumed a civil role with respect to marriage. That juridic change may be simply stated: the "let no one separate" of the Gospels (Mark 10:9; Matt 19:6) gave way to the "man *can not* put asunder" of the canons. That canonical law remains substantially unchanged today, so that, in distinction from the primitive Church, the only way for persons who are divorced and remarried to be reconciled to the Church is for them to repudiate their present spouse.

The bond arising from marriage is referred to constantly, but is defined or described only infrequently. Doyle, citing Urban Navarrette, gives the now-common theological and, therefore, canonical interpretation. "The bond is the unique relationship between a man and a woman by which they are constituted husband and wife."[8] The Second Vatican Council spoke of this bond in more personal language. "The intimate partnership [or relationship] of married life and love . . . is rooted in the conjugal covenant of irrevocable personal consent."[9] A philosophical delay over relationship will enable us to clarify the nature of the bond arising from a valid marriage.

The bond is a relationship, a category explained in, though in no way limited to, the philosophy of Aristotle and Aquinas. For our purposes here, we need focus only on one central teaching of that philosophy, the *praedicamenta,* or modes of being, specifically substance and accident. The essence of substance is to be in itself, *esse in se;* the essence of accident is to be in another in which it inheres, *esse in alio tamquam in subiecto inhaesionis.*[10] Relation is not a substance, an *esse in se,* neither a physical nor a spiritual substance and, therefore, it does not have autonomous existence. Relation is an accident, an *esse in alio;* it is a being in another, a being related to another. As an accident, it requires a subject in which to inhere, else it would have no existence. Since the bond arising from a valid marriage is a relation, it is an accident, requiring for its very existence a subject in which to inhere. Its subject is the two spouses, fashioned by marriage into one coupled-We or one biblical body-person.[11]

The bond arising from a marriage, therefore, is correctly called an ontological reality. It is not as correctly called "a separate reality,"[12] since no accident, existing as it does only in its proper subject, ever exists as a separate reality.[13] The bond arising from marriage comes into being from the loving relationship between a man and a woman, expressed in their lawfully manifested consent to "mutually give and accept one another for the purpose of establishing a marriage" (Can 1057.2). Their consent transforms a man and a woman into a husband and a wife, related, bonded, or obligated one to the other as spouses in an intimate consortium of the whole of life. A brief consideration of that consortium will further clarify the mutual relationship, bond, or obligation arising from marriage.

The Marital Bond and Consortium-Communion

> The marriage covenant, by which a man and a woman establish between themselves a *consortium* of their whole life, and which of its own very nature is ordered to the well-being of the spouses and to the procreation and upbringing of children, has, between the baptized, been raised by Christ the Lord to the dignity of a sacrament (Can 1055).

For our purposes, three things are to be noted in this canon. The first is that the marriage covenant establishes a *consortium* of the whole of life; the second is that the marriage covenant and the *consortium* it establishes are ordered to the well-being of the spouses and to the procreation and nurture of children; the third is that the covenant, and the *consortium*, has been transformed, in the case of the baptized, into sacrament. I shall consider each of these points in turn.

I have deliberately refrained from translating *consortium* only to consider Ladislas Orsy's opinion that "*consortium* is virtually impossible to translate correctly; it has no equivalent in English."[14] A distinction must surely be in order here. Orsy himself apparently does not believe that it is impossible to translate the word into English, for he immediately offers common translations from the Oxford Latin Dictionary: sharing, community life, partnership. I add another, from Lewis and Short's Latin Dictionary: fellowship or communion. I would argue, and I have no doubt that Orsy would agree, that all these translations are correct verbal translations of *consortium.* Such translation cannot be, therefore, what he deems virtually impossible. It is no more difficult to translate *consortium* than to translate any other word. Orsy must intend another difficulty, and we may isolate it by considering the history of Canon 1055.

A 1980 draft of a revised Code of Canon Law defined marriage as *communio,* communion or fellowship. In a 1982 draft, *communio* had given way to *consortium. Consortium* was preferred, it was stated without elaboration, as more suitable for a variety of cultural situations. It is at this point that we might attain the virtual impossibility of translation claimed by Orsy, a virtual impossibility of finding not a verbal translation, but a cultural one. Orsy himself reveals his mind by warning us that "we have to be careful not to make an exaggerated version of Western personalistic philosophy so absolute that the marriages of Christians living in another culture should be considered invalid."[15] That point is well made and I support it. The precise meaning of *consortium* has always been and should continue to be interpreted not by the law, but by the customs of a particular culture. A world-Church should avoid single-culture definitions which exclude or disregard all other cultures. That stated, I choose to translate *consortium,* absolutely correctly according to the accepted patterns of verbal translation, as fellowship or communion. We must consider that communion to understand the communion of the whole of life, which the spouses establish when they covenant one to the other in a marriage.

Communion is not a new word in the Catholic tradition. It translates the Greek word *koinonia,* which connotes two things: first, common possession and solidarity;[16] second, the mutual drawing of life from that solidarity. Jurgen Moltmann puts it well. In communion, "we give one another life and come alive from one another. In mutual participation in life, individuals become free beyond the boundaries of their individuality."[17] Though this description is couched in Western terms, it can be interpreted in other terms too. For Christians, indeed, *koinonia*-communion is exemplified in the earliest non-Western Church in Jerusalem which, we are told, devoted itself to "the Apostles' teaching and communion *[koinonia]*" (Acts 2:42) and "had everything in common *[panta koina]*" (Acts 4:32). Paul underscores the universality of such communion in the Church, telling us that the churches in Macedonia "have been pleased to make *koinonian*" for the church at Jerusalem (Rom 15:26; cf. 2 Cor 8:4). He indicates the personal cost of such sharing when he praises "the generosity of your *koinonias* for them" (2 Cor 9:13).

From its earliest history, then, as an official note from the Second Vatican Council explains, *koinonia*-communion "is an idea which was held in high honor in the ancient Church (as it is even today, especially in the East). It is understood, however, not of a certain feeling, but of an *organic reality* which demands a juridical form."[18] The notion and the reality of *koinonia*-communion derives not from "an exaggerated version of Western personalistic philosophy," but from the apostolic tradition itself. It made its way back into the Western tradition via the Second Vatican Council, whose guiding vision of Church was that of Church as communion.[19] That it is again a reality of the Catholic *Church* is proof enough that it is a reality also of Christian *marriage* that founds a "domestic Church."[20] We make a serious mistake, however, if we assume that the *koinonia-consortium*-communion which is marriage arises only from the covenanting or the "lawfully manifested consent of persons who are legally capable." Its root is prior to, and deeper in human reality, than that.

The Bond Arising from Love

Other human beings and I have the same needs: needs for trust, respect, safety, understanding, and acceptance of who I am. I commit myself to respond to the needs of selected others, and they commit to respond to mine. We are, we say, friends. Without friends, Aristotle wrote, "no one would choose to live, even if he had all other goods."[21] Friends journey through life together, revealing themselves to one another, sustaining one another, provoking one another to the realization of potential, rejoicing with one another when the potential is fulfilled. Friends will the good of one another; in an ancient word, they love one another.[22]

Aristotle distinguished three kinds of friendship. There is the friendship of pleasure, the friendship of usefulness, and the virtue-friendship of good, in which another is loved as pleasurable or as useful to me, or as good in herself or himself. Aquinas distinguishes love that is desire (*amor concupiscentiae*) and love that is friendship (*amor amicitiae*). In the former, I desire something as good for me; in the latter, I love someone who is good in herself or himself.[23] It is Aristotle's friendship of the good and Aquinas' love of friendship we intend predominantly, though never exclusively, when we say to another "I love you." Jules Toner calls it "radical love," love in which I affirm another as I affirm myself.[24]

Though feelings are frequently associated with it, feelings are not of the essence of this radical love. Loving, like knowing, is essentially doing something. It is essentially affirming the being, indeed, the well-being, of an other. It is willing the good of another. Though loving and knowing are both doing, the distinction between them is illuminating. "Knowledge is of things as they exist in the knower; the will is related to things as they exist in themselves."[25] To know is to receive into oneself. To love is to go out of oneself to another; love is ec-static.

My going out of myself to another, however, is not yet love in its fullest sense. Both Aristotle and Aquinas insist, correctly I believe, that love exists in its fullness only in mutuality. "Friendship requires mutual love, for a friend is a friend to a friend."[26] This mutual love between equally human selves creates between them the communion, the mutual bond, the mutual obligation that is the distinguishing characteristic of lovers. It is not that love *leads* to communion; true love *is* communion. That love creates an intense desire for the fullest possible communion, including the desire that it be for the whole of life, is obvious to every lover. But love itself, as mutual ecstatic affirmation, is already communion.

The location of love as doing, as willing good, affirming being raises the question: Is love free? The answer is yes, and no. An ancient maxim illustrates the no: *nihil amatum nisi praecognitum,* nothing is loved unless it is first known. The first movement of love is a response to knowledge, knowledge of the other's being, the other's goodness, beauty, and lovableness. To the extent that it is spontaneous response to what is judged to be loveable, love is not entirely free, not entirely active, but to some extent passive. However, the fact that I am not necessarily overwhelmed by this response of love illustrates the yes. I remain free to choose to attend to this response or not, to nurture it or not, to be persuaded by it or not. "I can take responsibility for my love—not just be carried away by it or victimized by it."[27] To the extent that I am responsible for it, love is free. It is something I do, as well as something that happens to me; it is action as well as passion.

A final point remains in this section, the consideration of which will both return us back to our theme and point us forward to other themes we must consider. As a freely willed act, love is a species of commitment, the giving of my word to do something. The commitment of love is the giving of my word to another to love her or him. The action in which my commitment is expressed is the symbol of both my love and my intention to love for the whole of life. This symbol relates me, bonds me, obligates me to the one I love. She or he can legitimately protest ever after: "But you promised." The symbol not only expresses to the one I love my intention to love for the whole of life, it also confirms me in that intention and in my love. As lovers, we commit to make our love permanent and to communicate it as permanent.

In reality, of course, though we can *intend* our love to be indissoluble, we cannot make it indissoluble at any given moment of our life, for our love stretches out with our life into an unknown future. What we can do, in Margaret Farley's words, is "initiate in the present a new form of relationship that will endure in the form of fidelity or betrayal." Commitment, she says, "is love's way of being whole while it still grows into wholeness."[28] This mutual commitment of love creates a relationship, a bond, an obligation which is morally binding in itself. It can be further bound by social ritual. In civil marriage, it is legally bound by civil law; in Christian marriage, it is religiously bound also by sacrament and the grace of God. From Christian marriage, then, arises an interpersonal, a civil, and a religious relationship, bond or obligation. None of this happens in any autonomous physical reality. It happens, really and ontologically, only in human reality, only in the interpersonal sphere of the human spirit. A consideration of this triple fact will lead us back to our opening.

The Bonds Arising from Marriage and Sacrament

For a valid marriage, as we have seen, only one moment of the ceremony counts, the moment of exchanging consent; "a marriage is brought into being by the lawfully manifested consent" (Can 1057.1). All present at a wedding hang on these solemn words. "I, Sean, take you, Kate, to be my wife. I promise to be true to you in good times and in bad, in sickness and in health. I will love and honor you all the days of my life."[29] When Kate has declared her consent in similar words, they are declared wedded, married, "husband and wife." If that moment of free consent is missing or seriously flawed, there is no valid marriage, no *marital* relationship, no bond arising from marriage. An annulment, a declaration that there never was a valid marriage in this case, could be given one, two, or twenty-two years after the flawed consent.

This marital commitment adds to the already-existing interpersonal commitment and bond of love a legal commitment and bond of law. Sean's and Kate's obligation is no longer only the obligation deriving from mutual love. They have enhanced their interpersonal commitment and bond of love by declaring their love publicly before their family and friends, and before the society in which they live, and by consenting to set it within the framework of marriage according to the laws prescribed for it by their society. They have related and bound themselves by legal ritual in a new law from which derives a new bond and a new obligation.

Their mutual love relates them to one another by an interpersonal relationship, bond and obligation, which they alone can absolve. Their wedding relates them to one another by a legal relationship, bond and obligation, which not they but only an authority beyond them can absolve. They have strengthened themselves in their love and commitment to one another "for all the days of their life," to paraphrase Canon 1134, by proclaiming it in a public ritual. Their ratified marriage, the Church teaches, is intrinsically indissoluble. That is, the spouses cannot dissolve it themselves, as they could, for instance, in ancient Rome simply by withdrawing their consent.

By committing themselves to marriage, spouses give a juridic form to the organic communion which already exists between them from the moment their love became mutual and fully real. When such a marriage is between two baptized Christians, the Catholic Church teaches, or between two believing Christians as I have insisted, it is also a religious sacrament. By committing themselves to sacrament, spouses give a religious dimension to their marriage; they locate it as a kingdom-reality informed by the grace of God.

Christians who commit themselves and their love to sacrament in marriage, and I repeat this can only be done by those in whom living faith informs love, are by this sacrament "strengthened and, as it were, consecrated for the duties and the dignity of their state" (Can 1134). Their mutual love binds them together in an interpersonal relationship, which is a bond and obligation of love. Their wedding binds them together in a civil relationship, which is a bond and obligation of law. Their marriage as sacrament binds them together in a religious relationship, which is a bond and obligation of divine grace. The uncovering of this triple relationship, bond, or obligation brings us to the conclusion of this section and leads us into the theological reflection of the next.

The Practice of the Catholic Church with Respect to the Bonds

The previous section demonstrated that when two Christians who love one another commit to one another in a marriage which they intend to be sacrament, they bind themselves together in an intimate communion of the whole of life by a triple bond of love, of law, and of sacrament. Since each succeeding bond strengthens the spouses in the preceding bond, the Church is correct in asserting that "in Christian marriage the spouses are by a special sacrament strengthened" (Can 1134). The questions for this section are about its further teaching that the spouses can dissolve the bond arising from love, that "a non-consummated marriage between baptized persons . . . can be dissolved by the Roman Pontiff for a just reason" (Can 1142), and that "a marriage which is ratified and consummated cannot be dissolved by any human power or by any cause other than death" (Can 1141).

It is no secret that the love between spouses sometimes ends, sometimes even is extinguished by the very spouses who wanted it to be, and publicly promised it would be, for the whole of life. The Catholic Church claims no control over the relationship, bond, or obligation arising from love. Canon 1152 exemplifies this posture.

> It is *earnestly recommended* that a spouse, motivated by Christian charity and solicitous for the good of the family, should not refuse to pardon an adulterous partner and should not sunder the conjugal life. Nevertheless, if that spouse has not either expressly or tacitly condoned the other's fault, he or she *has the right* to sever the common conjugal life.

The phrases I have underscored make the Church's position clear in the case of adultery, and by extension in every other case in which mutual love ends. When one of the spouses is guilty of adultery, the other has the canonical right to terminate conjugal life. This canon also prescribes that "within six months of having spontaneously terminated the common conjugal life, the innocent spouse is to bring a case for separation to the competent ecclesiastical authority" (Can 1152.3). In practice, however, this rarely happens. In the twenty-first century, Church authority has wisdom enough to recognize that the decision to live together in conjugal union is best left to free and personal decision and that any effort to impose the duty of conjugal union is unwisdom abounding.

The bonds arising from a valid marriage and from a valid sacrament are both regularly dissolved by the Catholic Church "in favor of the faith" (Can 1143.1) or "for a just cause" (Can 1142). I will explain each case in turn.

Canon 1143 specifies this. "A marriage entered into by two non-baptized persons is dissolved in virtue of the Pauline Privilege in favor of the faith of the party who has received baptism by the fact that a new marriage is contracted by the same party, provided the non-baptized party departs." This canon legislates the practice of the so-called Pauline Privilege, derived from Paul's ruling in his First Letter to the Corinthians (7:12-15). It is applicable only to the case of the marriage of two non-baptized persons. When it is applicable, it dissolves, by law and not by dispensation accorded by ecclesiastical authority,[30] a marriage that is accepted as valid. Since the marriage is dissolved, any bond or obligation of law arising from the marriage is also dissolved and the former spouses are free to remarry.

In the preceding, I referred to the "so-called Pauline Privilege" because it is not at all clear that what Canon 1143.1 legislates is exactly what Paul had in mind. "If the unbelieving partner separates *[chorizetai],*" he writes, "let it be so; in such a case the brother or sister is not bound" (1 Cor 7:15). Two things may be noted here about *chorizetai* which are important for a consideration of the so-called Pauline Privilege and of other Catholic privileges "in favor of the faith."

First, the verb is *chorizetai,* separate, an action which the agent does, not something that is done to him or her. Second, it includes no connotation whatsoever of the right to remarry. The Pauline Privilege as now legislated was introduced not by Paul but by the Church, which uses it to resolve all sorts of cases that go beyond the particular case cited by Paul.[31] Other privileges which grant the dissolution of a valid marriage in favor of faith, and which are gathered together under the misleading heading of "Petrine Privilege," though they have no direct connection to the apostle Peter, were even more clearly introduced by Peter's sixteenth-century successors.[32] The Catholic Church both believes and acts on the belief that there is a power in the Church to dissolve the relationship or bond or obligation arising from a valid marriage. It believes and acts also on the belief that there is a power in the Church to dissolve the relationship, bond, or obligation arising from a valid sacrament.

"A non-consummated marriage between baptized persons . . . can be dissolved by the Roman Pontiff for a just reason" (Can 1142). Since a marriage between baptized persons is also said to be a sacrament (Can 1055.2), at the moment of free consent there is both a valid marriage and a valid sacrament, both a bond and obligation arising from marriage and a bond and obligation arising from sacrament. Canon 1142 gives the force of law to the long-established practice of the Catholic Church that both these bonds and obligations can be dissolved by the Roman Pontiff at the request of either or both parties. A sacramental marriage and the bond and obligation arising from it can be, and are regularly, dissolved in the Church if the marriage is not consummated by sexual intercourse. That the Pontiff is said to proceed to such a dissolution "for a just cause" merely reflects the lawgiver's assumption that, in dispensing from the bond, he does so in virtue of his vicarious power, in the name of God under whose grace such a marriage stands. "He is dispensing from God's law not his own, therefore he is not entitled to act without a justifying cause."[33]

The Nature of Marital Consummation

The Catholic Church believes and acts on the belief that there is power in the Church to dissolve a valid marriage which is not a sacrament and a valid marriage which is a sacrament but not consummated. It further believes and enshrines in law that a marriage which is ratified, that is, correctly enacted as sacrament, and consummated "cannot be dissolved by any human power or by any cause other than death" (Can 1141).

The careful choice of language is to be noted; a ratified and consummated marriage cannot be dissolved *by any human power*. But there is in the Church a power which is more than human. The dissolution of sacramental, non-consummated marriages is an exercise of such power; so also is the forgiveness of sins and the celebration of Eucharist. Which leaves us with two final questions. First, what exactly is it that consummation adds to sacrament that makes the consummated sacramental marriage, and the bonds arising from it, immune to human power? Second, is the bond of a ratified and consummated marriage immune also to the more than human power that is daily exercised in the Church? I will deal with these questions in turn.

What is it that consummation adds to sacrament that makes the ratified and consummated marriage absolutely indissoluble? Pius XI suggests the answer is easily found, "if we seek reverently." It lies in "the mystical meaning of Christian marriage, which is found fully and perfectly in the consummated marriage between believers." That meaning is the meaning traditionally assigned to Christian marriage, namely, that "it refers to that most perfect union which exists between Christ and the church."[34] Though it does not specify as precisely as Pius that it is consummated marriage between Christian believers, presumed to be sacramental, that is indissoluble, the International Theological Commission offers the same reason for the indissolubility of Christian marriage. "The ultimate and deepest foundation for the indissolubility of Christian marriage lies in the fact that it is the image, the sacrament, the witness of the indissoluble union between Christ and the church."[35]

The two-in-oneness which spouses become in marriage is the most concrete image and symbol of the union, the two-in-oneness of Christ and his Church. This two-in-oneness, contrary to the evidence of modern psychology that sexual intercourse is not the only, and certainly not the most important, expression of marital communion, is assumed to be symbolized and effected most fully in their sexual two-in-oneness. The sexual union of the spouses, therefore, the consummation of their marriage, brings the image and the sacrament of the union of Christ and the Church to its perfection.[36] Both the marriage and the sacrament then become indissoluble. The answer to our first question, then, is this: What consummation adds to sacrament is that it relates the marital union of Christian spouses, expressed and perfected in their sexual union, so closely to the mystical union of Christ and his Church as sign and signified, as sacrament and sacramentalized, that the one union like the other becomes theologically, and therefore canonically, indissoluble. Canon 1141, which declares the dissolution of a ratified and consummated marriage beyond "any human power," legislates this prior theological connection.

This argument originated in the twelfth-century debates over whether consent or sexual intercourse makes a marriage,[37] and it controlled the Catholic tradition from the twelfth-century popes, Alexander III and Innocent III, to the Second Vatican Council. The council's teaching on marriage, followed twenty years later by the Code's prescription that, to be true, consummation must be *humano modo* (Can 1061.1), undermined its foundation. When Pius XI sought reverently in 1930, he took for granted the canonical tradition that dealt with marriage as a contract (Can 1012), that declared the object of the contract to be the exclusive and perpetual right to the body of the other for acts suitable for the generation of offspring (Can 1081.2), and that declared the ends of marriage to be primarily procreation and secondarily mutual help and the remedy of concupiscence (Can 1013). It is easy to see how, in such a legal and physical climate, a single act of sexual intercourse could be taken to be the definitive consummation of a marriage. It is not so easy to see in the changed theological and interpersonal climate in which the Second Vatican Council rooted its doctrine on marriage.[38]

The council teaches that the intimate partnership of life and love which is marriage "is rooted in the conjugal covenant of irrevocable personal consent," and "by that human act whereby the spouses mutually bestow and accept each other, a relationship arises which by divine will and in the eyes of society too is a lasting one."[39] Though faced with insistent demands to retain the juridical word *contract* as a precise way to speak of marriage, the council demurred, and chose instead the biblical, theological, and personal word *covenant*. This choice locates marriage as an *interpersonal* rather than as an exclusively *legal* reality, and brings it into line with the rich biblical tradition of covenant between God and God's People and Christ and Christ's Church. The council underscores the interpersonal character of marriage in its teaching that the spouses "mutually bestow and accept each other," firmly rejecting the reductionist view, set forth in the 1917 Code, that they mutually bestow only the right to the use of each other's body. It declares that the sexual intercourse in and through which the spouses symbolize their mutual gifts is to be *humano modo,* that is, "in a manner which is *truly human.*"[40] It is to be *actus humanus,* a human act, not just *actus hominis,* an act which a man or a woman does.

The council made another crucial change in Catholic teaching about marriage, which was later incorporated into the revised Code of Canon Law. That change is central to any modern theological discussion of consummation. Prior to the council, the traditional teaching on the ends of marriage was the primary end-secondary end arrangement articulated in Canon 1013. Despite insistent demands to reaffirm this hierarchical terminology, the council refused to do so. It taught explicitly that procreation "does not make the other ends of marriage of less account," and that marriage "is not instituted solely for procreation."[41] That this refusal to speak of a hierarchy of ends in marriage was not the result of a lapse of memory, but a deliberate choice, was confirmed when the council's teaching on ends was incorporated into the revised Code (Can 1055.1). As I noted in an earlier chapter, the council replaced the model of marriage as *procreative institution* with a model of marriage as *interpersonal union.*

This change of root perspective raises questions about the suitability of the claim that the spouses' first sexual intercourse is the definitive consummation of both their mutual self-gifting and their marriage. For instance, if the procreation of human life and the *consortium*-communion between the spouses are joint and equal ends of marriage, why should the act of procreation alone be the best symbol of the union of Christ and Christ's Church? Why should the broader marital communion, itself in part symbolized in sexual intercourse, not be the symbol? These questions have been exacerbated by the change in the way marital consummation is specified in the Code. A marriage is now said to be "ratified and consummated if the spouses have in a *human manner [humano modo]* engaged together in a conjugal act in itself apt for the generation of offspring" (Can 1061.1). The phrase I have underscored has placed Catholic teaching on conjugal sexuality, consummation, and indissolubility on hold theologically and, therefore, canonically, for the Church has not yet worked out a theology of sexuality that can elucidate what sexual intercourse in a human manner is. It cannot, therefore, say what consummates a ratified marriage and makes it permanent.

As early as 1973, the sub-commission drafting revisions of the Code's canons on marriage recognized the difficulty in including the phrase *humano modo* in the text. They questioned whether a marriage is consummated by *copula,* that is, physically complete but unconscious or extorted by force, and suggested that the affirmative answer to that question previously given in the Church[42] seemed "hardly consonant with [the teaching] of the Second Vatican Council on marriage, and specifically with its teaching concerning the marital act." They then proposed that "the law also state that consummation of marriage must be done *humano modo* if it is to be called true consummation," and noted the lack of a verifiable criterion "to prove that a consummating act has not been done in a human manner." Given that lack, they concluded with the unanimous recommendation that the words *humano modo* be included in the text within parentheses, "so that their doubts on the matter may be on record."[43]

When the revised Code was published in 1983, the parentheses recommended by the Commission had been removed and Canon 1061.1 simply specified that a marriage is "ratified and consummated if the spouses have *humano modo* engaged together in a conjugal act in itself apt for the generation of offspring." The problem noted by the commission—the lack of a verifiable criterion for non-consummation—remains unresolved today, leaving legislators with no sure criterion for verifying that a marriage has been truly consummated. As long, therefore, as the marriages of Christian spouses are held to be consummated and indissoluble only by sexual intercourse *humano modo,* there is no criterion to distinguish indissoluble from dissoluble marriages.[44] Neither, therefore, is there a sure answer to our first question: What is it that consummation adds to sacrament that makes the consummated sacramental marriage immune to human power? Until consummation in a human manner can be surely specified, the consummation and indissolubility of sacramental marriages in fact and in law continues quite untouched by sexual intercourse.

That lack of a sure criterion for the consummation and indissolubility of a sacramental marriage, fatally debilitating for the marital theory and practice of the Catholic Church though it be, is far from the only flaw in that theory and practice. If a marriage is conceived as an interpersonal process for the whole of life, then sexual intercourse within and consummation of the marriage ought to be thought of within that interpersonal process. If personal and marital identity are established diachronically, that is, across time, and they are, then so too must be sexual identity. Catholic ethicists argue today that decisions about morality or immorality ought to be based on interpersonal relationship and not on physical acts. Consummation, therefore, should no longer be conceived as one act of sexual intercourse but rather as an ongoing and developing interpersonal *consortium vitae.* More and more spouses are coming to experience their marriages as growth processes in time, "in which single acts have little meaning when they are cut off from an operational pattern."[45] That operational pattern, I suggest, is the growth of love into marital love and the growth of marital love into marital *consortium*-communion. Sexual intercourse fits in this pattern as both a sign and a cause of marital love and communion.

Theodore Mackin is correct, I believe, and he expresses the experience of the married when he asserts that to consummate a marriage means "to bring the marital relationship to its fullness."[46] It is legal and romantic nonsense, demeaning to marriage and to the married, to suggest that the consummation or perfection of marital love, of marriage, of *consortium*-communion is achieved in a first act of sexual intercourse. A marriage and, therefore, a sacrament of marriage reach perfection only when the faith-informed love that undergirds them reaches perfection, only when marital love has reached such fullness that the spouses would not place it second to any other human reality. To put it another way, a marriage is perfected or consummated and permanent or indissoluble only when the marital love in which it is founded is perfected or consummated and permanent or indissoluble. The sacrament of marriage becomes perfected and permanent only when the marriage which is its human matrix becomes perfected and permanent.[47]

Mutual love, marriage, sacrament, and the perfection of each, aptly expressed and facilitated in sexual intercourse though each may be, are all life-projects-in-the-making. In 1970, the Roman Rota, the Supreme Marriage Tribunal of the Roman Catholic Church, delivered a momentous judgment, in line with the change of perspective introduced by the Vatican Council. It ruled that "where conjugal love is lacking, either the consent is not free or it is not internal, or it excludes or limits the object which must be integral to have a valid marriage." It concluded that the "lack of conjugal love is the same as lack of consent."[48]

If consent makes marriage, the Rota argued, so also does conjugal love; if conjugal love *makes* marriage, I argue, so also does perfected conjugal love perfect or *consummate* marriage and sacrament. Although the moment of consummated conjugal love and communion will never be as clearly specifiable as the moment of the first sexual intercourse, consummation will take place and marriages will become indissoluble. Because of the inability to specify a moment of consummation, there will be a lack of clarity in judging when a marriage is completed and permanent, and lawyers will abhor that lack of clarity. Lacking a clear criterion to judge intercourse *humano modo,* however, lack of clarity is exactly what they presently have. Clear or not, consummation as perfected conjugal love and communion, rather than the moment of first sexual intercourse, is true to the experience of married couples. That is how law has always developed, not out of cold logic but out of warm human experience.[49] That is how conjugal *consortium*-communion is now an equal end of marriage with procreation in both the theology and the law of the Church.

The subjective dimension I have proposed as the criterion for the perfection or consummation of a marriage, perfected marital love and *consortium*-communion, is not without precedent in the Catholic tradition. In his careful study of Gratian, Alexander III, and Innocent III, John Noonan has demonstrated how they distinguished a true marriage, a *marital* union, from all other pre- and extra-marital unions on the basis of *affectio maritalis,* marital love, dealing with the spouse as a loved spouse. Prior to the Council of Trent, when there was no required canonical form, it was this marital love that served as evidence that marital consent had been given.[50] While I propose, however, the perfection of marital love as the perfection and consummation of marriage, I also fervently hope that Francis Morrisey's suggestion that "love can now enter into the canonical sphere under the heading of 'aptitude for the community of conjugal life'"[51] will be resisted. I know of no basis for confidence that law can appreciate or legislate marital love.

The second question for this section is whether the bond of a ratified and consummated marriage is immune to the more than human power that is daily exercised in the Church. Although that question is now moot until the consummation of a marriage in a human manner can be surely verified, I will still seek to show that the answer is no. We must first note that the question asks about extrinsic indissolubility, the immunity of a marriage to dissolution by an agent other than the spouses. There is universal agreement that a *marriage* (not merely a ratified and consummated marriage) is intrinsically indissoluble, immune to dissolution by the spouses. We must secondly note that the extrinsic indissolubility of a ratified and consummated marriage as prescribed in canon law is not a revealed truth. Louis Billot's opinion that it is *de fide catholica,* defined Catholic faith, has never found support;[52] most theologians judge it to be *doctrina catholica,* common Catholic teaching. Navarrette claims that Pius XI implicitly and Pius XII explicitly affirm that the ratified and consummated marriage cannot be dissolved, not even by the vicarious power of the Roman Pontiff.[53] I think he is exaggerating. Both popes did nothing more than cite without comment the teaching then legislated in Canon 1118. They added nothing that would elevate the teaching to a theological level higher than *doctrina catholica.*

The history of ratified and consummated marriage in Catholic teaching demonstrates four facts. First, the teaching is a compromise between the Roman perspective in which consent makes marriage and the northern European perspective in which sexual intercourse makes marriage. Second, the compromise emerged from a mixed cultural understanding of marriage, the southern culture of the Roman Empire and the northern culture of twelfth-century Europe. Third, the compromise was made necessary because of the Church's quest to understand and legislate marriage in changing cultural circumstances, a quest which has not yet ended. Fourth, the modern personalist culture from which the Vatican Council's revised doctrine derives is far removed from the twelfth-century legal and physical culture on which the current canonical practice is founded. There is no doubt that there have been changes over the course of history in both the Catholic Church's teaching on marriage and its practice based on that teaching. Neither is there any doubt for those who understand and value history that changes will occur again.

In 1973, the Congregation for the Doctrine of the Faith declared the obvious, that doctrinal formulae may sometimes bear the traces of "the changeable conceptions of a given epoch."[54] That is the inevitable result of historicity. With specific reference to the *de fide* doctrine of Chalcedon, Karl Rahner remarked that anyone who takes seriously the historicity of human truth "must see that neither the abandonment of a formula nor its preservation in a petrified form does justice to human understanding." History is not a beginning-anew; it is rather "a becoming-new which preserves the old, and preserves it all the more as old." Theology, therefore, must never cease the effort to release itself from a formula, "not so as to abandon it but to understand it."[55] It is precisely what the Church must do, and I seek to do here, with the medieval formula *ratified and consummated marriage.*

The Roman Catholic teaching on the marriages between Christians and the dissolution of these marriages is said to derive from the New

Testament teaching on marriage. And so it does, but only up to a point which I will now explain. It is definitely incorrect to speak of the New Testament *teaching* on marriage and divorce, because there are several New Testament *teachings* on marriage and divorce, and they are not all in agreement. Nor are they all derived from Jesus.

There is a well-remembered saying of Jesus, which scholars agree was probably originally reported in Luke 16:18: "Everyone who divorces his wife and marries another commits adultery." If that is what Jesus said, Bruce Malina argues, it has to be a parable. "When taken literally, it makes as little sense as 'you are the salt of the earth' or 'you are the light of the world,'" and "in the gospels of Matthew and Mark this teaching requires further, private explanation, a procedure these authors use for parables."[56] If it is a parable, it always needs interpretation for, and application in, the concrete circumstances in which its hearers find themselves. That interpretation in concrete circumstances is exactly what the New Testament authors provide.

Mark adds to Jesus' logion something that Jesus, a first-century Jew, would never have said to his Jewish audience, an addition that prohibits a wife from dismissing her husband (Mark 10:12). Matthew, good Jew that he is, adds his exceptive clause, except for *porneia,* whatever that meant for him (Matt 19:9). Paul contributes his own exception, covering the case in which an unbelieving spouse no longer wishes to live with a believing spouse (1 Cor 12:15). The Catholic Church continued this process of interpretation through the centuries, adding to and expanding the New Testament teachings as it faced new circumstances. The one major difference, however, between Mark, Matthew, and Paul and the historical Catholic Church is that the interpretations of the Church, including that on ratified and consummated marriage, are not gospel and definitive *de fide.* They are theological, canonical, and changeable *doctrina catholica.*

That is not to say that the teaching on ratified and consummated marriage is false, "for it is not from sacred scripture alone that the Church draws her certainty."[57] It is to say only that it is not irreformable, and to suggest that the agent of reformation is the same agent that introduced the teaching in the first place, that is, the magisterial Church, whose power extends to the binding and loosing of sin, to the transformation of bread and wine, and certainly to the reformation of a reformable Catholic doctrine. If a non-consummated marriage between baptized persons—a sacramental marriage which falls under God's law—"can be dissolved by the Roman Pontiff for a just reason" (Can 1142) in the name of God, a ratified and consummated marriage which falls under the Church's law can also be dissolved by the Roman Pontiff in the name of God for a similarly just reason.[58]

We have, then, an answer to the second question for this concluding section, a question which, remember, remains moot until a sure criterion for sexual intercourse *humano modo* is found. Is the bond of a ratified and consummated marriage immune to the more than human power that is daily exercised in the Church? No, it is not. That judgment concludes this essay.

Conclusion

I began by enumerating some things about marriage that I took for granted as a married theologian many years ago. I conclude by enumerating some things about marriage that I take for granted as a still-married theologian today. Any change in the enumeration derives from the intertwined modern development of the experience of both marriage and Roman Catholic theology.

First, the root bond in a marriage, the bond that requires constant nurture, is not the bond arising from marriage. It is the relationship, the bond, and the obligation arising from the mutual love in which a man and a woman affirm one another as good and equal selves, the very love that leads them to commit mutually in marriage to enhance their love and their selves for the whole of life. Second, a man and a woman may enhance and strengthen the bond arising from their love by affirming it before the society in which they live and by setting it within the framework of marriage as legislated by their society. Their marriage enhances and strengthens the bond arising from their love with a second bond, which is a relationship, a bond, and an obligation of law. Third, when a man and a woman are Christian believers, they can enhance and strengthen the bonds arising from their love and marriage by intending both as symbol-sacrament of the love and communion between Christ and Christ's Church. This sacrament enhances and strengthens the bonds arising from love and marriage with a third bond, which is a relationship, a bond, and an obligation of ecclesial sacrament and divine grace.

Over the centuries, the Catholic Church has assumed specific postures toward each of these three bonds. It leaves to the couple the task of nurturing or ending the bond arising from love. It prescribes that the bond arising from marriage between baptized persons, which is also a bond arising from sacrament, "can be dissolved by the Roman Pontiff for a just reason" (Can 1142) in the name of God. It further prescribes that, when the marriage is ratified and consummated, the bonds arising from marriage and sacrament "cannot be dissolved by any human power or by any cause other than death" (Can 1141).

Concerning this last prescription, this chapter raised two questions. First, what does consummation add to marriage and sacrament that makes them permanent when consummated? Second, is a ratified and consummated marriage truly immune to the more than human power that is daily exercised in the Church? It responded to the first question, with the theological tradition that what consummation adds to marriage and sacrament is that it refers them concretely to the perfect and permanent union between Christ and Christ's Church. It responded to the second question that the ratified and consummated marriage is not immune to the more than human power that exists in the Church, that it can be dissolved in the name of God by the very same power that regularly dissolves unconsummated sacramental marriages.

I argued further that, given the lack of a criterion for the verification of the canonically required intercourse *humano modo* (Can 1061), the definition of consummation as the first marital sexual intercourse is no longer acceptable as a criterion for the consummation or perfection of a marriage. I suggested that a better criterion of marital perfection or consummation in the personal context in which the Second Vatican Council dealt with Christian marriage, and in which Catholic ethicists deal with moral or immoral acts, is a personal criterion, which will never be pinpointed with the physical accuracy of first sexual intercourse. That criterion is this: both marriage and the sacrament of marriage reach their perfection or consummation and become permanent or indissoluble diachronically, across time, when the faith-informed mutual love of the spouses on which they are founded becomes perfect or consummated and permanent or indissoluble.

In 1968 Alexander Schmemann wrote of the machinery set up in the Roman Catholic Church to adjudicate the validity of marriages according to the canonical definition of a contract giving the right to bodily acts of reproduction. He complained, legitimately, that in this effort to achieve legal clarity both the personal elements in marriage and the supernatural context of sacrament were pushed into the background. "Where we in the Church should be speaking of the common life of two spouses who are children of God, we are probing in tribunal practice the conditions of a contract for bodily acts."[59] The good news for Schmemann, for the married, and for the Church is that this complaint is no longer legitimate. The personal and religious elements in marriages between Christians are now very much to the fore. In the long run, it is this transformation that this chapter has sought to demonstrate and to enhance.

Questions for Reflection

1. The word *relationship* is very common in current usage. What do you understand by the word?

2. What does it mean to speak of relationship as being also a *bond*? What are the implications of being bound in a relationship?

3. In a Christian marriage, the spouses are bound together by the interpersonal bond of love, by the legal bond of marriage, and by the religious bond of sacrament. Which of these three bonds, in your opinion, provides the surest foundation for a stable marriage for the whole of life?

4. What do you understand by "Pauline Privilege" and "Petrine Privilege?" Are you surprised to learn that the Catholic Church dissolves valid marriages; that is, in ordinary language, grants divorces?

5. Do you believe that a marriage is brought to its fullness and completion by a first act of sexual intercourse? How do you think a marriage is consummated?

Notes

[1] An earlier version of this essay appeared in *The Jurist* 55 (1955) 218–42. It is reprinted here with permission.

[2] Ladislas Orsy, *Marriage in Canon Law* (Wilmington, Del.: Michael Glazier, 1986) 47.

[3] *Epist. ad Diognetum* 5, PG 2.1173. See Athenagoras, *Legatio pro Christianis (Leg.)* 33, PG 6.965; Chrysostom, *Hom. 56 in Gen.* 29, PG 54.488; Ambrose, *De institutione virginis (Instit.)* 6, PL 16.316.

[4] See P. Fournier and G. LeBras, *Histoire des collections canoniques en Occident depuis les fausses decretales jusqu'au Decret de Gratien,* vol. I (Paris: Sirey, 1932) 127–232; Edward Schillebeeckx, *Marriage: Secular Reality and Saving Mystery* (London: Sheed and Ward, 1965) 246.

[5] Papal decrees of the fourth century required the *lower clergy* to have their marriages solemnized by a priest. See Schillebeeckx, *Marriage,* 255.

[6] Augustine, *De bono conjugali (Bon. conj.)* PL 40.378–9.

[7] See Michael G. Lawler, *Marriage and Sacrament: A Theology of Christian Marriage* (Collegeville: The Liturgical Press, 1993).

[8] See *The Code of Canon Law: A Text and Commentary,* ed. James A. Coriden et al. (New York: Paulist Press, 1985) 808.

[9] GS 48.

[10] Joseph Gredt, *Elementa Philosophiae Aristotelico-Thomistico,* vol. 2 (Barcelona: Herder, 1946) 121 and 135.

[11] See Lawler, *Marriage and Sacrament,* 38.

[12] *The Code of Canon Law,* ed. Coriden, 808.

[13] The single theoretical exception to that requirement is the case of the accidents of bread and wine which, after consecration, exist in Eucharist though not in their proper subject. In ST III, q. 77, a. 1, Aquinas appeals to a "miracle" to explain this exception.

[14] Orsy, *Marriage in Canon Law,* 51.

[15] Ibid., 51–2.

[16] Pier Cesare Bori, *Koinonia: L'idea della communione nell'ecclesiologia recente e nel Nuovo Testamento* (Brescia: Paideia, 1972) 107–19.

[17] Jurgen Moltmann, *The Spirit of Life: A Universal Affirmation* (Minneapolis: Fortress Press, 1992) 118.

[18] See Walter M. Abbott, *The Documents of Vatican II* (New York: America Press, 1966) 99, emphasis in original.

[19] See Gerard Philips, *L'Eglise et son mystère au IIe Concile du Vatican* (Paris: Desclee, 1966) vol. I:7, 59, and vol. II:24, 54, 159; Roman Synod (1985), Final Report, "The Church, in the Word of God, Celebrates the Mysteries of Christ," II.C.1; Michael G. Lawler and Thomas Shanahan, "The Church Is a Graced Communion," *Worship* 67 (1993) 484.

[20] LG 11.

[21] Aristotle, *Nichomachean Ethics* 8.1.

[22] ST I, q. 20, a. 1 ad 3.

[23] ST I-II, q. 26, a. 4.

[24] Jules J. Toner, *The Experience of Love* (Washington, D.C.: Corpus Books, 1968) 65–8.

[25] ST I, q. 19, a. 3 ad 6. M. Roland-Gosselin cites fifty similar citations throughout Aquinas' career. See his "Le désir du bonheur et l'existence de Dieu," *Revue des Sciences Philosophiques et Théologiques* 13 (1924) 163.

[26] *Nichomachean Ethics* 8.2; ST IIa-IIae, q. 23, a. 1.

[27] Margaret Farley, *Personal Commitments: Beginning, Keeping, Changing* (San Francisco: Harper & Row, 1986) 33.

[28] Ibid., 34.

[29] "Rite for Celebrating Marriage," *The Rites of the Catholic Church* (New York: Pueblo, 1976) 554.

[30] See, however, in *The Canon Law Digest* 8 (Chicago: Mundelein, 1978) 1177–83, the private Instruction from the Congregation for the Doctrine of the Faith, *Ut Notum Est,* which describes the conditions for a grant of dissolution by the pope "of marriage in favor of the faith, whether the petitioner is baptized or is a convert or is not" (1177). These norms enjoy the same force as the canons of the Code.

[31] See Peter Huizing, "La dissolution du mariage depuis le concile de Trente," *Revue de Droit Canonique* 21 (1971) 127–45.

[32] Michael G. Lawler, *Secular Marriage, Christian Sacrament* (Mystic, Conn.: Twenty-Third Publications, 1985) 106–8.

[33] Orsy, *Marriage in Canon Law,* 214.

[34] *Casti Connubii,* AAS 22 (1930) 552.

[35] "Propositiones de quibusdam quaestionibus doctrinalibus ad matrimonium Christianum pertinentibus," *Gregorianum* 59 (1978) 462.

[36] Aquinas had stated, without proof, that marriage, before consummation, signified the union of Christ and the individual soul and, after consummation, signified the union of Christ and Church. ST Suppl., q. 61, a. 2 ad 1.

[37] Lawler, *Secular Marriage, Christian Sacrament,* 38–9.

[38] See *The Code of Canon Law,* ed. Coriden, 740.

[39] GS 48.

[40] GS 49.

[41] GS 50.

[42] See, for example, *Canon Law Digest,* ed. T. Lincoln Bouscaren and James I. O'Connor, vol. 5:529–33.

[43] *Communicationes* 5 (1973) 79.

[44] Theodore Mackin, "Ephesians 5:21-33 and Radical Indissolubility," *Marriage Studies III: Reflections in Canon Law and Theology,* ed. Thomas P. Doyle (Washington, D.C.: Canon Law Society of America, 1985) 43.

⁴⁵ André Guindon, "Case for a Consummated Sexual Bond before a Ratified Marriage," *Eglise et Théologie* 8 (1977) 155–6.

⁴⁶ Theodore Mackin, *The Marital Sacrament* (New York: Paulist Press, 1989) 674.

⁴⁷ See Michael G. Lawler, "The Mutual Love and Personal Faith of the Spouses as the Matrix of the Sacrament of Marriage," *Worship* 65 (1991) 339–61.

⁴⁸ See Lawler, *Secular Marriage, Christian Sacrament,* 54.

⁴⁹ See Francis G. Morrisey, "Preparing Ourselves for the New Law," *Studia Canonica* 7 (1973) 117.

⁵⁰ John T. Noonan Jr., "Marital Affection in the Canonists," *Studia Gratiana* 12 (1968) 479–509.

⁵¹ Francis G. Morrisey, "Preparing Ourselves for the New Marriage Legislation," *The Jurist* 33 (1973) 345.

⁵² Louis Billot, *De Ecclesiae Sacramentis* (Roma: Pontificia Universitas Gregoriana, 1929) 440. The recent *Catechism of the Catholic Church* is in error when it asserts that "the marriage bond has been established by God himself in such a way that a marriage concluded *and consummated* between baptized persons can never be dissolved" (1640). The marriage bond, indeed, has been established by God. That the indissoluble bond comes into effect only when the marriage has been consummated has been established by the Church.

⁵³ Urban Navarrette, "Indissolubilitas Matrimonii Rati et Consummati: Opiniones Recentiores et Observationes," *Periodica* 58 (1969) 449.

⁵⁴ *Mysterium Ecclesiae,* AAS 65 (1973) 403. This declaration was, as is customary, "ratified and confirmed" by Pope Paul VI.

⁵⁵ Karl Rahner, "Current Problems in Christology," *Theological Investigations,* vol. I (London: Darton, Longman and Todd, 1965) 150.

⁵⁶ Bruce J. Malina, *The New Testament World: Insights from Cultural Anthropology* (Atlanta: John Knox, 1981) 118–21.

⁵⁷ DV 9.

⁵⁸ In an article already cited, "Indissolubilitas Matrimonii," Navarrette cites thirteen Catholic authors variously arguing this position. He dismisses them all gratuitously and inaccurately as lacking "scientific authority in the field of biblical exegesis, theology, history or matrimonial law" (445). The counter arguments he offers are equally gratuitous, and *quod gratis asseritur, gratis negatur.* There is no probative value in endlessly citing the present theory and practice. He does, however, raise a central question: "What is of primary interest is to know whether Christ established the law of the absolute indissolubility of the *consummated* Christian marriage" (464). The question is easily answered: no, he did not; the Church did. And if the Church has the power to establish a law, it also has the power to disestablish it. Jean Bernhard suggests "existential consummation and in faith," in "Indissolubilite du mariage et Droit Canonique," *Divorce et Indissolubilité du Mariage* (Paris: Cerf, 1971) 13–48.

[59] Alexander Schmemann, "The Indissolubility of Marriage: The Theological Tradition of the East," *The Bond of Marriage: An Ecumenical and Interdisciplinary Study,* ed. William W. Bassett (Notre Dame, Ind.: University of Notre Dame Press, 1968) 116.

5

Divorce and Remarriage in
the Catholic Church[1]

The United States is now a culture in which divorce rather than marriage is featured. Not only do some 40 percent of all marriages end in divorce (which means, of course, that some 60 percent end in stability), but divorce has become culturally acceptable. The earlier social stigma attached to it is greatly reduced if it has not entirely disappeared. Catholics are as enculturated as any other Americans, and there is no evidence to suggest their rate of divorce is significantly different from that of the general population. Many civilly divorced Catholics contract second marriages while their first spouse is still alive, making their second marriages invalid in the eyes of their Church. These remarried Catholics are banned from full participation in the sacramental life of the Church; specifically, they are banned from sharing communion. Many are pained by this ban and Catholic theologians, canon lawyers, ministers, and lay people are asking what, if anything, can be done for those in second marriages not sanctioned by the Church. In May 1977 the Conference of Catholic Bishops in the United States, the same body who imposed the penalty in the first place, dropped the automatic excommunication of divorced Catholics who remarry while their first spouse is still alive. That removed a major source of pain for many divorced and remarried Catholics. This chapter illuminates areas where more could be done.

My response to the question of what more can be done is developed in ten cumulative theses. Since several of the theses have already been explained in detail or will be explained later, the explications are of varying length. Since the argument is intended to be cumulative, no one thesis by itself resolves the disputes but, when taken together, they make a contribution for the Church to seriously consider.

Marriage between baptized believers is a sacrament, that is, a prophetic symbol of the union between Christ and the Church.

This is a thesis already fully explicated in the opening chapter and it can, therefore, simply be summarized here. Prophets, as we have seen, were fond of symbolic actions. Jeremiah bought an earthen pot, dashed it to the ground, and announced "Thus says the LORD of hosts: So will I break this people and this city, as one breaks a potter's vessel" (Jer 19:11). Ezekiel took a brick, drew a city on the brick, laid siege to the city, and declared the city Jerusalem and his action "a sign for the house of Israel" (Ezek 4:1-3; see also 5:5). Prophetic action-symbols reveal in representation the presence and action of God. Jeremiah's shattering of his pot and Ezekiel's destruction of his city is, in symbol, God's shattering of Jerusalem. The prophet Hosea portrayed marriage, the union of a man and a woman, as a prophetic symbol of the union between God and God's people, a reality not only of law but, more importantly, also of grace. On the one hand, it represents and expresses the covenanted love of a man and a woman; on the other hand, it also represents and expresses the covenanted love of God and God's people. This Jewish view of marriage, with a change of *dramatis personae,* became the Christian view. The Letter to the Ephesians taught that marriage is a prophetic symbol of the new covenant between Christ and Christ's Church; later Latin history taught that it was sacrament.[2]

A sacrament, then, is a prophetic symbol in which the Church reveals in representation the grace of God. To say that marriage is a sacrament is to say that it reveals simultaneously the intimate union of a man and a woman and the intimate union of Christ and Christ's Church. A couple entering any marriage says to one another "I love you and I give myself to and for you." A couple entering a sacramental marriage says that too, and more. Each says "I love you as Christ loves his Church, steadfastly and faithfully." From its beginning, therefore, a sacramental marriage is intentionally more than human covenant; it is *also* religious covenant. It is more than law; it is *also* grace. From its beginning, God and Christ are present in it, gracing it, modeling it, challenging and assisting it to faithfulness. This presence of God, grace in its most ancient Christian meaning, is not something extrinsic to Christian marriage but something intrinsic to it, something without which it would not be *Christian* marriage at all.

A previous chapter developed an important sacramental fact. A truly *Christian* marriage is not simply a marriage between two people who have been baptized; it is a marriage between two Christian *believers,* for whom the steadfast love of God and of God's Christ is consciously present as model for their mutual love. The love of faith-filled spouses is, indeed, the very matrix of the sacrament of marriage, for it is in and through the spouses' love that God and Christ are prophetically made present. It is a matter for empirical verification, however, that not all Christian marriages become permanent. Some die, and when they die it makes no sense to claim they are still binding ontologically, for the death of a marriage is as definitive as the death of a spouse. When a marriage dies, the Church traditionally deals with it in one of its many canonical processes. Its claim that it is precluded from doing otherwise by "fidelity to the words of Jesus" is not convincing in the honest light of its own ancient tradition.

The theology and practice of the Catholic Church with respect to divorce and remarriage are not as faithful to the New Testament as is claimed.

In October 1994, the Congregation for the Doctrine of the Faith sent a letter to the bishops of the world which purported to articulate Catholic doctrine concerning divorce and remarriage and claimed, citing Mark 10:11-12, "fidelity to the words of Jesus Christ."[3] The implication was that, since the doctrine in question is based on fidelity to the words of Jesus, it is irreformable. That argument might be true if the words of Jesus as cited from Mark were the only teaching in the New Testament on divorce and remarriage and the only one which the Church followed. That, of course, is not the case. Both Paul and Matthew contribute their own interpretation of and exception to Jesus' remembered command.

In his First Letter to the Corinthians, Paul answers questions posed to him by the Corinthian community. One of those questions was a question about divorce and Paul responds with a command from the Lord. "To the married I give this command—*not I but the Lord*—that the wife should not separate from her husband (but if she does separate, let her remain unmarried or else be reconciled to her husband)" (1 Cor 7:10-11). The custom of easy divorce was deeply rooted in the Greek tradition and it is not difficult to imagine Corinthians wanting to know what they were supposed to do now that they were followers of Jesus. Paul leaves them in no doubt: the wife is not to be separated from her husband and the husband is not to dismiss his wife.

Having responded to the question of divorce and remarriage in the case of two believing Christians, Paul then discusses a case of conscience that must have been prevalent in the earliest Christian communities, as it continues to be prevalent in mission territories today. The case asks about a marriage in which one spouse has become Christian and the other remains non-Christian, and asks specifically about divorce in such a marriage. Paul gives two pieces of advice, each of them hinging on the attitude of the non-Christian spouse. The first advice relates to the case in which the non-Christian spouse is willing to continue to live with the Christian. In that case, "if any believer has a wife who is an unbeliever, and she consents to live with him, he should not divorce her. And if any woman has a husband who is an unbeliever, and he consents to live with her, she should not divorce him" (1 Cor 7:12-13). Paul's instruction is firm: when the unbelieving spouse is willing to continue to live in marriage with the believer, he or she is not to be dismissed.

Paul's second piece of advice relates to the case in which the non-believer is unwilling to live with the Christian believer. "But if the unbelieving partner separates, let it be so; in such a case the brother or sister is not bound. It is to peace that God has called you" (1 Cor 7:15). It is the nonbelieving spouse who separates himself or herself; he or she is not to be dismissed by the believer. There is no suggestion that the marriage between a believer and a nonbeliever is not valid; there is no suggestion that Jesus' instruction does not apply. There is only the suggestion that Paul is making an exception: "*I say*—I and not the Lord" (7:12). For Paul, the preservation of peace, it would appear, is a greater value than the preservation of an unpeaceful marriage. The Roman Church sanctioned this approach to dissolving a valid marriage in the twelfth century, enshrines it in its law today, and calls the process the Pauline Privilege (Can 1143).

Matthew also nuances Jesus' words with his own Jewish exception (5:32; 19:9). Again, there is Jesus' remembered logion: "Therefore what God has joined together, let no one separate" (Matt 19:6). And, again, there is an interpretive nuance: "Whoever divorces his wife, *except for porneia,* and marries another commits adultery" (19:9). The meaning of that exceptive phrase, "except for *porneia*," predictably, has been endlessly disputed. I will not enter into that debate in this book, since I agree with Collins that "its meaning is not self-evident to modern inter-preters."[4] I raise here a different question: Does the exceptive clause originate in the teaching of Jesus or of Matthew? Is it rooted in that stratum of the Gospel which faithfully records the words of Jesus, or is it from that stratum which derives from Matthew in light of the needs of his first-century Jewish community? I accept the majority scholarly opinion that the latter is the case, given Matthew's acknowledged penchant for adding to the words of Jesus for his own purposes, and given the absence of the phrase in Paul, Mark, and Luke. I wish to underscore only one conclusion from that. Matthew did not hesitate to add to the words of Jesus in light of the needs of his own Jewish-Christian Church, that is, a Church composed of Jews who had been "converted" to Christianity but who still adhered to the Jewish law, including the law of divorce for *erwat dabar* or *porneia* (Deut 24:1-4).

There are, then, divergent accounts of Jesus' saying about divorce and remarriage because divergent Christian communities had divergent concerns about marriage and divorce that needed to be addressed. The nuancing of the words of Jesus on the basis of contextual need, validated by the early Church, was continued in the later Church by Gratian in respect to what consummates a marriage as indissoluble (1140), and by the misnamed and misleading Petrine Privileges of Popes Paul III (1537), Pius V (1561), and Gregory XIII (1585) with respect to the circumstances of polygamy and slavery.[5] This consistent and acknowledged nuancing of the words of Jesus in the Church makes any argument based exclusively on the words of Jesus at best incomplete and at worst dishonest.

This brief consideration of the traditional data on divorce and remarriage leads to several important conclusions. First, it is incorrect to speak of the New Testament *teaching* on divorce and remarriage, as if there was only one. There are several *teachings* and they do not all agree. Second, not all these teachings derive from Jesus, as the Catholic Church ahistorically insinuates. Third, diverging accounts of divorce and remarriage are an integral part of the New Testament and later Christian traditions because the diverse cultural followers of Jesus sought to translate the meaning of his life, death, and resurrection into the circumstances of their concrete lives. Fourth, though popular unwisdom later singled out one element in those diverging accounts, namely the demand for indissoluble marriage, and allowed that one element to override all the others, that fact should not be allowed to obscure either the original or the ongoing divergence.

The solemn teaching of the Council of Nicea is intimately related to the Church's teaching on divorce and remarriage, and has much to say to its pastoral practice today.

There is a veneration in the Church of Ecumenical Councils, most especially of the first of them, the Council of Nicea (325), whose creed established the doctrinal basis of the Christian faith. Canon 8 of that council goes to the very heart of the question of divorce and remarriage.

> As regards those who define themselves as the Pure and who want to join the Catholic and Apostolic Church, the holy and great Council decrees that they may remain among the clergy once hands have been imposed upon them. But beforehand they will have to promise in writing to comply with the teachings of the Catholic and Apostolic Church and to make them the rule of their conduct. That is to say, they will have to communicate both with *those who married a second time [digamoi]* and with those who failed under persecution but whose time has been established and whose moment of reconciliation has arrived. They will, therefore, be bound to follow the teaching of the Catholic and Apostolic Church completely.[6]

According to this Canon, the "Pure," those who belonged to the rigorous sect called Novatians,[7] had to promise in writing to accept the teaching of the Catholic Church before they could be reconciled with it. Specifically, they had to accept to live in communion with those who had been married twice *(digamoi)* and those who had apostatized during persecution but who had completed their penance and had been reconciled to the Church. We are concerned here only with those *digamoi* who have done penance and have been reconciled to the Church.

Novatian teaching excluded from penance and reconciliation those who were guilty of certain sins "leading to death," among them *digamia*, which refers to remarriage either after the death of a spouse or after a divorce. Since, however, remarriage after the death of a spouse was not considered a sin leading to death until long after the Council of Nicea, the council's *digamoi* must be those who have remarried after a divorce or repudiation. That "sin," according to the council, can be forgiven and reconciliation with the Church can be achieved after a period of suitable penance. Acutely relevant is the fact that neither the Church before Nicea nor the council itself, in keeping with the proscriptions of Deuteronomy 24:1-4, which was binding in the Church before Nicea and which forbade a husband to take back his repudiated wife after she had married another,[8] required the repudiation of the new spouse as a

prerequisite for forgiveness and reconciliation. Basil explicitly reports
the treatment of a man who had abandoned his wife and remarried,
who had "done penance with tears," and who, after seven years, had
been accepted back "among the faithful."[9] The man's second marriage is
accepted and neither the repudiation of his second wife nor his taking
back of the first is demanded as a prerequisite for full communion. This
teaching of Basil is the foundation for the teaching and practice of the
Orthodox Church known as *oikonomia,* which I will consider in my
final thesis.

*The Catholic Church has never practiced what is enshrined in its law,
namely, that "the essential properties of marriage are unity and indissolubility" (1983 Can 1056). The actual number of marriages the Church holds
to be canonically indissoluble is, in reality, very limited.*

If the Church truly believed that indissolubility was an essential
property of *marriage,* and not just of *Christian marriage,* and that by
the will of God "from the beginning" (Mark 10:6; Matt 19:4), then it
would treat all marriages as indissoluble. It does not and never has. The
Church accepts the marriages of the non-baptized as valid when they
have been performed according to the laws which govern them and yet,
utilizing the Pauline Privilege, it regularly dissolves them "in favor of the
faith of the party who received baptism" (Can 1143). It has further
extended the Pauline Privilege, as already noted, to embrace the dissolution of valid marriages utilizing the misnamed and, therefore,
misleading Petrine Privilege. An official commentary from the Canon
Law Society of America apparently recognizes, but does not identify, the
problem. It explains the obvious discrepancies between Canon 1056
and Catholic practice by declaring that "the essential properties of marriage, unity and indissolubility, must be understood in the context of
sacramental marriage defined as the intimate community of the whole
of life."[10] Canon 1056, however, does not say that the essential properties of *sacramental marriage* are unity and indissolubility but that the
properties of *marriage* without qualification are unity and indissolubility. If *marriage* is indissoluble, then every marriage is indissoluble. That
is never what the Catholic Church has practiced, and it is not what it
practices today.

In Christian marriage, Canon 1056 adds, indissolubility is said to ac-
quire "a distinctive firmness by reason of the sacrament" (Can 1056). We
can presume that it is on this statement that the Canon Law Society's com-

mentary cited above is based. Yet, in practice, this is no more true than the preceding statement. Valid sacramental marriages which have not been consummated are dissolved "by the Roman Pontiff for a just reason, at the request of both parties or of either party" (Can 1142). Long-standing Church practice with respect to the dissolution of valid marriages demonstrates anything but a belief that an essential property of marriage in general or of sacramental marriage in particular is indissolubility.

The official doctrine of the Church on the indissolubility of marriage demonstrates that fidelity to the words of Jesus is not the only criterion for ecclesiastical judgments about divorce and remarriage. Only that marriage "which is ratified (as sacrament) and consummated cannot be dissolved by any human power other than death" (Can 1141). The two conditions which make a marriage indissoluble in the eyes of the Church, that it be both sacramental and consummated, are not conditions ever mentioned by Jesus or any of the New Testament writers. They are both the result of historical nuancing long after Jesus, despite the ahistorical and egregiously incorrect teaching of the recent *Catechism of the Catholic Church* that "the marriage bond has been established by God himself in such a way that a marriage concluded *and consummated* between baptized persons can never be dissolved" (n. 1640, my emphasis). That marriage was created by God no Catholic theologian would debate. That the marriage bond becomes indissoluble, even in a sacramental marriage, only when the marriage is consummated is a nuance added by Gratian in the twelfth century to resolve the debate between the Roman and Northern European opinions about what makes a marriage.

Jesus' logion about marriage in the Gospels declares "what God has joined together, let no one separate" (Mark 10:9; Matt 19:6). For the first thousand years of Catholic history, the Church interpreted this logion as a moral demand; man *should not* put asunder. In the twelfth century, again under the influence of Gratian, the moral demand began to be spoken of as an *ontological* reality. The *should not* gave way to *cannot*, as in "a ratified and consummated marriage *cannot* be dissolved by any human power or for any reason other than death" (Can 1141). That progression from the words of Jesus, from the moral demand, to the philosophical words of the Church, to the ontological reality, is clearly another nuance the Church added to the words of Jesus. Notice, however, that it is again not *marriage*, but *sacramental and consummated* marriage, that cannot be dissolved. We shall consider that particular question in the next section.

The Catholic Church, which teaches that the only marriage which is indissoluble is the sacramental and consummated marriage, today has no criterion for judging when a marriage has been consummated and therefore made indissoluble.

A theological question is consistently raised about the Catholic teaching on the effect of consummation: What is it that consummation adds to sacrament that makes the consummated sacramental marriage immune to dissolution? Pius XI suggested the answer lies in "the mystical meaning of Christian marriage," namely, its reference to that "most perfect union which exists between Christ and the church."[11] Though it does not specify as precisely as Pius that it is the consummated sacramental marriage that is indissoluble, the International Theological Commission offers the same reason for the indissolubility of Christian marriage. The ultimate basis for the indissolubility of Christian marriage lies in the fact that it is the sacrament, the image, of the indissoluble union between Christ and the Church.

But questions remain. When Pius XI wrote in 1930, he took for granted the 1917 Code of Canon Law that dealt with marriage as a contract (Can 1012), that declared the object of the contract to be the exclusive and perpetual right to the body of the other for acts suitable for the generation of offspring (Can 1081.2), and that declared the ends of marriage to be primarily procreation and secondarily mutual help and the remedy of concupiscence (Can 1013). In such a legalist and physicalist context, it is easy to see how a single act of sexual intercourse could be taken to be the consummation of a marriage. It is not so easy to see in the changed theological and personalist climate in which the Second Vatican Council rooted its doctrine on marriage.

The council teaches that marriage "is rooted in the conjugal covenant of irrevocable personal consent."[12] Despite insistent demands to retain the legal word *contract* as a precise way to speak of marriage, the council demurred and chose instead the biblical, theological, and personal word *covenant*. Though the legal effects of contract and covenant are identical, this choice locates marriage as a primarily interpersonal rather than legal reality, and brings it into line with the rich biblical tradition of covenant between God and God's people and Christ and Christ's Church. The revised Code also preferred *covenant* to *contract* (Can 1055.1), though it relapses into contractual language some thirty times.

The council made another change to Catholic teaching about marriage, which is central to any modern theological discussion of consummation and which was later also incorporated into the revised Code.

The traditional teaching on the ends of marriage was the primary end-secondary end hierarchy between procreation and spousal love (1917 Can 1013). Despite insistent demands to reaffirm this hierarchical terminology, the council refused to do so. It taught explicitly that procreation "does not make the other ends of marriage of less account," and that marriage "is not instituted solely for procreation."[13] That this refusal to speak of a hierarchy of ends in marriage was not the result of oversight but a deliberate choice was confirmed when the council's teaching on ends was incorporated into the revised Code (Can 1055.1).

This change of perspective raises questions about the claim that the spouses' first sexual intercourse is the consummation of their mutual self-gifting and marriage. If the procreation of human life *and* the *consortium-communion* between the spouses are equal ends of marriage, why should an act of sexual intercourse alone be the symbol of the union of Christ and Christ's Church? Why should the diachronic interpersonal union between the spouses, the traditional marital *consortium*, itself symbolized in sexual communion among other things, not be the symbol? I have dealt with this at length in the preceding chapter and I will not repeat the argument here. I will note only that this question has been exacerbated by the change in the way consummation is specified in both the council and the revised Code. A marriage is now said to be "ratified and consummated if the spouses have in a *human manner [humano modo]* engaged together in a conjugal act in itself apt for the generation of offspring" (1983 Can 1061.1). The phrase I have underscored has placed Catholic teaching on consummation and indissolubility on hold theologically and canonically, for as yet a theology of sexuality elucidating what sexual intercourse *humano modo* means has not been elaborated. Since marital intercourse *humano modo* cannot be precisely defined, neither can the marital consummation it is said to effect. And since the consummation of a marriage cannot be precisely defined, neither can the radical indissolubility of the marriage which hinges on it. Many more valid marriages than heretofore ever imagined are, therefore, now open to dissolution in the Church.

The Code's claim that "a valid marriage contract cannot exist between baptized persons without its being by that very fact a sacrament" (Can 1055.2) contradicts the Catholic dogma that faith is necessary for the reception of grace and salvation.

This thesis has been explicated at length in Chapter 3 and need only be summarized here. The Code presumes something that can never be theologically presumed for free adults, namely, that all that is required for the *sacrament* of marriage is prior baptism and a valid marriage contract. That presumption stands in contradiction to the long tradition about the necessity of personal faith in Catholic teaching. The Gospels record that Jesus both complained about the absence of faith and praised its presence (Matt 8:5-13, 23-27; 9:2, 20-22; 17:19-21; 21:18-22; Mark 5:25-34; 6:1-6). Paul vehemently defended the necessity of personal faith for salvation (Rom 1:16-17; 3:26-30; 5:1; Gal 3:6-9). That tradition of the necessity of faith continued in the Church and flowered on both sides of the Reformation controversies.

Martin Luther made his stand on "faith alone." Though wishing to combat the Lutheran teaching that faith *alone* was necessary for salvation, the Council of Trent left no doubt about the necessity of personal faith: "Faith is the beginning of man's salvation, the foundation and source of all justification, 'without which it is impossible to please God' (Heb 11:6)."[14] Baptism is "the sacrament of faith, without which no man has ever been justified."[15] The Latin text makes clear that "without which" *(sine qua)* qualifies faith and not sacrament or baptism, both of which would require *sine quo.* There is no doubt that the Fathers of Trent wished to affirm solemnly the primacy of active, personal faith for salvation. So also did both the First and Second Vatican Councils: faith is an act by which "a man gives *free* obedience to God by cooperating and agreeing with his grace, which can be resisted";[16] faith is an act by which "man entrusts his whole self *freely* to God, offering 'the full submission of intellect and will to God who reveals,' and *freely* assenting to the truth revealed by him."[17] That free, cooperating personal faith is required for salvation is a solemn dogma of the Catholic Church.

Convinced of the necessity of faith for the validity of baptism, Augustine sought to make good the lack of faith in infant baptism by arguing that *ecclesia fidem supplet,* the Church supplies for the infant's lack of the faith required.[18] That argument cannot be applied in the case of marriage, a sacrament for adults who are required to have an active faith to participate in any sacrament. Aquinas never doubted that "every sacrament remains a sign and a proclamation of personal faith. Whoever receives it without believing in his heart places himself in a violent state of 'fiction' and deprives himself of sacramental grace."[19] Bonaventure agrees: the sacrament of marriage can be distinguished only by personal faith.[20]

The 1980 Synod of Bishops gave quasi-unanimous support (201 *placet*, 3 *non placet*) to the following proposition: "We have to take into

account the engaged couple's degree of faith maturity and their awareness of doing what the church does. *This intention is required for sacramental validity.* It is absent if there is not at least a minimal intention of
believing with the church" (my emphasis). Sacramental intention is critical in sacramental theology. To intend to participate in a sacrament, the
participant must intend what the Church intends in the sacrament. The
theological question is: Can a person have a real intention to participate
in a sacrament without at least minimal personal faith?

Aquinas has no doubt: "Faith directs intention, and without [faith]
intention cannot be right" *(fides intentionem dirigit, et sine ea non potest
esse . . . intentio recta).*[21] The International Theological Commission
continues that tradition: the real intention is born from and feeds on
living faith.[22] One cannot have a right sacramental intention without at
least a minimum of personal faith. When personal faith is absent, so too
is right sacramental intention; when right intention is absent, as the tradition universally holds, the sacrament is not valid. No personal faith-no
right intention is a well-founded theological judgment. The conclusion
that flows from it is equally well founded: without faith no one can
enter into a valid sacramental marriage.

The intention required to participate in a sacrament, as distinct from
a mere physical rite, is the intention to participate in a rite that offers
salvation, a God-in-Christ, Christ-in-Church, and believer-in-God,
Christ, and Church event. Neither God-in-Christ nor Christ-in-Church
can be intended, however, without being at least minimally known and
embraced in faith. The connection of personal faith to valid sacrament
is particularly relevant today when Catholic theology distinguishes the
baptized as *baptized believers,* those who have been baptized and have
been nurtured into active faith, and *baptized nonbelievers,* those who
have been baptized and not nurtured into active faith.[23] The two should
never be confused in law. If they are confused in law, as they are presently
in Canon 1055.2, no legal pronouncement will ever make up for the
lack of personal faith that is necessary for valid sacrament.

*The Code's claim that "a ratified and consummated marriage cannot be
dissolved by any human power" (Can 1141) ignores the more-than-human
power in the Church capable of dissolving such marriages.*

Though the question of the consummation of a marriage is now
moot until the meaning of *humano modo* can be defined, there is still a
more-than-human power in the Church to dissolve a failed ratified and

consummated marriage. Two things are to be noted. First, the question asks about extrinsic indissolubility, the immunity of a marriage to dissolution by an agent other than the spouses. There is universal agreement that a *marriage* (not only a ratified and consummated marriage) is intrinsically indissoluble, that is, immune to dissolution by the spouses, as it was, for instance, in ancient Rome. Second, the extrinsic indissolubility of a ratified and consummated marriage as prescribed in the Code is not a revealed truth. Billot's opinion that it is defined, infallible Catholic faith *(de fide catholica)* has never found support;[24] most theologians judge it to be undefined, general Catholic teaching *(doctrina catholica)*. Urban Navarrette's claim that Pius XI implicitly and Pius XII explicitly affirm that the ratified and consummated marriage cannot be dissolved, not even by the vicarious power of the Roman Pontiff, is an exaggeration.[25] Both popes do no more than cite without comment the legislation then current in Canon 1118. They add nothing that would elevate the teaching to a theological level higher than *doctrina catholica.*

The history of the doctrine and law about ratified and consummated marriage in the Catholic tradition demonstrates three facts. First, it is a compromise between the Roman law in which free consent makes a valid marriage and the northern European custom in which sexual intercourse makes a valid marriage. As we have noted several times already, the compromise, offered by Gratian, the Master of the University of Bologna, in the twelfth century, was that consent initiates a valid marriage and intercourse *consummates* it (Can 1061). Second, the compromise emerges from a mixed cultural understanding of marriage, the southern culture of twelfth-century Europe, which emphasized legal consent, and the northern culture, which emphasized sexual intercourse leading to the required fertility. Third, it is not defined Catholic faith; it is undefined, general Catholic teaching. That is not to say that it is not true; it is to say only that it is not irreformable. The agent of reformation is surely the same agent that introduced the teaching in the first place: not God, not Jesus, but the magisterial Church. There is a power in that Church that extends to the binding and loosing of sin and to the transformation of bread and wine. That momentous power surely extends also to the reformation of a reformable doctrine the Church itself inaugurated. If a non-consummated marriage between baptized believers, that is, a sacramental marriage which falls under God's law, "can be dissolved by the Roman Pontiff for a just reason" (Can 1142), a ratified and consummated marriage which falls under the Church's law can also be dissolved by the Roman Pontiff for a similarly just reason. The bond of a ratified and consummated marriage is far from immune to the much-more-than-human power daily exercised in the Church.

The argument that Catholics who are divorced and remarried civilly without annulment are "in a situation that objectively contravenes God's law . . . consequently they cannot receive holy communion as long as this situation persists,"[26] is contrary to the universal law of the Catholic Church, obedience to which takes precedence over obedience to a Roman dicastery.

Among the most serious and pervasive pastoral problems facing the Catholic Church in the Western world today is the problem of Catholics who, after their own or their current spouse's divorce, have civilly remarried in contravention of the Church's law. Their remarriage places them in an irregular situation in the Church and they are, consequently, banned from the reception of Holy Communion as long as their irregular situation persists. With respect to this situation, basing himself on interviews with priests working with alienated Catholics in Boston, New York, Providence, and Wilmington (Del.), Kenneth Himes comments that "the single biggest reason people cease active participation in the Church is that they have found themselves in irregular marital situations and feel themselves unwanted by the Church."[27] After a five-year study of divorced and remarried Catholics in England, Buckley reaches a similar conclusion. He reports that the consensus of bishops, priests, and people is that "something is seriously wrong with the present teaching and that more than that it is a scandal."[28] The situation of divorced and civilly remarried Catholics is clearly a pressing and painful pastoral problem.

In July 1993, the bishops of the Upper Rhine province in Germany issued a statement of pastoral principles with respect to this situation. In their statement they outlined a differentiated pastoral approach by which some civilly divorced and remarried Catholics, whose subjective state had been judged to be not gravely sinful after serious discussion with a competent pastor, might be allowed to share Holy Communion. The approach suggested by the Bishops was not a blanket approach by which every civilly divorced and remarried Catholic could share communion; it was a differentiated, case-by-case approach by which *some* Catholics, in certain situations and under certain conditions, could be permitted to share communion.[29] In September 1994, the Congregation for the Doctrine of the Faith (CDF) issued a response to the German bishops which strongly affirmed the exclusion of divorced and remarried Catholics from Holy Communion.

The CDF argued as follows:

> If the divorced are remarried civilly, they find themselves in a situation
> that *objectively contravenes* God's law. Consequently, they cannot receive
> Holy Communion as long as this situation persists. . . . This norm is not
> at all a punishment or a discrimination against the divorced and remar-
> ried, but rather expresses an objective situation that of itself renders im-
> possible the reception of Holy Communion.[30]

The argument is clear. The exclusion of the civilly divorced and remarried from communion is based on the objective, presumed grave, sinfulness of their remarriage contrary to the laws of the Church. The CDF
is an authoritative voice of the Catholic Church and, therefore, should
be listened to carefully. It is, however, neither the only nor the prime
Catholic authority pertaining to the reception of Holy Communion in
the Catholic Church. The prime authority is the Code of Canon Law,
and the matter is clear from Book IV, Title III, Chapter I, Article 2 of the
Code, "Participation in the Blessed Eucharist."

The relevant canons prescribe the following: "Any baptized person who
is not forbidden by law may and must be admitted to Holy Communion"
(Can 912); "those upon whom the penalty of excommunication or interdict has been imposed or declared, and others who obstinately persist in
manifest *grave sin,* are not to be admitted to Holy Communion" (Can
915, my emphasis); "anyone who is conscious of *grave sin* may not celebrate mass or receive the Body of the Lord without previously having
been to sacramental confession" (Can 916, my emphasis).

Since the first part of Canon 915 does not apply to Catholics who
have been divorced and civilly remarried without annulment, because
they are neither excommunicated nor placed under interdict, that leaves
only the question of *grave sin* or *mortal sin* in the terms of Canons 915
and 916. The question can be put succinctly: Does grave sin in the
Catholic tradition, and therefore in the mind of the legislator, follow
from the fact that an action "objectively contravenes God's law" or constitutes gravely sinful matter? The answer can be put just as succinctly:
in Catholic moral theology an objectively gravely sinful action does not
ipso facto result in grave sin. In addition to objectively grave matter,
grave sin requires both full consciousness of the sinfulness of the action
and full, free consent to the action. The civil remarriage of the divorced
Catholic without annulment may constitute grave matter in the eyes of
the Church; it may even, on occasion, constitute grave sin. But it constitutes *grave* sin only when there is full awareness and full, free consent.

Those Catholics who have attempted remarriage after divorce without obtaining an annulment, and especially those who have been unable to obtain an annulment for some formal reason, do not all *necessarily* have the required full awareness and free consent to commit grave sin. They are not, therefore, all guilty of grave sin and are not all, therefore, prohibited by law from receiving Holy Communion.

Those who are not guilty of grave sin because the traditional conditions for grave sin—objectively grave matter, full consciousness, and free consent—have not all been met (and whether or not the conditions have been met can be decided only on a case-by-case basis in discussion with a competent pastor), *must* be admitted to Holy Communion according to the universal law of the Catholic Church (Can 912). No undifferentiated pronouncement of any Roman dicastery, or even of the Bishop of Rome,[31] can bar them from the communion to which they are entitled by faith and by law. And no minister of the Church should either be put in or assume the invidious position of refusing them, at the risk of destroying their good name and defaming them, the Holy Communion to which they are entitled.

In 1995 Fr. Patrick Travers published an essay in which he offered an argument similar to the one I offer here,[32] with a notable exception. While my argument is essentially *theological*, hinging on the traditional theological meaning of the phrase *grave sin*, Travers' argument is essentially *canonical*, according to "the 1983 Code of Canon Law." Travers' essay drew criticism from canon lawyers, directly for the "flawed" canonical methodology it followed and indirectly for its consequent conclusions,[33] and he later published a "revisitation" of his earlier essay.[34] In that revisitation, he convincingly defended himself and his original methodology against the criticisms leveled at it, but he presented also a reassessment and a retraction of his previous conclusions. The reassessment and retraction, he writes, were not occasioned by the criticisms of his earlier essay but by a declaration of Pope John Paul II to the Pontifical Council for the Family subsequent to his earlier essay.[35] I note these facts only to record that I find Travers' retraction of his previously sound *canonical* conclusions supremely unconvincing, so obviously unconvincing that one is forced to wonder about the source of his reassessment and retraction.

Travers' original essay examined the effect under the 1983 Code of Canon Law of the publication of the CDF's "Letter to the Bishops of the Catholic Church Concerning the Reception of Holy Communion by Divorced and Remarried Members of the Faithful," to which I drew attention earlier. The essay raised questions about whether the prescriptions of the letter

> in certain circumstances might contrast with the provisions of canons 915 and 916 of the 1983 Code, which prescribe limits on the reception of Holy Communion by certain persons living in specified sinful circumstances, and with canon 912, which requires that any baptized person not prohibited by law be admitted to Holy Communion.[36]

The conclusion that *some* Catholics who had attempted marriage after civil divorce could be admitted to Holy Communion *under certain conditions* hinged on the argument that such Catholics could not be barred from communion in a blanket way on the basis of the CDF's judgment that "they find themselves in a situation that objectively contravenes God's law."[37] The grave sin, or mortal sin, of canons 915 and 916, as I have argued, theologically requires not only gravely sinful matter, like attempted marriage after divorce, but also full knowledge and full, free consent. On this basis, Travers' original essay concluded that, under the prescriptions of canons 912, 915, and 916, there was the possibility that the requirements of the Code and of the CDF's letter could conflict, and the possibility that, under certain conditions, some Catholics who had attempted remarriage after divorce could be permitted to share Holy Communion. Exactly what I have also argued.

What caused Travers to reassess and retract this conclusion? He says it was the address of Pope John Paul II to the Pontifical Council on the Family which "resolved these questions in a decisive manner."[38] We are entitled to ask how John Paul resolved "these questions," which ask about the meaning of "grave sin" in canons 915 and 916, specifically does "grave sin" mean only the objectively sinful situation or does it include also the traditional subjective requirements of full knowledge and free, full consent? Travers' answer is that the Pope "strongly prescribed the categorical exclusion of Catholics who have attempted remarriage after divorce from reception of the Holy Eucharist and of the sacrament of penance, based solely on the objective fact of their attempt at such remarriage."[39] He did this simply by repeating what he had already said in *Familiaris Consortio* and in the *Catechism of the Catholic Church* (n. 1650), and what the CDF had said in its Letter, namely, that the state of life of the divorced and remarried "objectively contradict that union of love between Christ and the Church which is signified and effected by the Eucharist."[40]

The difference John Paul's address makes to any previous interpretation, Travers argues, is that in this address, for the first time since the publication of the new canons, a pope is making an authentic interpretation of Canons 915 and 916 as their "legislator."[41] The Pope's address, according to Travers, changes the meaning of "grave sin" in Canon 915 while leaving it with its traditional meaning of mortal sin in Canon 916. In Canon 915, grave sin no longer means what it has meant theologically for centuries, namely, mortal sin with all its subjective requirements; it now means, for the first time ever in Catholic history, "gravely sinful matter, the external, objective element accessible to the minister of Holy Communion."[42] This conclusion is so extraordinary, and so contrary to the received tradition about grave sin, that Travers is obliged to confess that "it is, of course, highly remarkable that the 1983 Code uses a single term, *peccatum grave*, in immediately adjacent canons to express two realities which, while related, differ in critically important ways."[43] Highly remarkable, indeed, and highly improbable and unconvincing; so unconvincing that one is left again to wonder about the source for such reassessment and retraction.

I believe Travers is exaggerating. In his address, John Paul is doing no more than citing without legislative comment the teaching that civilly-divorced and remarried Catholics are in a situation which *objectively* contravenes God's law and is, therefore, *objectively* sinful. He makes no comment whatever, either explicitly or implicitly, about their *subjective* situation or sinfulness. Travers' reassessment of the meaning of "grave sin" in Canon 915 is so wide of the long established theological and undebated requirements for "grave sin" that it must be judged to be in theological error. The theological argument I offered in this section, and the argument Travers offered in his original essay, stand: those who are not subjectively guilty of grave sin, because the objective *and* subjective requirements for grave sin have not all been met, *must* be admitted to Holy Communion according to the law of the Catholic Church (Can 912).

The scandal insinuated in both papal and dicasterial statements if divorced and civilly remarried Catholics are admitted to communion is no different from the scandal one could insinuate in solutions approved by the Church.

Pope John Paul II specifies the scandal that might ensue if civilly divorced and remarried Catholics were admitted to communion: "the faithful would be led into error and confusion regarding the Church's teaching about the indissolubility of marriage."[44] The CDF repeats his judgment without commentary.[45] The implication is that, if civilly divorced and remarried Catholics were admitted to communion, people might believe that the Church no longer teaches that fidelity is required in marriage and that marriage is indissoluble. No one should ever underestimate the possibility of scandal, but neither should anyone overestimate it. No one, in fact, should ever estimate it at all, for real scandal is a fact which can be clarified empirically. Real scandal is in the same category as real sin; it can, and therefore must, be clarified on a case-by-case basis.

There are two cases in which the Church permits the civilly divorced and remarried to approach communion. The first is the case in which a couple has received the necessary annulment(s) to be free to marry; the second is the case in which a couple agrees to live continent as brother and sister. Neither case removes the threat of scandal.

The brother-sister case, in which the couple lives together publicly as husband and wife but abstains from all sexual intercourse, provides the same threat of scandal as the case of a couple not living as brother and sister, for no modern adult conscious of the ways of men and women would ever presume sexual celibacy in a couple living together as husband and wife. Kevin Kelly notes the obvious: "Unless a couple had a 'brother and sister' logo on their doorstep, neighbors and fellow parishioners would be none the wiser and so the alleged scandal would presumably still be given."[46] Given these obvious empirical considerations, it is astonishing to see the pope[47] and the new *Catechism* (n. 1650) presenting the brother-sister solution as a genuine pastoral option, completely ignoring the weight of theologians and canonists who teach that this option is full of danger and should be employed rarely and almost never.[48] The case of annulment runs the same peril. Unless a couple publicized their annulment from the sanctuary, most fellow-parishioners would never know about its existence. Today, indeed, when annulment has become so commonplace, those fellow parishioners would simply assume that the couple had been granted annulment(s) and think no more of it. Most of them would take the same approach to the divorced and civilly remarried approaching communion.

The scandal given in the case of civilly divorced and remarried Catholics may lie not with the remarried but with the Church which bars them from full communion. Recall Himes's American report that "the single biggest reason people cease active participation in the Church is that they have found themselves in irregular marital situations and feel unwanted and rejected by the Church,"[49] and Buckley's English report that the consensus of bishops, priests, and people is that "something is seriously wrong with the present teaching and that more than that it is a *scandal*."[50] Cardinal Newman wrote of the general consensus of the faithful which senses error and "at once feels it as a *scandal*."[51] Sound empirical connection to Newman's sense of error and scandal among the faithful in the United States is provided in a 1992 survey, in which only 23 percent of Catholics agreed that the Magisterium *alone* should decide the morality of a divorced Catholic remarrying without an annulment, and 72 percent agreed that divorced and remarried Catholics should be able to receive communion.[52] In 1999, only 20 percent of Catholics agreed the Magisterium alone should decide the morality of a divorced Catholic marrying without an annulment.[53] The faithful's sense of scandal and non-scandal could not be empirically clearer.

The Roman Catholic Church should embrace the Orthodox practice of oikonomia, *declared by the Council of Trent to have certain claim to the gospel and to the name Christian.*

Questions raised by divorce and remarriage confront all the Christian churches in the United States today. Not one of them escapes. What should the churches do about divorce and remarriage? They should, I suggest, pay close attention to the ancient Orthodox practice of *oikonomia*. Oikonomia flourishes within a context of spirit and grace, not of law. It grows out of the powerful Orthodox faith in the continuing benevolent and merciful action in the Church of the Spirit of God and of Christ. *Oikonomia* refers to the order of salvation in Christ. In that order of salvation, God is the benevolent and merciful Father of the household *(oikos)*; Jesus is the Good Shepherd who leaves ninety-nine good sheep for a time to lead to salvation one that is lost (Luke 15:3-7); the Holy Spirit is the omnipresent comforter who makes possible in the household every good; the Church is the householder, as benevolent and merciful as the father of the household (Luke 6:36; Matt 5:44-48). *Oikonomia* is embedded in a context of grace, not of law. It heeds the Gospel injunction that "the letter kills, but the Spirit gives life" (2 Cor 3:6). *Oikonomia* cannot exist without great faith in the Father and Spirit of the *oikos*, and of the Christ they continue to send.

How does *oikonomia* relate to the question of divorce and remarriage? While holding firmly to the belief that the Gospel presents to Christians a demand for indissoluble marriage, the Orthodox churches also acknowledge that men and women sometimes do not measure up to the gospel. They acknowledge that marriages, even Christian marriages, die and, when they die, it makes no sense to argue they are still binding. When a marriage is dead, even if the spouses still live, *oikonomia* impels the Church to be not only sad, for the death of a marriage is always "the death of a small civilization,"[54] but also compassionate, for the Church represents the merciful God. This compassion extends to permitting the remarriage of an innocent or repentant spouse. The liturgy differentiates the second marriage from the first, highlighting that grace is always threatened by sin, that Christian ideal is always at the mercy of human frailty. It lacks the joy of the first marriage; it ritually proclaims that no one in attendance, including the priest, is without sin. It is in just such an economy that the householder-Church is summoned to minister compassionately on behalf of the compassionate God.

A reasonable Christian objection arises at this point. Should not what the churches do about divorce and remarriage be based on the tradition of Jesus mediated to them in the New Testament? Yes, it should, and we considered that tradition briefly and found diverging accounts of divorce and remarriage in the New Testament as culturally diverse followers of Jesus sought to translate the meaning of his life, death, and resurrection into their diverse cultural lives. That early process of interpreting the Lord's command concerning divorce and remarriage continued in the churches of both East and West. The East developed its doctrine of *oikonomia* related to marriage, the West developed its law related to marriage which continues in force today.

In the twelfth century, the Bologna canonist Gratian developed two pieces of legislation which continue to be a central part of Roman Catholic law. The first was a continuation of Paul's exception, now called the Pauline Privilege, which remains today one of the bases on which the Catholic Church grants the dissolution of a valid marriage (Can 1143). The Pauline Privilege, as noted earlier, has been much extended beyond what Paul ever envisioned by the so-called Petrine Privilege. The second piece of legislation was a compromise solution between the Roman and northern European answers to the question of when a valid marriage came into existence. "Marriage is initiated by betrothal (consent), perfected (or consummated) by sexual intercourse."[55] These two pieces of legislation became enshrined in the law of the Roman Catholic Church with respect to the indissolubility of marriage. That Church regards as indissoluble only that marriage which is both sacramental *and* consummated by sexual intercourse (Can 1141). It holds all other marriages to be dissoluble and it dissolves them on occasion "for a just reason" (Can 1142) or "in favor of the faith" (Can 1143).

Several things are clear. First, despite every claim to follow only the Lord's command, the Catholic Church also follows Paul, Matthew,

Gratian, and medieval popes in interpreting and extending that command for their ongoing situations. Second, it is not true that the Roman Catholic Church never grants divorces. It grants them regularly in valid marriages which are not sacramental or not consummated, though it obscures that fact by naming the process dissolution rather than divorce. Third, though there is no warrant in the New Testament for such canonical processes, there is ample warrant for *oikonomia,* a fact to which the Council of Trent attested. Despite hewing to a rigid line on the question of the indissolubility of marriage, the council steadfastly refused to condemn the practice of *oikonomia* or to declare that it did not have equal claim to the gospel tradition and to the name Christian.[56]

The 1980 Synod of Bishops presented to Pope John Paul a request that the Orthodox practice of *oikonomia* be studied for any light it might shed on a pastoral approach to Catholics who are civilly divorced and remarried. Many of those second marriages have become so stable, and the families nurtured by them so Christian, that they cannot be abandoned without serious spiritual, emotional, and economic harm. The Catholic Church must discern whether its understanding of the Gospel precludes the development of an *oikonomia* approach to the care of its members in second marriages. It is summoned to Gospel *oikonomia* as a way to alleviate the suffering of those thousands of Catholics divorced and remarried without sin and as a way to attain the ecclesial peace and communion to which God has called all Christians (1 Cor 7:15).

There is strong support in every sector of the Church for reassessment of the pastoral practice related to divorce and remarriage, especially among women who know that women frequently suffer most from divorce.[57] The theological question for assessment can be clearly stated. Can the Catholic Church continue to claim fidelity to the total economy revealed by the compassionate and merciful God and continue to permit one element of that economy, its reading of Jesus' words on divorce and remarriage, to override all others. The question does not admit of an easy answer. But a Church faithful to the Gospel, and to the Spirit who continues to reveal its meanings in contemporary context, can face it secure in the belief that the Spirit will lead it into the truth of God as surely today as at any time in the past.

Questions for Reflection

1. What fidelity to the words of Jesus do Paul and Matthew practice? What fidelity to the words of Jesus does the Catholic Church practice when it dissolves valid marriages on the basis of the Pauline Privilege and the Petrine Privilege?

2. The Catholic Church teaches that the only marriage that is indissoluble is the marriage that is both sacramental and consummated. When did Jesus teach this? If Jesus did not teach this doctrine, why does the Catholic Church follow it?

3. Thesis 8 argues that the claim that Catholics who are civilly divorced and remarried without the annulment of their first marriage are in an objective situation that contravenes God's law and, therefore, cannot receive Holy Communion is contrary to the law and moral practice of the Catholic Church. What do you think? What does this thesis have to say generally about morality and conscience?

4. Do you think that Catholics who are divorced should be allowed to remarry in the Church and to share communion? What scandal would be given to ordinary people by this practice?

5. What do you understand by the Orthodox practice of *oikonomia*? Do you think it is in accord with the Gospels?

Notes

[1] This essay is a revised version of one that appeared in *New Theology Review* 12 (1999) 48–63. It is reprinted here with permission.

[2] Michael G. Lawler, *Symbol and Sacrament: A Contemporary Sacramental Theology* (Omaha: Creighton University Press, 1995) 5–62.

[3] Congregation for the Doctrine of the Faith, "Concerning the Reception of Holy Communion by Divorced and Remarried Members of the Faithful," *Origins* (October 27, 1994).

[4] Raymond F. Collins, *Divorce in the New Testament* (Collegeville: The Liturgical Press, 1992) 205.

[5] See Michael G. Lawler, *Marriage and Sacrament: A Theology of Christian Marriage* (Collegeville: The Liturgical Press, 1993) 92–3.

[6] J. D. Mansi, ed., *Sacrorum Conciliorum Nova Collectio,* vol. II (Paris: Welter, 1903–27) 672, my emphasis.

[7] Charles J. Hefele, *A History of the Councils of the Church,* vol. I (Edinburgh: Clark, 1883) 410.

[8] See Origen, PG 13.1237; and Jerome, PL 22.563.

[9] Basil the Great, *Epistola LXXVIII,* PG 32.804–5.

[10] James A. Coriden, Thomas J. Green, and Donald E. Heintschel, eds., *The Code of Canon Law: A Text and Commentary* (Mahwah, N.J.: Paulist Press, 1985) 742.

[11] AAS (1930) 552.

[12] GS 48.

[13] GS 50.

[14] DS 1532.

[15] DS 1529.

[16] DS 3010, my emphasis.

[17] DV 5.

[18] *Epist. 98, The Fathers of the Church,* vol. 18 (New York: Fathers of the Church, 1953) 133–8.

[19] Louis Villette, *Foi et sacrement: De Saint Thomas à Karl Barth* (Paris: Bloud et Gay, 1964) 40.

[20] *IV Sent.,* d. 26, a. 2, q. 1. *Opera Omnia,* 6.215.

[21] *IV Sent.,* d. 6, q. 1, a. 3 ad 5.

[22] Richard Malone and John Connery, eds., *Contemporary Perspectives on Christian Marriage: Propositions and Papers from the International Theological Commission* (Chicago: Loyola Press, 1984) 15.

[23] Ibid., 14–21.

[24] Louis Billot, *De Ecclesiae Sacramentis* (Rome: Universitas Gregoriana, 1929) 440.

[25] Urban Navarette, "Indissolubilitas Matrimonii Rati et Consummati: Opiniones Recentiores et Observationes," *Periodica* 58 (1969) 449.

[26] Congregation for the Doctrine of the Faith, "Concerning the Reception of Holy Communion by Divorced and Remarried Members of the Faithful," *Origins* 24 (October 27, 1994) 339.

[27] Kenneth Himes and James Coriden, "Notes on Moral Theology 1995: Pastoral Care of the Divorced and Remarried," TS 57 (1966) 118.

[28] Timothy J. Buckley, *What Binds Marriage? Roman Catholic Theology in Practice* (London: Chapman, 1997) 178.

[29] The Bishops' document "Respekt vor der Gewissensentscheidung," was first published in *Herder-Korrespondenz* 47 (1993) 460–7. An English translation appeared later in *Origins* (March 10, 1994) 670–6.

[30] Congregation for the Doctrine of the Faith, *Epistola ad Catholicae Ecclesiae Episcopos de Receptione Communionis Eucharisticae a Fidelibus Qui post Divortium Novas Inierunt Nuptias* (Rome: Libreria Editrice Vaticana, 1994) n. 4, my emphasis. An English translation appeared in *Origins* (October 27, 1994) 338–40.

[31] See John Paul II, AAS 74.185.

[32] Patrick J. Travers, "Reception of the Holy Eucharist by Catholics Attempting Remarriage after Divorce and the 1983 Code of Canon Law," *The Jurist* 55 (1995) 187–217.

[33] See Michael Manning, "Reception of Holy Communion by Divorced and Remarried Catholics," *Canon Law Society of Great Britain and Ireland Newsletter* 111:3 (1997) 63–71; and John J. Myers, "Divorce, Remarriage, and Reception of the Holy Eucharist," *The Jurist* 57 (1997) 485–516.

[34] Patrick J. Travers, "Holy Communion and Catholics Who Have Attempted Remarriage after Divorce: A Revisitation," *The Jurist* 57 (1997) 517–40.

[35] John Paul II, Address to Members of the Plenary Session of the Pontifical Council for the Family, AAS 89 (1997) 482–5. This address was also published in *Origins* (February 20, 1997) 583–4.

[36] Travers, "Holy Communion and Catholics Who Have Attempted Remarriage," 520.

[37] Congregation for the Doctrine of the Faith, Letter, n. 4.

[38] Travers, "Holy Communion and Catholics Who Have Attempted Remarriage," 524.

[39] Ibid., 525.

[40] FC 84.

[41] Travers, "Holy Communion and Catholics Who Have Attempted Remarriage," 528.

[42] Ibid., 530.

[43] Ibid.

[44] FC 84.

[45] "Concerning the Reception of Holy Communion," n. 4.

[46] Kevin T. Kelly, "Divorce and Remarriage: Conflict in the Church," *The Tablet* 248 (1994) 1374.

[47] AAS 74.186.

[48] B. Sullivan, *Legislation and Requirement for Permissible Cohabitation as Invalid Marriages* (Washington, D.C.: Catholic University Press of America, 1954) viii.

[49] Himes and Coriden, "Notes on Moral Theology 1995," 118.

[50] Buckley, *What Binds Marriage?* 178.

[51] John Henry Newman, *On Consulting the Faithful in Matters of Doctrine* (London: Collins, 1986) 73.

[52] William V. D'Antonio et al., *Laity American and Catholic: Transforming the Church* (Kansas City, Mo.: Sheed and Ward, 1996) 53.

[53] William V. D'Antonio, "The American Catholic Laity in 1999," *National Catholic Reporter* (October 29, 1999) 12.

[54] Judith S. Wallerstein and Sandra Blakeslee, *Second Chances: Men, Women, and Children a Decade after Divorce* (New York: Ticknor and Fields, 1989) xxi.

[55] Gratian, PL 187.1429 and 1406.

[56] DS 1807.

[57] See the statistics reported in *Time* (June 22, 1992) 64–5 and in *National Catholic Reporter* (October 29, 1999) 12–20.

6

Interchurch Marriages:
Theological and Pastoral Reflections[1]

For the past thirty years I have taught a course on the theology of marriage at a Catholic university. As a result, I have been called upon regularly to give advice to young couples planning to marry, some 35 percent of them these days in the United States of two different Christian denominations. Like all young people in the culture of divorce in which Americans now live, they have questions about commitment, lifelong marriage, divorce, and children. If they are of two different denominations, they also have particular questions about the interchurch marriage they are planning, for they have heard that heterogamous marriages are less stable than homogamous marriages.[2] Two approached me last semester, I shall call them Sarah, who claimed to be a Catholic, and Philip, who was a Presbyterian. What follows is a brief overview of our conversations.

Theological Considerations

An important first item is how to talk about their marriage. At our first meeting Sarah and Philip used a traditional term, *mixed marriage*. In 1917, the Catholic Church's Code of Canon Law proscribed mixed marriages. "The church everywhere most severely prohibits the marriage between two baptized persons, one of whom is a Catholic, the other of whom belongs to a heretical or schismatic sect" (Can 1060). No one in

1917 could be in much doubt: in the eyes of the Catholic Church, and in many other churches, a mixed marriage was something evil and to be avoided. In 1983, however, the Code was specifically revised in the matter of "mixed marriages." It now reads: "Without the express permission of the competent authority, marriage is prohibited between two baptized persons, one of whom was baptized in the Catholic Church . . . the other of whom belongs to a Church or ecclesial communion not in full communion with the Catholic Church" (Can 1124). The softening of the language was obvious to Sarah and Philip, especially the language referring to Philip. No longer is he described negatively as a heretic or schismatic; he is now described positively as a Christian of another church. This softening of the language furthers the matter of terminology.

Several terms are used to describe religiously heterogamous marriages. The broadest are *interreligious marriage,* which emphasizes the different religions involved, and *interfaith marriage,* which emphasizes the different belief systems involved. I believe that both terms are not specific enough to describe the marriage of a Christian married to another Christian of a different denomination and are best reserved for the marriage between a Christian and someone of another religion. The Code's description of Philip as a Christian belonging to another Church points toward a term which has become common: *interchurch marriage.* This term describes the marriage between spouses from two Christian denominations, in which each spouse participates in her or his own Church and, to some degree, in the spouse's Church, and in which both spouses take an active part in the religious education of their children.[3] This definition has the disadvantage that it embraces only a small percentage of interchurch couples, those at the high end of the religiosity spectrum,[4] but it has the advantage of being the term coming into common usage. Interchurch marriage is the term I will use throughout this essay. I will use it in its broadest sense, however, to embrace every marriage in which the spouses belong, however loosely, to two different Christian churches or denominations.

When I explained to Sarah and Philip the Code's abandonment of the term *mixed marriage,* they asked what caused such a sea-change. The answer to this question is the answer also to another question: What do a Catholic woman and a Presbyterian man have in common that might provide a good basis for a Christian married life together? The answer to both questions is their Christian baptism. Baptism is no longer looked upon as an exclusively confessional matter in the divided Christian churches. No one is baptized exclusively into the Catholic Church or the Presbyterian Church; one is baptized into the one, holy, catholic (universal), and apostolic church of Jesus Christ. In spite of intense pressure to repeat the teaching of Pope Pius XII that this Church of Christ is identical with the Roman Catholic Church, the Second Vatican Council in 1964 refused to accept that identity and taught instead that the Church of Christ "*subsists* in the Catholic Church."[5] The Church established by Christ, that is, is imperfectly embodied in but is not identical with the Catholic Church; it is also imperfectly embodied in but is not identical with the Presbyterian Church or any other Protestant Church. While each and every Christian is incorporated into and nurtured in the Church of Christ through faith and baptism in a specific Christian denomination, baptism is never to be thought of as incorporating them into *only* that denomination. Though, in ecumenical theology, each local Church or denomination is wholly Church, none of them is the whole Church.

Today all the major Christian denominations accept that those who believe in Christ and have been properly baptized are brought into a certain union with the Catholic Church, and with the Presbyterian Church, and so on. They accept baptism in one another's churches as incorporation into the one universal church of Christ, and hence they do not re-baptize anyone who changes religious affiliation from one Christian denomination to another. The degree of communion between believers of different denominations may not be perfectly clear in any given case, any more than the degree of communion within any given denomination is clear, but it is certain, and has been recently reaffirmed by Pope John Paul II: "All those justified by faith through baptism are incorporated into Christ. They therefore have a right to be honored by the title of Christian, and are properly regarded as brothers and sisters in the Lord by the sons and daughters of the Catholic Church."[6] No longer does the Catholic Church look on Presbyterian Philip as a heretic or schismatic; he is a Christian and a brother. There is a foundational Christian union in the Lord between Sarah and Philip that results from their shared baptism and their shared Christian faith. This foundational communion shared in the Christian Churches through baptism is one reason the Catholic Church has radically mitigated its language about "mixed marriages." One mutual resolution Sarah and Philip should make is not to permit their Christian, faith-filled, and baptismal unity to be obscured by less foundational confessional divisions.

The union in Christ between Sarah and Philip through their shared faith in and baptism into Christ, the Christian bond between them if you like, is further solidified by three other bonds: their mutual love unites them in an interpersonal bond of friendship; their wedding unites them publicly and legally in the bond of marriage; their celebration of their marriage in the Lord unites them in a religious bond of sacrament. Their marriage in very deed becomes, to paraphrase the Second Vatican Council, "an intimate partnership of love, life, and religion,"[7] which establishes them in a union so close that the Bible describes it as "one flesh" (Gen 2:24). I choose to describe their union as a coupled-We to intimate the bonds which bind Sarah and Philip together. So close is their communion of love, life, and religious faith that the Catholic Church has established their marital communion as the sacrament or symbol of the steadfast communion between Christ and his Church. The unity Sarah and Philip achieve in their church-blessed marriage places them under the gospel injunction, "What God has joined together, let no one separate" (Matt 19:6). It was reflection on their blessed communion and on this gospel injunction that drove Presbyterian Philip to raise a question. "If Sarah and I are united in baptism and marriage blessed by both our Churches," he asked, "how can those same churches separate us for the Holy Communion of the Lord's table?"

Shared Communion

I let this section stand by itself because the question of shared communion is the neuralgic question for many interchurch couples. They argue exactly as Philip did. We are made one in Christ in faith and baptism; we are made one body in Christ in marriage; we desire to celebrate and enhance our unity and one-bodiness in Christ in the sacrament of communion, Holy Communion with the Lord and one another at the Lord's table. How can the churches who have celebrated our oneness turn around and say we are not and cannot be one in Holy Communion? For many interchurch couples, the inability to share communion is a serious challenge to their Christian life together and sometimes a challenge also to their marital life together. That creates a serious pastoral challenge for the churches.

There are two major Catholic documents relevant to the question, the Code of Canon Law (1983) and the *Directory for the Application of Principles and Norms on Ecumenism* (1993). No Christian—Protestant or Catholic—should expect any Catholic minister to go beyond the principles and norms embodied in these two foundational documents, for no Catholic minister can go beyond them and still claim to be giving a distinctively Catholic witness. Neither, however, should any Catholic, clerical or lay, impose restrictions beyond what is embodied in these two documents. The main text of canon law sounds not only prescriptive but also restrictive. "Catholic ministers may lawfully administer the sacraments to Catholic members of the Christian faithful only and, likewise, the latter may lawfully receive the sacraments only from Catholic ministers with due regard for 2, 3, and 4 of this canon" (Can 844.1). Due regard for Can 844.2, 3, and 4 requires understanding of the exceptions and conditions enunciated therein and serious interpretation of their possible application in any given case.

> "Whenever necessity requires or a *genuine spiritual advantage commends* it . . . Christ's faithful for whom it is physically or morally impossible to approach a Catholic minister, may lawfully receive the sacraments of penance, eucharist, and anointing of the sick from *non-Catholic ministers in whose churches these sacraments are valid*" (Can 844.2).
>
> "Catholic ministers may lawfully administer the sacraments of penance, eucharist, and anointing of the sick to members of the oriental churches which do not have full communion with the Catholic Church, if they *ask on their own* for the sacraments and are properly disposed. This holds also for members of other churches, which in the judgment of the Apostolic See are in the same condition as the oriental churches as far as these sacraments are concerned" (Can 844.3).
>
> "If there is a danger of death or if, in the judgment of the diocesan Bishop or of the Episcopal Conference, there is *some other grave and pressing need,* Catholic ministers may lawfully administer those same sacraments to other Christians not in full communion with the Catholic Church, who cannot approach a minister of their own community and *who spontaneously ask for them,* provided that they *demonstrate the Catholic faith in respect of these sacraments* and are properly disposed" (Can 844.4).

The *Directory* is just as clear: "In certain circumstances, by way of exception, and under certain conditions, access to these sacraments [including Holy Communion] may be permitted, or even *commended,* for Christians of other churches and ecclesial communities" (n. 129). The *Directory* raises the question of shared communion with non-Catholic Christians, thereby suggesting, *ipso facto,* that extraordinary shared communion is a possibility. The conditions under which a Catholic minister may administer the Eucharist to a baptized, non-Catholic Christian are specified as fourfold: "the person be unable to have recourse for the sacrament desired to a minister of his or her own church or ecclesial community, ask for the sacrament of his or her own initiative, manifest

Catholic faith in this sacrament, and be properly disposed" (n. 131). Catholics may ask for the sacrament of Eucharist "only from a minister in whose church these sacraments are valid or from one who is known to be validly ordained according to the Catholic teaching on ordination" (n. 132). All of these conditions are the ones I have underscored at various points in the above discussion of Canon 844.

What is to be noted here is that exceptions and conditions, though carefully defined and delimited, are listed and never retracted. The problem is that not all official Catholic interpreters interpret the exceptions and conditions in the same way. Some interpret them rigidly to the letter; others, equally competent, interpret them more broadly. Predictably, this difference of interpretation causes discontent, confusion, hurt, and frequently anger among both Catholic and Protestant spouses. That anger, and the division induced among interchurch families at the Lord's table, as the German Bishops note in their document on Eucharistic Sharing (1997), can easily lead to "serious risk to the faith life of one or both partners"; it can "endanger the integrity of the bond that is created in life and faith through marriage"; it can lead to "an indifference to the sacrament and a distancing from Sunday worship and so from the life of the Church."[8] These considerations highlight shared communion as a specific example of what Pope John Paul II said to interchurch couples gathered in York Cathedral in 1982: "You live in your marriage the hopes and the difficulties of the path to Christian unity." They highlight also the interchurch marriage as a situation requiring special pastoral care.

Since I have introduced the German Bishops' document on Eucharistic Sharing, we can start there in our examination of how principles must be, can be, and are interpreted. The document, as the title indicates, is focused on the sharing of communion in interchurch marriages, and because of that focus gets immediately to concretizing the principles of Canon 844 and the *Directory.* "Families in interchurch marriages may experience '*serious (spiritual) need*' in certain situations . . . [and] in situations of pastoral need the married partners living in interchurch marriages may be admitted to receive communion in the Catholic Church under certain conditions."[9] Everyone familiar with the Code and the *Directory* will know the provenance of that statement.

The practical question is how is "spiritual need" to be assessed and who is to assess it? The bishops give a pastoral and obvious answer.

> Since pastorally the establishment of objective criteria for "serious (spiritual) need" is extremely difficult, ascertaining such a need can as a rule only be done by the *minister* concerned. Essentially, this must become

clear in pastoral discussion. Does the couple concerned (and any children) experience being separated at the Lord's table as a pressure on their life together? Is it a hindrance to their shared belief? How does it affect them? Does it risk damaging the integrity of their communion in married life and faith?[10]

It is a good pastoral rule, a discussion between the couple and the minister on the spot, usually a priest, who might best understand their situation. There are many interchurch families who could establish their "serious (spiritual) need" in such an open pastoral discussion.

Two years earlier, in 1995, the Catholic Archbishop of Brisbane issued a document entitled *Blessed and Broken: Pastoral Guidelines for Eucharistic Hospitality,* which contained a section on interchurch marriages. Noting that "the Directory of Ecumenism states that eucharistic sharing for a spouse in a mixed marriage can only be exceptional," the archbishop agrees with his German brothers that the verification of the required conditions and dispositions is best assessed in pastoral discussion. "It is sufficient for the presiding priest to establish, by means of a few simple questions, whether or not these conditions are met." Of great moment in the Brisbane document is the recognition that some interchurch couples "could well experience a serious spiritual need to receive communion each time he or she accompanies the family to a Catholic mass,"[11] and that this need can be met. Though the Roman *Directory* states that shared communion for interchurch spouses can only be exceptional, a spouse in an interchurch marriage could well experience exceptional ongoing need for shared communion. There is, in some though probably not all interchurch marriages, not only the exceptional, one-time case but also the exceptional, ongoing case. The ongoing spiritual need in this ongoing interchurch case, again, can be assessed in pastoral discussion between the local priest and the couple, but has to be referred to the archbishop for the authorization of exceptional, but ongoing, shared communion.

An example of a different interpretation of the foundational principles, exceptions, conditions, and circumstances is the document published jointly in 1998 by the Catholic Bishops of Great Britain and Ireland under the title *One Bread, One Body.* This document does not focus exclusively on interchurch marriages and the question of shared communion. As its subtitle asserts, it is a teaching document which sets forth, first, "the teaching of the Catholic Church on the mystery of the eucharist" (n. 2), and then norms "to govern sharing of the sacraments between Catholics and other Christians in our countries" (n. 8).[12] I cannot deal with the first part here, since focus and space prohibit it, but it is a rich exposition of the contemporary Catholic theology of Eucharist in an ecumenical context. It should be read meditatively by everyone, Catholic and Protestant alike, who wishes to understand the Catholic approach to the Eucharist and why that approach mandates shared communion as an *exceptional,* rather than a *normal,* reality for the Catholic Church.

The second part of the document, the norms on sacramental and eucharistic sharing, is of major interest to us. The bishops adopt two interesting strategies. While acknowledging the general norm which allows shared communion in exceptional circumstances "when strong desire is accompanied by shared faith, grave and pressing spiritual need, and at least an implicit desire for communion with the Catholic Church" (n. 77), they introduce a shift from the category of *need* to the category of *pain.* This enables them to point out, correctly, the brokenness of the Body of Christ, the pain that results from a broken body, and the fact that taking away the pain (in this case by the palliative of shared communion) does not necessarily achieve healing. Healing is achieved only by dealing with the underlying problem.

In the case of interchurch families, however, the pain of being unable to share communion is not the point. The point on which all the discussion of shared communion turns is the more radical *serious (spiritual) need* felt by interchurch spouses who already share communion in baptism, communion in marriage, and, above all, communion in the intimate partnership of life, love, and faith. Their shared communion in all these facets of life, inchoate and imperfect as it may sometimes be, creates the inter-spousal *need* for the shared communion of Eucharist. When unfulfilled, that need certainly causes pain, as unfulfilled hunger causes pain. But it is the need not the pain, as it is the hunger not the pain, that must be satisfied. It is not palliative but authentic pastoral care that is required.

The second strategy the bishops adopt is one found nowhere in the Code, the *Directory,* or any other Vatican document: the transposition of the exceptional *case* to the exceptional *unique occasion,* "an occasion which of its nature is unrepeatable, a 'one-off' situation which will not come again" (nos. 106, 109). Examples of such unique occasions are baptism, confirmation, first communion, ordination, and death. Though they have earlier employed the classical Catholic language about marriage, "a partnership of the whole of life" *(consortium totius vitae),* the bishops betray no understanding of what that might mean in practice in the case of committed married couples, interchurch or same-church. The Christian "partnership of the whole of life" is not about unique and occasional events; it is about the seamless whole of life.

The *consortium totius vitae* language derives from ancient Roman definitions of marriage, like the one found in Justinian's *Digesta* (23.2.1), which controlled every discussion of marriage in the West. "Marriage is a union of a man and a woman, and a communion of the whole of life, a participation in divine and human law." The phrase *communion of the whole of life (consortium totius vitae)* is ambiguous, open to two separate but not separable interpretations. It can mean as long as life lasts ("until death do us part"), and then implies that marriage is a life-long covenant. It can mean everything that the spouses have ("all my worldly goods"), and then implies that nothing is left unshared between the spouses. Over the centuries in the West, the two meanings have been so interwoven that marriage is considered the union of a man and a woman embracing the sharing of all goods, material and spiritual, as long as life lasts.[13]

A marriage which lasts as long as life lasts is certainly a unique event in the modern world, but it is a diachronic unique event. Any couple journeying through life together can attest to the fact that marriage is an ongoing situation, much more than a "one-off" wedding, much, much more that a "one-off" baptism or ordination. A marriage is not a one-off wedding; it is, to repeat, a partnership of the whole of life. The "unique [one-off] occasion" confuses wedding and marriage, legal ceremony and diachronic, lifelong partnership. If married people allow it to stand unchallenged, there can be no exceptional but ongoing sharing of communion, though the German, Australian, and South African norms, which I have not yet mentioned,[14] all interpret such ongoing exception as possible because of ongoing "serious (spiritual) need." Again, discontent, confusion, hurt, and anger, possibly damaging to both marital and ecclesial communion. To conclude this section, I wish to return to the four conditions under which a Catholic minister may administer communion to a baptized person: the person is unable to have recourse to a minister of his or her own church, must ask for communion on his or her own initiative, must manifest Catholic faith in the sacrament, and must be properly disposed. Since these conditions are required of all Catholics for the reception of Eucharist, it is not surprising to find them required also of all non-Catholics. The requirement of proper disposition, required of all who approach Holy Communion, needs no comment; the other three do.

The South African Directory explicates the inability to have recourse to a minister of one's own Church. This inability "need not be one that exists over a period of time but could arise out of the nature of the situation in which the petitioner finds himself or herself." They offer as example "when spouses in a mixed marriage attend a eucharistic celebration together."[15] It is a good and obvious point. Again, it is not about a unique occasion, but about an exceptional but ongoing situation in which an interchurch wife and husband participate together in the Lord's Supper, have a serious need to share communion together, and cannot have recourse on that situation to his or her own minister. If all the other conditions are fulfilled, then on each and every situation, by authoritative interpretation of the norms, the non-Catholic spouse may share communion in the Catholic Church. It is worth noting that the first version of this South African Directory did not obtain Vatican approval and that Roman "suggestions" were incorporated into a revised version released in January 2000. The language of the second version is more precise, more accurately reflects the present discipline, but yields nothing on exceptional practice. What was in the original version explicitly continues to be in the new version implicitly.

This leads to the requirement that a person ask for communion on his or her own initiative. Why, we may ask, establish such a requirement? To respect individual conscience and, in these ecumenical times, to avoid all suspicion of proselytizing. In earlier times, it was common for some churches to *invite* all baptized Christians who shared their faith in Eucharist to share communion with them. Others suggested this approach could be taken as an invitation to the person to disobey the rules of his or her own Church. When my mother, for instance, "invited" me to do the dishes, I always knew I was in trouble if I did not accept the "invitation." It is difficult to argue that I was completely free. It has become common, therefore, to replace *invite* with *welcome* to the Lord's table, as is done, for instance, in most Anglican churches worldwide today. *Welcome* does not invite anyone to go beyond the rules of his or her own Church to share communion, but it does respect the consciences of those who believe they can and must go beyond those rules. The initiative is always with the person involved; there is no proselytism; all that is offered is Christian hospitality and welcome when a person has come to his or her own decision.

And what of the requirement to share Catholic faith in the sacrament? The German bishops summarize that faith briefly: "The crucified and risen Lord Jesus Christ gives himself to us in person in the eucharist as Giver and Gift in bread and wine and so builds up his Church" (n. 4). Three essential Catholic elements are contained in that summary: the connection between Eucharist and the paschal sacrifice of Christ, the real presence of Christ in Eucharist, and the connection between Eucharist and Church. Any Christian who accepts those three realities in faith is manifesting Catholic faith. Christoph Cardinal Schonborn, Archbishop of Vienna, has offered a short-form statement of the Catholic faith required for sharing communion in a Catholic Church. "Everyone who can in good conscience say 'Amen' to the eucharistic prayer of the Catholic mass may take communion in a Catholic Church."[16] There are many Protestant Christians, and specifically many interchurch spouses, who can readily say "Amen" to that.

A final point is essential in this discussion. With respect to the requirement of sharing Catholic faith, the South African Directory, citing without acknowledgment Pope John XXIII's instruction to the Fathers at the opening of the Second Vatican Council,[17] notes the "crucial distinction between the substance of the faith and the way in which it is expressed."[18] Believing in the substance of defined Catholic eucharistic *faith* is one thing; accepting the undefined Catholic *theology* which seeks to explain that faith is quite another. The British and Irish bishops employ this distinction in their own way by explaining Catholic faith in the eucharistic presence of Jesus without any reference to the word which was once the touchstone of Catholic explanation, *transubstantiation,* a word they relegate to a footnote.

Contrary to popular unwisdom, this word was never part of Catholic faith about Eucharist. The Council of Trent, frequently cited as defining *transubstantiation* as Catholic faith, simply asserted that the change that takes place in bread and wine is "most aptly *[aptissime]*" called transubstantiation.[19] The bishops acknowledge the non-substantive nature of the word by relegating it to a brief footnote. The South Africans bishops insist that, when it comes to judging the substance of the faith that is present, "due cognizance must be taken of those ecumenical agreements that display the existence of a substantial agreement in faith." They offer as an example the agreement reached by the Anglican Roman Catholic International Commission (ARCIC) regarding the Eucharist and have no hesitation in stating that, "in the light of that agreement, members of the Anglican communion may be presumed to share the essentials of eucharistic faith with us [Catholics]" (n. 6.3.8).

We began this section with a quotation from the Code of Canon Law, noting that it "sounds prescriptive." After our journey through the

Code, the Roman *Directory on Ecumenism,* and various authoritative interpretations of both, it now appears as much permissive as prescriptive. "The purpose of every law in the Church," asserts Ladislas Orsy, one of the Church's most distinguished canon lawyers, "is to open the way for God's unbounded love." For that to happen, he notes, quoting Pope Paul VI, "we need not so much new legislation as a 'new attitude of mind.'"[20] That new attitude of mind, I suggest, needs to be ecumenical, it needs to realize that there are other Christians besides Catholics, that all of them are united to the Catholic Church through the bonds of baptism, and that some of them are further united to the Catholic Church through the bonds of sacramental, covenantal marriage to a Catholic.

The Catholic tradition about sacraments is that they not only signify grace but they also cause it instrumentally.[21] The aphorisms are well-known; sacraments "effect what they signify," "cause by signifying," are "efficacious signs of grace." The full and intimate communion achieved in marriage between a non-Catholic Christian and Catholic spouse, and the communion achieved directly and indirectly between them and the Catholic Church, can be signified in shared eucharistic communion. More importantly, those two interconnected communions can also be "caused," effected, enhanced, deepened, and broadened in shared communion. Sacraments, the Second Vatican Council taught, "not only presuppose faith, but by words and objects they also nourish, strengthen, and express it."[22] That they do this, and do the same with love and communion, is a frequently ignored factor in the debate over shared communion. The council taught, with its usual care, that "the expression [or signification] of unity generally forbids common worship. Grace to be obtained sometimes commends it."[23] The overall argument of this section, and of authentic episcopal teachers of the Church, is that the serious spiritual need experienced by interchurch couples is an exceptional but ongoing "sometimes" that commends it.

Pastoral Considerations

When I explained to them that their growing communion in love had been long preceded by their baptismal communion in Christ, Sarah and Philip told me this was the first time they had ever heard that. This points to a serious problem that contemporary couples in interchurch marriages frequently have to face, namely, their ignorance of the beliefs not only of their partner's Church but also of their own Church. In a recent ecumenical group with pastors from six different Christian denominations, I was horrified to hear pastors admit openly they did not know much about the teachings of one another's churches. If pastors do not know what their brothers and sisters in Christ believe, how will their congregations ever know? But Sarah and Philip, and every other interchurch couple, must know if they hope ever to grow together religiously in marriage. Each must understand not only her and his own tradition but also that of the other, so they can come to understand and appreciate one another as fully as possible and respond to their children's questions about their two churches. For this to happen, both need to be educated ecumenically, not just in the few weeks preceding their wedding but also throughout their married life together. As the incidence of interchurch marriage continues to increase, the demand for this kind of religious education will increase accordingly. Mutual ignorance is not a good basis for any marriage, least of all an interchurch marriage.

It is now widely recognized that theology cannot be done in isolation from the cultural context in which it is done; a contemporary theology of interchurch marriages cannot be done without hard scientific data about interchurch marriages. To obtain this data, a national, randomized study of same-church and interchurch marriages was conducted by the Center for Marriage and Family at Creighton University in 1997. Approximately one-third of all respondents were in interchurch relationships at the time of their engagement,[24] a significant percentage. Fewer interchurch than same-church respondents reported they had any marriage preparation and, of those who had marriage preparation, fewer interchurch reported it addressed religious issues related to their relationship and the raising of their children. In an earlier Center for Marriage and Family study of the impact of marriage preparation, interchurch couples, who randomly composed 39 percent of that study population, complained that the marriage preparation offered to them minimally sought to prepare them for the challenges of a specifically interchurch marriage.[25]

Marriage preparation is a key learning moment, a natural rite of passage in a couple's life. It can also be a key religious moment. In the culture of divorce which presently holds sway in the western world, the churches are challenged to make interchurch couples, now a significant number of all marrying couples, a priority population. Only 24 percent of interchurch respondents who reported that religious issues were addressed in their marriage preparation reported having received specific material dealing with their different religious backgrounds. Those engaged in the marriage preparation of interchurch couples must do better to tailor their educational approach to the interchurch character of a couple's relationship. Programs should highlight religious faith and practice as an important part of marriage, as indeed it is,[26] and provide couples with strategies to deal with their religious differences. Such marriage preparation may be done best when the denominations of the two partners are both represented. The continuing and scandalous Christian problem is not that Christians of different denominations are falling in love and marrying in large numbers, but that the Christian Church continues to be rent into different, sometimes unseemly competing, denominations. Only when Protestant and Catholic congregations come to understand and truly respect each other's faith and teachings will they be in a position to provide the marriage preparation interchurch couples require for their marriage to be successful.

In his 1981 letter On the Family, Pope John Paul II urged the Catholic Church to "promote better and more intensive programs of marriage preparation to eliminate as far as possible the difficulties many married couples find themselves in, and even more to favor the establishing and maturing of successful marriages" (n. 66). All the churches, not just the Catholic Church, are challenged to promote marriage, to prepare young people for their marital vocation, and to do all in their power to uphold the permanence of marriage. They are specifically challenged by interchurch couples to create preparation programs that make diverse Christian faith and practice an ongoing part of their marriages. That this is an important challenge for the churches is evident from the fact that the faith of parents is a critical factor in the religious education of their children. It is an even more critical factor in the religious education of interchurch children.

One other factor obliges the churches to a greater commitment to interchurch marriages. The Creighton interchurch study joined a growing list of studies demonstrating that interchurch couples are at greater risk than same-church couples for marital instability. Same-church respondents had a statistically significant lower percentage of divorce (12.7 percent) than interchurch respondents (20.3 percent). Two things, however, are to be noted here. The first is that, though the percentage of divorce was higher for interchurch than for same-church respondents, both percentages were significantly lower than the percentages commonly reported for the study's time frame, that is, approximately 40 percent.[27] Since every respondent in the study identified with a Christian denomination at the time of engagement, the sample may be more religiously oriented than the general married population. Since religious affiliation is associated with a lower risk of divorce,[28] the greater religiousness of the sample may account for the lower percentage of divorce. There is another message here for marriage preparation providers: religion makes a difference in a marriage, even when there are two different churches involved, as there are in an interchurch marriage. Religion can be a bonder in a marriage, binding the spouses together as a coupled-We; or it can be divisive, keeping the spouses apart from the joint religious activities they ought to share. Here is another place where genuinely ecumenical marriage preparation can help.

The second thing of note in the divorce statistics above is that, when a long list of other variables was taken into account, being in an interchurch marriage per se was not a major predictor of marital instability. This suggests that it is not interchurch marriage that puts interchurch couples at greater risk for marital instability, but other factors that may accompany the interchurch status of the marriage. Three such factors were found to be major: the religious differences between interchurch couples, the limited joint religious activities they shared, and their families' approval or non-approval of their choice of spouse. If churches wish to contribute to the improvement of the declining attractiveness, quality, and stability of marriage, these findings suggest three concrete areas where they might profitably concentrate their efforts in marriage preparation and enrichment programs: the managing of religious differences, the promotion of joint religious activities, and the managing of parental influence. Religious differences and joint religious activities are areas of focus for both same-church and interchurch couples, but they are especially critical for interchurch spouses since they tend to report greater religious differences and fewer joint religious activities.

Two other findings by the Creighton study should be noted by the churches. The first is that interchurch respondents had, on average, lower religiosity scores than same-church respondents.[29] Religiosity, or level of religious attitude and practice, was assessed by a variety of factors: personal faith, personal church involvement, joint religious activities, sense of belonging to a local congregation, strength of denominational identity, religion as a strength in the marriage, emphasis on religion in raising children, commitment to Christ, and having participated in adult religious education. The *average* scores of interchurch respondents on all these items, both individually and collectively, were lower than the average scores of same-church respondents. I underscore *average* here to introduce an important caveat. Neither same-church nor interchurch individuals are homogeneous groups. Not all churches are alike, not all lawyers are alike, and not all interchurch or same-church individuals are alike. When respondents were divided into groups of high, medium, and low religiosity, there were interchurch individuals in the high religiosity group and same-church respondents in the low religiosity group, though only 15 percent of interchurch were in the high religiosity group compared to 40 percent of same-church respondents. It is evident, nevertheless, that the pervasiveness of religiosity differences shows that churches have much work to do to bind interchurch families to them.

The preceding conclusion is supported by the second item to be noted. Fewer interchurch than same-church respondents were very satisfied with the clergy with whom they came in contact. Satisfaction with clergy was related to clergy awareness of needs, sensitivity to people of other denominations, and commitment to helping interchurch couples deal with their marital and religious lives. This suggests three areas where churches and their clergy need to examine their attitudes and behaviors. Clergy need to welcome interchurch couples when they attend Church services or other activities, and they need to invite them to attend more than simply Church services.

The family is the first and most vital cell of any society; the Christian family is the first and most vital cell of the Church. The future of both society and Church, in John Paul's felicitous phrase, "passes through the family."[30] It is in the family, which Chrysostom urged spouses "to make a church"[31] and Augustine called "domestic church" and "little church,"[32] that children learn to value or not to value Christ, Christ's gospel, and Christ's church. If for no other reason than the honest religious nurture of their children, interchurch couples need to strive to understand and respect each other's faith as fully as possible. Only when they mutually understand and respect both faiths can their children consult both of them on both faiths, eliminating the divisive strategy of consulting mother on one faith and father on the other. Understanding and respecting the other spouse's faith might also ensure that nothing explicitly or implicitly derogatory about that faith will ever be said around the children. There are enough sources of potential conflict in marriage without multiplying them.

When we were talking about the children they hoped one day to have, Sarah surprised me with a sudden outburst of anger, blurting out that she would not agree to have Philip sign any document promising their children would be raised Catholics. Her father, she added, who was and still is a Lutheran, had to sign such a document when he married her Catholic mother and had been very angry at the Catholic Church, and her mother, ever since. She was astonished when I told her that neither she nor Philip would have to sign anything. When her parents were married in 1969, it was the law of the Catholic Church that such a written promise be given by the Protestant partner. It is no longer the law. In 1970, Pope Paul VI freed the non-Catholic partner of every declaration and promise concerning children born of the marriage. The Catholic partner is now required to promise *orally* "to do all in my power" to share her or his faith with the children by having them baptized and raised as Catholics. This promise is simply an assurance given by the Catholic partner that she or he understands the obligations; it makes explicit in a human fashion, *humano modo,* an obligation already existing by the fact that they are Catholics. Sarah retained a certain amount of anger and unease at the fact that such a promise is required, but both Pope Paul VI and Pope John Paul II have words to soothe her.

After having stated that the Catholic partner in an interchurch marriage is obligated "*as far as possible* to see to it that the children are baptized and brought up" in the Catholic faith, Paul VI added what the Catholic Church takes for granted: the question of the children's faith is not a question for the Catholic partner alone. Their children's education is a responsibility of both parents, "both husband and wife are bound by that responsibility," Paul VI teaches, "and may by no means ignore it."[33] John Paul II reiterates the difficulty that arises here between interchurch couples and reaffirms the Catholic Church's modern celebration of religious freedom. This freedom could be violated, he teaches, "either by undue pressure to make the partner change his or her beliefs or by placing obstacles in the way of the free manifestation of these beliefs by religious practice."[34] John Paul here is simply repeating the Second Vatican Council's reaffirmation of an ancient Catholic teaching that "parents have the right to determine, in accordance with their own religious beliefs, the kind of religious education their children are to receive."[35]

The Catholic Church acknowledges the education of children is the right and duty of *both* parents and is not to be reserved to one parent over the other, even if that parent happens to be a Catholic. The promise now required of a *Catholic* partner in an interchurch marriage specifies that she or he "*will do all in my power*" to ensure that children are raised Catholic. It does not, because it cannot, guarantee that they *will in fact* be raised Catholic. Every decision about children in every marriage, including the decision about their religious upbringing, is a decision, the Catholic Church teaches, for both parents, never for the Catholic parent alone. Why then, Sarah wanted to know, did she still have to promise to do all in her power to ensure the children were raised Catholic? So that both she and Philip would be fully conscious of her obligations as a Catholic, not so that Philip would be required to surrender his parental rights.

There is another group of people to be considered in the project of an interchurch marriage: the parents of the prospective bride and groom. All of us derive from a family of origin and all of us are marked by that family, no matter how free and individual we believe we are. I cannot tell you how often I have heard the comment, "My parents would never approve me marrying a Catholic or Presbyterian or a whatever." This perceived tension between parents and an adult child frequently is one more source of stress in premarital decisions, and marriage, interchurch or not, is not a state that needs any more stressors in this modern age. Something must be done to reduce that stress before it becomes intolerable. Parents may have concerns about the differences between churches and, therefore, also between their child and the one she or he is marrying. They may fear loss of faith through change of religious affiliation or indifference. They may worry about where the wedding will take place, what church the couple will attend, what faith their grandchildren will be reared in. They may cause great irritation, both before and after the wedding, by trying to convert the spouse not of their denomination. They need a good talking with to dispel their doubts, their fears, their worries, their tensions.

Since they do not always keep up with change, parents frequently need to have explained to them the change in attitudes between the Christian churches. They need to have explained to them the importance of their different faiths to the prospective spouses and that each not only loves the other but also respects the faith of the other. They need to know their children have already discussed the things that are bothering them, have come to mutually acceptable and respectful decisions about them, and want their parents to join them and support them in the project that is their marriage. Sarah told me that, when she told her parents she was going to marry Philip, they responded that she was facing a difficult task but they would do everything they could to be supportive. Philip, on the other hand, told me his father was very unhappy he was planning to marry a Catholic. Their very different levels of tension provided me with concrete evidence of the importance of embracing families of origin into the process of choosing an interchurch partner.

If there is one thing I have learned over the years of working with couples, it is that a stable and successful marriage takes time. It takes time for two individuals to come to know, appreciate, and respect one another; it takes time for them to come to value one another; it takes time for them to attain mutual love and communion; it takes time for them to become one body. If I was given the opportunity to offer one piece of advice to an interchurch, or any other, couple, it would be this: give your marriage time. I once asked a Missouri Synod Lutheran woman, who had been married to a Catholic for thirty-eight years, what was the most rewarding or most difficult time in her marriage. Her reply surprised me: "It depends what stage of marriage you are talking about." She explained that in the beginning of their marriage, she and her husband had wasted endless hours trying to convert one another, then had gradually come to understand and respect one another's commitment to religion, and had finally come to love one another precisely as *Lutheran* and *Catholic*. "I grew to understand," she said, "that loving John meant loving a Catholic." There is a wise message for all of us, and perhaps also for all of our churches, in that comment.

I have already cited Pope John Paul's 1982 comment to interchurch couples in York cathedral, "you live in your marriages the hopes and the difficulties of the path to Christian unity." His comment can stand as overall summary of everything that can currently be said about interchurch marriages. Marriage is always a time of hope and difficulty, a time of gift and challenge, a time when families lovingly unite or angrily divide. John Paul suggests that interchurch marriages mirror the hopes and the difficulties of the churches as they come to know, appreciate, and respect one another as Catholic, as Presbyterian, as Baptist. I agree they do that and suggest they also do more. Interchurch couples who take the time required to know, appreciate, love, and respect one another, and thus become one "coupled-We," not only mirror the paths of the churches as they too seek to become one but they also mark out the path by which the churches can reach their goal. The path is not an easy one, for it is not a path that leads necessarily to the conversion of one spouse to the denomination of the other, though about 43 percent of spouses in the Creighton study did change religious affiliation to become same-church. Rather, it is a path that leads to mutual respect, mutual appreciation, mutual trust, mutual love, and mutual unity in diversity. That is the only path that will lead to the fulfillment of Jesus' great prayer for humankind: "That they may all be one" (John 17:21). Oneness for all couples, all churches, all nations is a challenging goal; it is a goal that takes time. It is also a goal toward which many interchurch couples are now mapping out the way. "Let anyone with ears listen" (Matt 11:15; Mark 4:9; Luke 8:8).

Questions for Reflection

1. Do you see any real difference between the terms "mixed marriage" and "interchurch marriage?" In the current context of mutual ecumenical respect, which do you think is preferable? Why?

2. What do you think of Philip's argument: "If Sarah and I are united in baptism and marriage blessed by both our churches, how can those same churches separate us for the Holy Communion of the Lord's Table?" Would you be scandalized in any way if Christian churches, who shared the same faith in the presence of Jesus in Holy Communion, shared communion at the Lord's Table?

3. The Catholic Church has established four conditions for the sharing of Holy Communion with other Christians: the person is unable to have recourse to a minister of his or her own Church, must ask for communion on his or her own initiative, must manifest Catholic faith in the sacrament, and must be properly disposed. How do you understand and evaluate these conditions?

4. It is well established by research that interchurch marriages have a greater risk of instability than same-church marriages. If this is true, what should the churches do about interchurch marriages?

5. Do you believe that marriage preparation is a key learning moment in a couple's life? If it is, how should the couple approach it, and how should the churches approach it, especially in the case of interchurch marriage?

Notes

[1] This essay is a revised version of one that appeared in *INTAMS Review* 6 (2000) 199–214.

[2] Howard M. Bahr, "Religious Intermarriage and Divorce in Utah and the Mountain States," *Journal for the Scientific Study of Religion* 20 (1981) 251–61; Dean R. Hoge and Kathleen M. Ferry, *Empirical Research on Interfaith Marriage in America* (Washington, D.C.: United States Catholic Conference, 1981); Tim B. Heaton, Stan L. Albrecht, and Thomas K. Martin, "The Timing of Divorce," *Journal of Marriage and the Family* 47 (1985) 631–9; Tim B. Heaton and Edith L. Pratt, "The Effects of Religious Homogamy on Marital Satisfaction and Stability," *Journal of Family Issues* 11 (1990) 191–207; Larry L. Bumpass, Teresa Castro Martin, and James A. Sweet, *Background and Early Marital Factors* (Madison, Wisc.: Center for Demography and Ecology, 1989); Evelyn L. Lehrer and Carmel U. Chiswick, "Religion as a Determinant of Marital Stability," *Demography* 30 (1993) 385–404.

[3] See George Kilcourse, *Double Belonging: Interchurch Families and Christian Unity* (New York: Paulist Press, 1992).

[4] See Center for Marriage and Family, *Ministry to Interchurch Marriages: A National Study* (Omaha: Creighton University, 1999) 20–34.

[5] LG 8.

[6] John Paul II, *That They May Be One* (Washington, D.C.: United States Catholic Conference, 1995) n. 13.

[7] GS 48.

[8] "Eucharistic Sharing in Interchurch Marriages and Families: Guidelines from the German Bishops," *Journal of the Association of Interchurch Families* 6 (1998) 10.

[9] Ibid., n. 2, my emphasis.

[10] Ibid., n. 5.

[11] *Blessed and Broken: Pastoral Guidelines for Eucharistic Hospitality* (Brisbane: Archdiocese of Brisbane, 1995) 7.

[12] *One Bread, One Body: A Teaching Document on the Eucharist in the Life of the Church and the Establishment of General Norms on Sacramental Sharing* (London: Catholic Truth Society, 1998).

[13] See Michael G. Lawler, *Marriage and Sacrament: A Theology of Christian Marriage* (Collegeville: The Liturgical Press, 1993) 7–12.

[14] *Directory on Ecumenism for Southern Africa.* This document may be found at www.sacbc.org.za/dir.html.

[15] Ibid., n. 6.3.7.

[16] *The Tablet* (October 16, 1999).

[17] AAS 54 (1962) 792.

[18] *Directory on Ecumenism for Southern Africa*, n. 6.3.8.

[19] DS 1652.

[20] Ladislas Orsy, "Interchurch Marriages and Reception of Eucharist," *America* (October 12, 1996) 19.

[21] Peter Lombard, *Liber Sententiarum* 4, d. 1, c. 4; Thomas Aquinas, ST III, q. 60, a. 1; Michael G. Lawler, *Symbol and Sacrament: A Contemporary Sacramental Theology* (Omaha: Creighton University Press, 1995) 33–5; LG 1.

[22] SC 59.

[23] UR 8.

[24] *Ministry to Interchurch Marriages,* 15.139. This percentage was replicated in the more recent Center for Marriage and Family study: *Time, Sex, and Money: The First Five Years of Marriage* (Omaha: Creighton University, 2000). See also *Catholic Engaged Encounter Renewal: 1999 Follow-Up Project* (Washington, D.C.: Georgetown University, 1999) 3.

[25] *Marriage Preparation in the Catholic Church: Getting It Right* (Omaha: Creighton University, 1995).

[26] S. L. Albrecht, H. M. Bahr, and K. L. Goodman, *Divorce and Remarriage* (Westport, Conn.: Greenwood Press, 1983); Vaughn R. A. Call and Tim B. Heaton, "Religious Influence on Marital Stability," *Journal for the Scientific Study of Religion* 36 (1997) 382–92; Heaton and Pratt, "The Effects of Religious Homogamy," 191–207; Lehrer and Chiswick, "Religion as a Determinant of Marital Stability," 385–404.

[27] Theresa Castro Martin and Larry Bumpass, "Recent Trends in Marital Disruption," *Demography* 26 (1989) 37–51; Andrew J. Cherlin, *Marriage, Divorce, Remarriage* (Cambridge, Mass.: Harvard University Press, 1992); Norval D. Glenn, *Closed Hearts, Closed Minds: The Textbook Story of Marriage* (New York: Institute for American Values, 1997).

[28] See the works cited in n. 26 above.

[29] This finding was replicated independently for a different sample population in Center for Marriage and Family, *Time, Sex, and Money.*

[30] FC 75.

[31] Chrysostom, *Homiliae in Genesim (Hom. Gen.)* 6, 2, PG 54.607.

[32] Augustine, *Epistola 188,* 3, PL 33.849.

[33] *Matrimonia Mixta,* AAS 62 (1970) 259.

[34] FC 78.

[35] DH 5.

7

Friendship and Marriage

The connection between friendship and marriage has been illuminated anew in an excellent contemporary study of what makes good marriages succeed. Judith Wallerstein and Sandra Blakeslee uncovered a consistent explanation: friendship between the spouses makes good marriages succeed. One woman explained that she and her husband "like each other, we trust each other, we have mutual respect." She went on to explain that love is important but that what gives love solidarity is "a basic sense of real trust, of really knowing where that other person is at, and knowing that whatever they're going to do is going to be in your best interests as well as theirs."[1] Friendship between spouses is a good recipe for a good marriage. Philosophers in all ages have given a great deal of attention to friendship, but Christian theologians, for a reason I will explain later, have given it scant attention, and they have never listed it among the Christian virtues. This essay seeks to redress that situation. It deals with friendship in three steps: it examines the meaning of friendship, the relationship between friendship and love, and how friendship founds a good marriage.

Friendship

Even the most egocentric of persons recognizes that he or she cannot survive without other people. If I do not associate with others, interact with them, assist them, see to their needs, and let them do the same for me in return, then I will fail to become a fully integrated human being. Born of a woman, I am classified as human, but that names only my physiology. Without other human persons in my life, without emotional intimacy, intellectual stimulation, personal and social connectedness, I will never develop toward full humanity.

I will not, of course, allow everyone into my life, that project is too vast; and not everyone will allow me into their lives. Those few I do let into my life, and who reciprocate by letting me into theirs, will be apart from the general crowd, special, and specially named. They will be called *friends,* without whom, Aristotle wrote, "No one would choose to live, even if he had all other goods."[2] A contemporary theological and philosophical commentator agrees. Pope John Paul II teaches that "man *[sic]* cannot live without love. He remains a being incomprehensible for himself, his life is senseless, if love is not revealed to him, if he does not encounter love, if he does not experience it and make it his own, if he does not participate intimately in it."[3] The special love and relationship friends share is called friendship.

Aristotle bears witness to the fact that friendship is deeply rooted in human history. He distinguishes three kinds of friendship: of pleasure, of usefulness, and of good. In the first, some quality in another person, Aristotle suggests wit, gives *me* pleasure. In the second, the other person is perceived as useful to *me.* In the third, I am attracted to and love something good in the *other person.* In each of the three friendships, it is something good that is loved, for good is always the object of love, but in each of the three it is a different good that is loved. When I seek friendship with others because they amuse me or because I see them as useful to me, it is *my* good I seek; when I love others because of the good that is in them, it is *their* good I seek. The difference lies in willing good for my sake or for the sake of another. Aristotle judges that, though all three loves may be called friendship, only the third, what he calls the friendship of virtue, is true friendship.[4] Everyone who has experienced true friendship knows that it takes time to develop. "It is impossible for men to know one another before they have eaten salt together," Aristotle says, "nor can they admit each other to intimacy nor become friends before each appears to be worthy of friendship and confidence." To be perfect, Aristotle and Aquinas agree, friendship must be reciprocal.[5]

Aristotle suggests three reasons why we need friends and why our lives would not be complete without them. First, friendship is a crucial source of self-understanding. The best way to come to an honest appraisal and understanding of myself, Aristotle knew before any modern psychologist, is not by looking directly at myself in my own self-reflecting and self-deceiving mirror, but by seeing myself reflected indirectly in the unedited mirror of a friend unafraid to reflect the truth. Second, friendship supports us against loss of interest in and commitment to even the most necessary activities, including the pursuit of good. In Aristotle's opinion, the flourishing human life is a life of morally and intellectually good activities, and such a life is never possible alone. I need friends of virtue with whom I can share good activities, and by whom I can be reassured that I am not alone, that others care about the things I care about. Every life activity—physical, intellectual, moral—is enhanced when I share it with others. Third, and perhaps most obviously, I cannot become morally good except in relation to another self, a friend, because virtue cannot be attained alone. If the performance of good deeds is the mark of a good and virtuous man, then a good man will need other selves to whom he can do good.[6] A contemporary commentator makes the same point: the moral life always begins in an encounter with another who calls forth my response.[7] I will return to these reasons for needing friends when I deal with living with a best friend in marriage.

Aristotle was not the only ancient to write about friendship. The Roman author Cicero also wrote about it, and his *De Amicitia* became the most influential book about friendship. The Roman, however, agrees with the Greek. Friendship, "a complete accord of feeling on all subjects, divine and human, accompanied by kindly feeling and attachment,"[8] is to be preferred "to all human possessions."[9] True friendship is possible only for the virtuous who pursue good, only for those who live in such a way that "their honor, their integrity, their justice, and their liberality are approved, so there is not in them any covetousness, or licentiousness, or boldness, and they are of great consistency."[10] Friendships based on desire for gain, prestige, power, or wealth, or those based on carnal or erotic pleasure, are not true friendships. These benefits may derive from true friendship, but they are not its motivation. A rule of friendship is this: "We expect from our friends only what is honorable and for our friends' sake do only what is honorable."[11] All of this, Cicero adds, requires probation. The prudent man checks "the impetus of his kindly feeling as he would his chariot, that we may have our friendships, like our horses, fully proved."[12] Hypocrisy, Cicero judges, is the death of friendship, "for it destroys all truth, without which the name of friendship can avail nothing."[13]

Christian writers in later years sought to advance Cicero and to Christianize him. In his *Confessions,* Augustine of Hippo reflects on the death of a dear friend, a man "sweet to me above every sweetness," and confesses that their early friendship was not a true friendship. True friendship "cannot be unless you solder it together in those who unite to one another by the love poured forth in our hearts by the Holy Spirit who is given to us."[14] True friendship for Augustine is a gift from God, is rooted in God, transformed by God, and brought to its full perfection in eternal friendship with God.[15] For Aristotle and Cicero, friends are brought together by the good or virtue they see and value in one another. For Augustine, friends are brought together by God, and they grow together in God until they reach true friendship. By receiving friendship as a gift of God, by rooting it in the love of God, by living it in imitation of Christ the Son of God, friendship is transformed into Christian universal neighbor-love. This point will be further developed below.

The twelfth-century Cistercian monk Aelred of Rievaulx made an even more concerted effort than Augustine to Christianize Cicero's work on friendship. In his *Spiritual Friendship,* Aelred follows Cicero's and Aristotle's threefold division: there are carnal, worldly, and spiritual friendships. "Carnal friendship is created by an agreement in vices, while hope of gain spurs worldly friendship, and similarity of character, goals, and habits in life makes for a bond of friendship among good people."[16] This last is spiritual friendship, Aelred's true friendship. It develops when other persons are loved not for what they can offer in terms of erotic pleasure or material usefulness, but for what they are in themselves, images of God and reflections of the love of Christ.[17] As for Augustine, the love of God is the foundation, the principle, and the goal of Christian friendship, and that love is communicated to friends in Christ. Spiritual friendship is not the opposite of carnal or worldly friendships but their perfection, for frequently friendship begins as carnal or worldly and progresses to true spiritual friendship.[18] As for Cicero, true friendship is possible only for the virtuous, those who pursue good, and it finds its epitome in those who seek good to the fullest. "Friendship can arise among the good, it can progress among the better, but it can reach its highest point only among the best."[19]

There are four steps in the ascent to the perfection of true friendship. "The first is choice, the second is testing, the third is acceptance, the fourth is 'the highest agreement on both human and divine affairs, combined with good will and mutual esteem.'"[20] Notice that the last is Cicero's definition of true friendship. There are two things to look for when choosing a friend, vices that make friendship impossible and virtues that are congenial to it. Among the vices, Aelred lists reproach, "which extinguishes the flame of Christian love";[21] pride, "that makes a person bold to commit injury in the first place and too haughty to accept correction";[22] betrayal of a friend's secrets, which "ruins a friend's trust";[23] and slander, "a poison to friendship."[24] There was no disagreement at the time, nor will there be much more today, with Aelred's judgment that the greatest vice on this list is the betrayal of a friend's secrets.

Among the virtues conducive to friendship Aelred lists faithfulness, "the nurse and the guardian of friendship";[25] intention, to ensure the other is looking for nothing except "God" and "mutual friendship";[26] judgment, that the other "not be ignorant of the obligations and demands of friendship";[27] and patience, "to make sure the other is not grieved by correction and does not despise or hate the one who corrects him."[28] Each of these virtues would have been congenial to Cicero, but they do not yet fully reflect Aelred's concept of true spiritual friendship. What distinguishes true, spiritual friendship is another virtue that underlies faithfulness, intention, judgment, and patience; namely, the love of God.[29] Because God is its foundation, principle, and goal, true friendship is eternal and, if it ever ceases to be, it was never true friendship at all.[30] Aelred is so convinced of the eternal character of true friendship that he dares to transpose the consecrated biblical phrase "God is love" *(agape)* (1 John 4:16) into "God is friendship" *(philia)*.[31] When all these vices and virtues have been tested and a person has passed the test, he or she can then safely be admitted to friendship and two friends can live in "the highest agreement on both divine and human affairs." They can be true, Christian friends.

Love and Friendship: Agape *and* Philia

If friendship was such a significant aspect of virtue and goodness for pagan Aristotle and Cicero, why has it never been a significant part of virtue for Christians? The answer lies in an interpretation of the words of Jesus reported in the Gospels: "Love *[agape]* your enemies and pray for those who persecute you, so that you may be children of your Father in heaven. . . . If you greet only your brothers and sisters, what more are you doing than others? Do not even the Gentiles do the same?" (Matt 5:44-47). There are two Greek words for love: *agape* and *philia,* translated in English as love (charity) and friendship.[32] The nineteenth-century Anglican theologian Jeremy Taylor explained what happened to *philia* and *agape.* "When friendships were the noblest things in the world," as in the days of Aristotle and Cicero, "charity *[agape]* was little."[33] When

Christianity created a shift in the culture of Europe, charity became the noblest thing in the world and friendship was demoted. The problem lies in the understanding of the two words.

Philia, the word Aristotle uses for friendship, is the particular, preferential, and reciprocated love of a friend over all others. And there is the Gordian knot: *philia* is particular and reciprocal love. *Agape* is the universal, non-preferential, and not necessarily reciprocated love of others, the love commanded by Jesus: "love your neighbor as yourself" (Mark 12:31) and "love your enemies" (Matt 5:44). *Agape* is what God shows when God makes the "sun rise on the righteous and on the unrighteous" (Matt 5:45); *agape* is what God is said to be in the metaphor "God is love" (1 John 4:8). *Philia* is a reciprocally preferential love based on the valued goodness of the individual friend; *agape* is non-preferential and universal love, love that is to be shown even to an enemy who can never be expected to reciprocate. *Philia* is a love subject to change, as every forgotten friendship verifies, though it can be argued, as Aelred argues, that friendship that ends was never true friendship. *Agape,* by definition, is love that "never ends" (1 Cor 13:8). Though there is evidence that the early Christians referred to themselves as "friends *[philoi]* of God," perhaps applying to themselves what Isaiah said of Abraham (Isa 41:8), it was not a designation that stuck. It was quickly superseded by "children of God," which might have been judged to be more familial and intimate.[34]

The relationship between *philia* and *agape* became problematic when the latter was promoted as Christian love, the love that makes perfect "as your heavenly Father is perfect" (Matt 5:48), leaving *philia* to languish as a lesser love that does not measure up to all that is required of the Christian. Friendship may be a good and powerful love, as Aristotle and Cicero argue; it may be necessary and very useful in every human life. It is just not specifically Christian and does not lead to God as does *agape.* Søren Kierkegaard enunciated the standard argument in two statements. "Love of one's neighbor . . . is self-renouncing love, and self-renunciation casts out all preferential love just as it casts out all self-love."[35] Christianity has misgivings about erotic love and friendship because "preference in passion or passionate preference is really another form of self-love."[36] There, in a nutshell, is the problem as Kierkegaard enunciates it. Neighbor-love is Christ-like selflessness; friendship-love is disguised selfishness and, therefore, anathema to followers of the Christ. Kierkegaard's fellow Scandinavian Anders Nygren occupied the same high ground, arguing that *agape,* the very center of Christianity, "overleaps such limits [and] is universal and all-embracing."[37]

In his seminal treatment of *agape* as equal regard, Gene Outka takes a less restrictive approach, arguing that *agape* permits "special relations" as long as they do not violate the demands of equal consideration for all.[38] In his excellent analysis, Edward Vacek also takes a less restrictive approach, arguing that "equality is an empty criterion when it comes to the positive practice of care. Something more akin to proportionality becomes relevant."[39] It may not be as clear, then, as Kierkegaard and Nygren argue, that *agape* and *philia* are separate and unconnected. Augustine certainly does not think so.

For Cicero, friends are brought together by virtue and goodness; for Augustine they are brought together by God. Each is a gift of God to the other, and each is to be loved in God. Marie Aquinas McNamara suggests that this is "the heart of Augustine's conception of friendship and his great innovation":[40] we do not choose our friends, God does. When friends respond to their friendship as a gift of God, root it in God, and live it as disciples of God incarnate in Christ, their friendship leads them to God as surely, it is as salvific, as *agape*. Indeed, when accepted as gift of God and lived in Christ, *philia* leads to *agape*, for when friends learn to love whom God loves, they learn to love all God's children, not as strangers but as friends. Continuing this tradition, John Henry Newman will later argue that "the best preparation for loving the world at large, and loving it duly and wisely, is to cultivate an intimate friendship and affection toward those who are immediately about us."[41] Augustine's ideal, McNamara suggests, "was to have the unity which is an integral part of individual friendship reign among all men in fraternal charity" [*agape*].[42] Friendship has a twofold function for Augustine: it teaches men and women to love particular friends, and it teaches them to love their universal neighbors. Gilbert Meilaender comments that "*philia* is transcended in *caritas [agape]* but not destroyed, for the intensely personal sharing which friendship involves is added to charity [*agape*] as its internal fruition."[43] Far from being opposed, *agape* and *philia* are truly inseparable.

Aelred agrees with Augustine. Acknowledging his debt to Cicero, he seeks to go beyond Cicero to ask what friendship might mean for the Christian. Friendship is a great good, he cannot imagine life without it: "In *human* affairs there is no goal that is holier than friendship, nothing more useful, nothing more difficult to find, nothing sweeter to experience, nothing more enjoyable to maintain."[44] Aristotle and Cicero speak of the friendship of *natural* goodness and virtue as the only true friendship. Aelred speaks of *spiritual* friendship, one in which friends are brought together in the *supernatural* virtue of love of God, as the only true friendship.

For Christian friends true friendship is, indeed, the result of virtue, but of supernatural not natural virtue, namely the love of God. In loving one other in preference to all other creatures, Christians love God as well; indeed, they love God above all. In growing together in this preferential love, they grow also in the love of God, which is the foundation, the principle, and the goal of Christian friendship. It is not surprising that Aelred begins his work with the pregnant phrase: "Here we are, you and I, and I hope that Christ makes a third with us."[45] Christ is always present as a third partner in true Christian friendship, and so too, therefore, is God.

The problem in history, especially in post-Enlightenment history, is that *agape* was enthroned as the norm of all love and *philia* did not measure up to that norm. *Agape*, however, is not the norm of love; God is the norm of all love, both *agape* and *philia*. Friendship by itself is not a non-Christian love; friendship without God and Christ is a non-Christian love. Human friendship-love and neighbor-love both originate in and are images of the love of God. Paul Wadell puts it well. "Once it is acknowledged that both Christian friendship and *agape* originate in the same love, not only are they reconcilable they are also inseparable . . . we not only know why *agape* is not opposed to friendship, we also know why it is friendship's most perfect expression."[46]

If friendship leads to a Christ-like life, it leads to God as surely as *agape*. A friend is not just another step in the journey toward God but, recalling Aristotle's reasons why we need friends, a source of self-revelation for me on the journey, a support on the journey, and a challenge to me to do good on the journey to all children of God. A Christian friend is not only a permanent source of self-revelation for me, he or she is also a permanent source of the revelation of God for me, "a necessary complement to the soul in its movement to God."[47] "God is love" *[agape]*, John tells us. All very well as metaphor, but metaphors require interpretation. Surely, however impossible it is to describe dogmatically the inner relationships of the divine Trinity, it is equally impossible to imagine a divine love that is not particular and reciprocal benevolence between the three divine persons. It is impossible to imagine, that is, a love that is not also friendship and mutual communion between Father, Son, and Holy Spirit. In God, deep and lasting *philia* must surely coexist with and particularize *agape*. If that is true in God, there is no reason to think it is not true also in humans made in God's image (Gen 1:26).

Philia, Aristotle's love of reciprocal benevolence, and *caritas-agape*, Aquinas' love of universal benevolence, so mutually enrich and nourish one another that, as I noted at the beginning of this essay, the mature

Aquinas is led to identify them.[48] He claims what Aristotle had thought the unthinkable, namely, that "charity *[agape]* signifies not only love of God but also a certain friendship *[philia]* with God, which consists in a certain familiar colloquy with God." That friendship with God happens "in this life by grace and will be perfected in the future life by glory."[49] As always for Aquinas, as for the entire Catholic tradition,[50] grace makes possible what is impossible for men and women left to themselves, in this case reciprocal love, communion, and communication with God. To be friends with God, or to love God as a friend, is possible only because God has first loved us as friends (1 John 4:19). Left to our own devices, as Aristotle knew, hoping for friendship with God is hoping for too much. But the Christian tradition believes firmly that we are not left to our own devices; we are left to God and God's grace which makes possible charity *(agape-caritas),* which is also friendship *(philia).* Citing John 15:15, where Jesus calls his disciples "friends," Aquinas also suggests that the paradigmatic friendship-love is that of Jesus for his disciples.[51]

Although *philia* and *agape* may not be identical for the philosophers, for Christian theologians they are not totally separate and unrelated, and there is no reason for judging true friendship-love inferior to agapaic-love as a path to God. This question of the relationship of friendship-love and agapaic-love is one of several questions where the mature Aquinas parts company with the young Aquinas. As Fergus Kerr notes, he may well have been reacting to the over-exaltation of *agape-caritas* that led to the ludicrous situation of loving all so impartially that no one was loved in particular.[52]

Psychiatrist Ignace Lepp, in full agreement with Aristotle and Aquinas, writes that "the most universal and, in our opinion, the noblest of all forms of interhuman communication, the only one capable of dissolving our loneliness, is friendship."[53] It is also, I suggest, under the gentle influence of grace, the noblest of all forms of divine-human communication, so that not just any relationship with God is acceptable but only a relationship of friendship-love. That friendship-love with God, as already noted, is necessarily reciprocal because "God first loved us" (1 John 4:19). Aelred's transposed metaphor, after all, is not over-reaching: "God is friendship." And friendship, therefore, in equal metaphor, is God.

Friendship and Marriage

Norman Geisler echoes Newman already cited: "The love of all comes best when the love for those one is next to comes first."[54] To be grasped fully, this judgment needs to be contextualized within the debate about the nature of Christian love just rehearsed. Is Christian love essentially universal, non-preferential, and not necessarily reciprocated love, embracing all persons *qua* persons? Or is it essentially particular, preferential, and reciprocated love, embracing those special persons one is next to: spouse, children, parents, friends, fellow believers? Or is it both particular and universal, so that "the love of all comes best when the love for those one is next to comes first?" Evidently I have argued for the third option, and I shall argue now for the view that this option was and is the dominant Christian approach. My investigation of this approach will focus it specifically on friendship and marriage.

Christianity is a "textualized religion,"[55] that is, it gives prominence to its canonized writings. Both inclusive and exclusive love, *agape* and *philia*, are extolled in those writings. Jesus summed up Torah in the commandments to love God and to love *(agapeseis)* one's neighbor as oneself (Mark 12:29-31; Matt 22:37-40; Luke 10:27). That double commandment is the sacred root of the Christian demand for universal neighbor-love *(agape)*. John reports, however, that Jesus, the paradigmatic neighbor-lover, called his disciples friends *(philoi)* (15:15), and loved Lazarus so particularly and so obviously that onlookers could comment "see how he (Jesus) loved *[ephilei]* him" (11:36). I have already suggested that John 15:15 was a decisive factor leading Aquinas to identify *caritas-agape* and *philia*.[56] The demands of universal neighbor-love do not displace or negate particular friendship-love and the special relationship it implies. Rather, *agape* and *philia* are related and mutually nourish one another.

The tension between the universal, inclusive love of all and the particular, exclusive, or preferential love of some is retained in the Pauline instruction to the followers of Jesus in Galatia: "Whenever we have an opportunity, let us work for the good *[agathon]* of all, and especially for those of the family of faith" (Gal 6:10). Christian love is both universal ("all") and legitimately particular ("especially"). The particularity is made even more exclusive, the relation even more preferential, in Timothy's post-Pauline community: "Whoever does not provide for relatives, and especially for family members, has denied the faith and is worse than an unbeliever" (1 Tim 5:8). Christian love is both universal *(agape)* and particular *(philia)*; it requires inclusive and exclusive covenants, and neither the abstract universal nor the concrete particular dimension excludes the other. The universal love of all comes easiest when the particular love of some—spouse, parents, children, fellow-Christians—comes first.

Newman is correct: "the best preparation for loving the world at large, and loving it duly and wisely, is to cultivate an intimate friendship and affection toward those who are immediately about us."[57]

The developing Christian tradition held firmly to this Pauline tradition. Augustine accepted the demand for universal love, but he also specified who ought to be loved, and affirmed the root of this judgment in 1 Timothy 5:8. A man "ought to make this endeavor on behalf of his wife, his children, his household, all within his reach. . . . For the law of nature and of society gives him readier access to them and greater opportunity of serving them."[58] Aquinas also hews to the Pauline tradition. He writes that, although *caritas-agape* requires us to love all, by nature we are bound to love some neighbors more than others, to love those nearer to us more than those who are better than them, and to love our relatives more than others.[59] He, too, cites 1 Timothy 5:8 to substantiate his judgment.[60] We recall his explicit identification of *philia* and *agape* on the basis of John 15:15. In the eighteenth century, Bishop Butler maintains that same tradition, teaching that "the care of some persons, suppose children and family, is committed to our charge by nature and providence."[61] Stephen Post's comment is accurate: "The moral agent is a social animal. . . . Because there are degrees of relatedness and proximity, [universal] Good Samaritanism provides only a partial vision of love."[62] Consistently in the tradition, *agape* is only one facet of the love to which Christians are called.

Two great preachers have given American voice to this ancient tradition, albeit from different perspectives. Jonathan Edwards interpreted the harmony he perceived in nature as communion or mutual love between the various parts of nature, and from that perception he derived a theory of love as communion. "Love in heaven is always mutual [reciprocal]. It is always met with answerable returns of love. . . . [Love] will always be mutual and reciprocated."[63] Love in heaven, in other words, will be *philia*. Martin Luther King teaches that *agape* is "love seeking to preserve and create community. It is insistence on community even when one seeks to break it. *Agape* is a willingness to go to any length to restore community."[64] Community is preferential, mutual, reciprocal love, or *philia*. It is *agape* longing for communion, King adds, that impelled God toward the cross, which is now the symbol "of the length to which God will go to restore broken community,"[65] or foundered friendship. I am in full agreement with Margaret Farley when she argues that mutuality or reciprocity is central to the covenant tradition because God's commitment to humans "has mutuality [friendship] as its goal."[66]

   This emphasis on love as mutual communion or community is what brings us specifically to marriage. The Second Vatican Council defined marriage as "a community of love . . . an intimate partnership of life and love" (*Gaudium et Spes* 47–8). *Community* derives from the Latin *communis,* and is defined as common or reciprocal sharing, common or reciprocal ownership, common or reciprocal responsibility. In his analysis of the meaning of love, Robert Johann paraphrases Aristotle and Aquinas, summarizes much of what I have been arguing, and adds a new dimension:

> For friendship, it is not enough to love another directly as myself; to be friendship, my love of benevolence must be explicitly reciprocated. Friendship exists only between those who love one another. Thus it is conceived as adding to a one-sided love of benevolence *[agape]* a certain society of lover and beloved in their love.[67]

For the majority of modern men and women, the interpersonal partnership or community created by love continues to be publicly formalized in marriage and, in the community between spouses, marital love includes the reciprocal responsibility to maintain and grow the friendship-love that founded communion in the first instance. Spousal love cannot be only *agape,* it must be also *philia.* It must be also, of course, affection *(storge)* and sexual love *(eros)* but, to maintain focus on the questions at issue, I am not dealing with these here.

   The communion between spouses in marriage has no obvious models in our world other than itself. It is not a monarchy, which is about unequal individuals; it is not a democracy, which is about equal but separate individuals. It is about equal individuals who are so united that they can truly be said to be "two in one body" (Gen 2:24), a small community, a relational and coupled-We. Without models all we can say, with the Second Vatican Council, is that marital communion is an intimate community of love in which one self and another self, an I and a Thou, become a coupled-We, and mutually share their experiences, their feelings, their thoughts, their joys, their sorrows, their love, and their lives. When such love is Christian, as we have seen, it is a school for learning *philia,* particular, preferential, and reciprocal friendship-love of another and others, and *agape,* universal, non-preferential, and unconditional neighbor-love of all. If Wallerstein and Blakeslee are right, and the social-scientific evidence suggests they are, preferential *philia* is the best lasting foundation of a good marriage, because it cements with mutual virtue the community and communion marriage is. Steadfast marital love is a rich blend of friendship-love and unconditional neighbor-love, and also of affection and sexual love. Catholics look upon this rich, many-splendored love as such a gift of, and a way to, God that they hold marriage as the sacrament, the symbol in the world, of the friendship and self-sacrificing love between God and God's people and Christ and Christ's Church.[68]

Communion is not a new word in the theological tradition. A note from the Second Vatican Council explains that communion "is an idea which was held in high honor in the ancient Church (as it is even today especially in the East)."[69] We make a mistake, however, if we assume that the communion which exists between spouses in marriage arises only from their marriage. Its root is prior, and deeper in human reality, than that.

The opening section of this essay documented a fact which does not really need documenting; namely, that humans have needs: needs for trust, respect, safety, understanding, acceptance. I commit myself to respond to the needs of particular others and they commit to respond to mine. We are friends, we say, without whom "no one would choose to live, even if he had all other goods."[70] Friends journey through life together, revealing themselves to one another, sustaining one another, provoking one another to the realization of potential, mutually rejoicing when the potential is realized, mutually sorrowing when it is not. Friends wish one another well; in an ancient word, they love one another.[71] Though feelings are frequently associated with love, feelings are not of its essence. Loving is essentially doing something. It is affirming the being, the very well-being, of another. To love is to will the good of another.

As I have insisted several times, willing the good of another is not yet friendship-love; that occurs only when my love is reciprocated by another, who wills my good in return. This mutual friendship-love between equal selves creates between us the communion, the reciprocal bond that is the distinguishing mark of lovers, the fertile root through which we draw life from and give life to one another. Reciprocal love does not *lead* to communion; reciprocal love *is* communion. It is true that love creates an intense desire for fuller communion, including the desire for friendship for the whole of life, but love is itself already communion, a relationship, a bond which is morally binding. Love can consent to bind itself further by social ritual. In marriage, it consents to bind itself legally by law; in sacrament, it consents to bind itself religiously by the grace of God. In a marriage between Christians, therefore, three bonds arise: an interpersonal bond of love between the spouses, a legal bond of marriage, and a religious bond of sacrament.[72]

Though, as a Catholic theologian, I might be tempted to declare the bond of sacrament the most fundamental of these three bonds, it is not.

The most fundamental bond is the bond of mutual love, the bond forged by both friendship and unconditional neighbor-love, because it is the root of the other two. It is the bond ritualized in both marriage and sacrament. Only if this root is healthy and strong can the bonds of marriage and sacrament flower as lasting bonds of satisfying and stable commitment. It is not difficult to understand why spouses who maintain friendship-love, who like each other, trust each other, and respect each other, should maintain satisfying, happy, and stable marriages. When the root friendship-love, through which the spouses give marital life to and draw marital life from one another, is healthy, so too are the marriage and sacrament which draw sustenance and flower from the root.

Every reader of this essay will have been to a wedding. In the hustle and bustle that surrounds weddings, however, everyone might not have noticed that only one moment in the ceremony truly counts, the moment of giving free consent. "Marriage is brought about through the consent of the parties, legitimately manifested" (Can 1057). Only after the free consent of the parties has been exchanged, "I, Sean, take you Kate, to be my wife. . . . I, Kate, take you, Sean, to be my husband," are they declared married, husband and wife. If that moment is lacking or in any way flawed, there is no valid marriage, no marital relationship, no bond arising from marriage, and no bond arising from sacrament. If that moment is valid, then there is a valid marriage, a valid marital relationship and bond is added to the interpersonal relationship of friendship-love also present. In addition to the interpersonally related and coupled-We, there is now also legally related and coupled-We.

It may appear that, in the previous paragraph, I have switched from a broadly relational to a narrowly juridical focus. I have not. The bond of friendship-love which brought two people into relationship in the first instance, and which brought them to formalize their relationship publicly in marriage and sacrament in the second instance, shapes the consent which makes their prior interpersonally coupled-We also a legally coupled-We. In other words, the mutual consent which makes their marriage and, under the appropriate conditions,[73] also their sacrament, is necessarily shaped by the defining characteristics of the related and coupled-We who consent.

The characteristics of a friendly, agapaic consent are: (1) a decision that one's own personal well-being is permanently linked to the well-being of one's friend-spouse; (2) a commitment to yield rights to make individual decisions and to make those decisions henceforth in mutual consultation; (3) a judgment to be perceived personally, socially, legally, and religiously as no longer two individuals but one related and coupled-We; (4) a commitment to a shared interpersonal identity which involves reshaping and redefining individual identities as part of a related and coupled-We; (5) a decision to invest the individual autonomies of both friends-spouses in a new autonomy of the enlarged coupled-We.[74] That consent is "an act of the will by which a man and a woman by an irrevocable covenant mutually give and accept one another for the purpose of establishing a marriage" (Can 1057) provides an important clue. *Agape* can mandate the individual consent to love, but only *philia* can mandate the reciprocal consent to love. For one self and another self, an individual I and an individual Thou, to become a truly related and coupled-We, the mutual and reciprocal benevolence of friendship-love must be strong; for the coupled-We to remain stable and satisfied, that love must remain steadfast over the length of a lifetime.

One last question remains: Why would a man and a woman freely choose to yield their individual rights and become a coupled-We for life? A short answer is because they wish to be best friends for life. A more extended answer developed in the Christian tradition from the consideration of the ends or purposes of marriage. Those ends are traditionally two: the mutual love of the spouses and procreation. As long as marriage was viewed as a procreative institution to ensure the birth of children and their nurture into functioning adulthood, it was traditional to view procreation as the *primary* end of marriage and the love of the spouses as a *secondary* end. When marriage came to be viewed in the twentieth century as an interpersonal union between the spouses, even the Catholic Church adjusted that hierarchical arrangement and established the two ends as equal ends of Christian marriage.[75] I shall conclude this chapter by considering these two ends of marriage along with a third frequently forgotten end: the Christian life of friendship-love of those near to you and unconditional neighbor-love of all.

The bedrock of every friendship, including the friendship called marriage, is generativity, the capacity to generate and nurture life beyond one's own. The first life generated in a marriage, and the life on which all other lives in the marriage depend for their viability, is the life of the spouses together, their two-in-one-bodiness, their coupled-We. Pope John Paul II argues:

> The first communion is the one which is established and which develops between the husband and wife. By virtue of the covenant of married life, the man and the woman are no longer two but one flesh and they are called to grow continually in their communion through day to day fidelity.[76]

The loving communion of the spouses is an important end of their marriage, indeed the very end for which they decided to marry in the first place.

A friend who is also a spouse, as Aristotle argued, daily reflects to me an honest appraisal of myself; she offers me support against the constant temptation to loss of interest in and commitment to our ongoing consent to be a coupled-We; she provides me with daily opportunities to do good and to grow in virtue. As other to be responded to in steadfast love, she calls me to constant virtue and moral behavior in and out of marriage.[77] All of that, and more, is generated, first, by mutual fidelity to our ongoing consent to be a preferential communion of best friends forever. However, precisely because the communion of best friends in marriage is founded on preferential criteria—beauty, intellect, strength of character, shared interest, and the like—and because preferences can ebb and flow, marriage is always fragile. And that is where *agape* is necessary, as universal support for particular preference. The communion between the spouses, therefore, is both friendly and agapaic communion, and it fashions the stable foundation on which is built "the broader communion of the family."[78]

Most parents will agree with the Vatican Council's claim that "children really are the supreme gift of marriage and contribute substantially to the welfare of their parents,"[79] and so we need not spend time establishing procreation as an end of marriage. We do, however, given the physical, emotional, and social fate of children in contemporary families,[80] need to spend some time underscoring that the generativity and fruitfulness of a marriage are not achieved by the biological generation of children. To be parentally fruitful requires not only the momentary act of intercourse but also the long-term nurture of the children resulting from that intercourse into functioning adulthood. Maternity and paternity may generate children; only motherhood and fatherhood, the long-term nurture of those children, generate functioning adults. It is the generation of functioning adults that has always been the desired end of the act of procreation, and it is certainly functioning adults that are required today in both society and Church.

There is a third end of specifically *Christian* marriages which is frequently forgotten. Christian marriage requires Christian spouses to live their marital life in imitation of Jesus, whom they confess as the Christ. Though biologically childless, Jesus was enormously fruitful, generating and nurturing all those called by his name, *Christians.* He nurtured them specifically to call upon God as *Abba,* Father (Mark 14:36), and, therefore, to look upon all the children of God as brothers and sisters and friends. For a marriage to be genuinely Christian, it must generate and nurture Christian life and communion, not only between the spouses, not only within their immediate family, but also within the human community in which they live. The end of marriage sought by Jesus is a friendship-love and a neighbor-love, not only inside but also outside marriage.

To be truly fruitful as *Christian* spouses, as a Christian partnered-We, spouses must generate and nurture a world of love, care, compassion, reconciliation, justice, and peace for their neighbors, especially for those poor neighbors who exist on the margins of modern societies, so that they can pass on to their and all children a world in which they are not only biologically generated but also socially nurtured into fruitful life and functioning adulthood.[81] In this way Christian spouses fulfill the injunction of the Letter to Timothy to "provide for [their] relations, and especially for family members" (1 Tim 5:8); in this way they fulfill the Augustinian and Thomistic injunctions to love all within their reach[82] and those nearest to them most of all.[83] In this way, too, in John Paul II's words, they make their "first and fundamental contribution to society,"[84] so that their families can truly become "the primary vital cell of society."[85]

Conclusion

This essay sought to bridge a gap in the Christian approach to friendship, and to show that it is a gift of God both to have friends and to be united in the intimate partnership of marriage with a best friend for life. All I have written, of course, will seem philosophically cold and calculating to friends and lovers when compared to the warmth and spontaneity of their intimate friendship-love. Friends and lovers, inside or outside marriage, will recognize that emotional and physical bonding is a more central part of friendship-love than philosophical or theological analysis. There is joy and sadness in friendship, laughter and tears, celebration of communion and grief when communion is threatened; there is sensual delight, growing affection, deepening commitment; there is mutual respect, honesty, trust, understanding, empathy, support, compassion, forgiveness, frequent reconciliation. There is risk, however, always risk, no matter how extensive has been the probation (*pace* Aelred), for to love is to go out of oneself to another self, to entrust oneself to her or to him, and that cannot be done without accepting the risk that one may be rejected, hurt, or betrayed.

Cicero already hinted at the essential other-ness of friendship by describing the friend as a second self, "one to whom you can speak on all subjects as to yourself."[86] Wallerstein and Blakeslee agree. The intimate connectedness, the two-in-one-bodiness, of a good marriage "includes knowing enough about the other so that at critical times one can take an imaginative leap inside the other's skin."[87] Taking an imaginative, loving, and empathetic leap inside another's skin might be a good, modern definition of friendship-love, a personalized equivalent of Cicero's philosophical "complete accord of feeling on all subjects, divine and human, accompanied by kindly feeling and attachment." I end this essay by offering both definitions as powerful prescriptions for good, satisfying, and stable marriages.

Questions for Reflection

1. What do you think of Cicero's definition of friendship: "A complete accord on all subjects, divine and human, accompanied by kindly feeling and attachment"? What do you think of Aristotle's claim that friendship is to be preferred "to all human possessions"? Does this judgment apply in marriage?

2. What do you think of Aelred's judgments that God is the foundation of friendship and that true friendship is possible only for the virtuous? Does this apply in marriage?

3. Do you experience *philia* and *agape* in your life? Explain the difference between them. What do you think of Aelred's suggestion that "God is friendship" rather than love?

4. What do you think of Geisler's suggestion that "the love of all comes best when the love of those we are next to comes first"? Does this apply in marriage and family?

5. Reflect on and explain the three ends of marriages discussed in this chapter. Do any of these ends surprise you?

Notes

¹ Judith S. Wallerstein and Sandra Blakeslee, *The Good Marriage: How and Why Love Lasts* (New York: Houghton Mifflin, 1995) 169–70.

² Aristotle, *Nichomachean Ethics* 8.1.

³ *Redemptoris Hominis* 10, AAS 71 (1979) 274.

⁴ Aristotle, *Nichomachean Ethics* 8.3.

⁵ Ibid.; Aquinas, *In III Sent.,* d. 27, q. 2, a. 1, ad 8: *"amicitia est redamantium"* (friendship is between those who love reciprocally).

⁶ The ideas expressed in this paragraph are indebted to the excellent essay by John M. Cooper, "Aristotle on Friendship," *Essays on Aristotle's Ethics,* ed. Amelie Oksenberg Rorty (Berkeley: University of California Press, 1980).

⁷ Enda McDonagh, *Gift and Call* (St. Meinrad, Ind.: Abbey Press, 1975).

⁸ Cicero, *Friendship* (Chicago: Albert and Scott, 1890) 17.

⁹ Ibid., 15.

¹⁰ Ibid., 17.

¹¹ Ibid., 30.

¹² Ibid., 40.

¹³ Ibid., 56.

¹⁴ Augustine, *The Confessions,* trans. John K. Ryan (Garden City, N.J.: Doubleday, 1960) 97.

¹⁵ See Marie Aquinas McNamara, *Friendship in Saint Augustine* (Fribourg: University Press, 1958) 196–7.

¹⁶ Aelred of Rievaulx, *Spiritual Friendship,* trans. Mark F. Williams (Scranton: University of Scranton Press, 1994) 1:38.

¹⁷ Ibid., 3:3, 1:1, 2:20.

¹⁸ Ibid., 1:44.

¹⁹ Ibid., 2:38. Cf. 3:1.

²⁰ Ibid., 3:8.

²¹ Ibid., 3:23.

²² Ibid., 3:24.

²³ Ibid., 3:25.

²⁴ Ibid., 3:28.

²⁵ Ibid., 3:62.

²⁶ Ibid., 3:61.

²⁷ Ibid.

²⁸ Ibid.

²⁹ Ibid., 3:5, 54.

³⁰ Ibid., 1:21.

³¹ Ibid., 1:69.

³² There are four Greek words for love: *storge* (affection), *philia* (friendship), *eros* (love of another for my sake), and *agape* (love of another for the other's sake, translated in English usually as charity), but I am concerned here only

with *philia* and *agape.* See C. S. Lewis, *Four Loves* (New York: Harcourt Brace Jovanovich, 1960).

[33] Jeremy Taylor, "Discourse on the Nature and Offices of Friendship," *Works,* vol. 1, ed. R. Heber, revised and corrected C. P. Eden (London: Longman, Green, Longman, Roberts, & Green, 1847) 72.

[34] See Adolph Harnack, "Friends," *The Mission and Expansion of Christianity* (New York: Harper Torchbooks) 421.

[35] Søren Kierkegaard, "You Shall Love Your Neighbor," *Other Selves: Philosophers on Friendship,* ed. Michael Pakaluk (Indianapolis: Hacket Publishing, 1991) 242.

[36] Søren Kierkegaard, *Works of Love: Some Christian Reflections in the Form of Discourses,* trans. Howard and Edna Long (New York: Harper & Row, 1964) 65–6.

[37] Anders Nygren, *Agape and Eros* (New York: Harper & Row, 1969) 63.

[38] Gene Outka, *Agape: An Ethical Analysis* (New Haven, Conn.: Yale University Press, 1972). See also his "Universal Love and Impartiality," *The Love Commandments: Essays in Christian Ethics and Moral Philosophy,* ed. Edmund N. Santurri and William Werpehowski (Washington, D.C.: Georgetown University Press, 1992).

[39] Edward Collins Vacek, *Love: Human and Divine* (Washington, D.C.: Georgetown University Press, 1994) 173. See also Martin C. D'Arcy, *The Mind and Heart of Love, Lion, and Unicorn: A Study in Eros and Agape* (New York: Holt, 1947).

[40] McNamara, *Friendship in Saint Augustine,* 202.

[41] John Henry Newman, *Parochial and Plain Sermons* (San Francisco: Ignatius Press, 1987) sermon 5, 258.

[42] Ibid., 221.

[43] Gilbert Meilaender, *Friendship: A Study in Theological Ethics* (Notre Dame, Ind.: University of Notre Dame Press, 1981) 17–8.

[44] Aelred of Rievaulx, *Spiritual Friendship,* 2:9.

[45] Ibid., 1·1.

[46] Paul J. Wadell, *Friendship and the Moral Life* (Notre Dame, Ind.: University of Notre Dame Press, 1989) 83.

[47] Adele M. Fiske, *Friends and Friendship in the Monastic Tradition* (Cuernavaca: Centro Intercultural de Documentación, 1970) 2–3.

[48] ST Ia-IIae, q. 23, a. 1.

[49] ST IIa-IIae, q. 65, a. 5.

[50] See the Council of Carthage (418), DS 225–7; the Second Council of Orange (529), DS 373–95; and Caesar of Arles, DS 396.

[51] See Anthony W. Keaty, "Thomas' Authority for Identifying Charity as Friendship: Aristotle or John 15?" *The Thomist* 62 (1998) 581–601.

[52] See Fergus Kerr, "Charity as Friendship," *Language, Meaning and God: Essays in Honour of Herbert McCabe,* ed. Brian Davies (London: Chapman, 1987) 1–23.

[53] Ignace Lepp, *The Ways of Friendship* (New York: Macmillan, 1966) 21.

[54] Norman L. Geisler, *The Christian Ethic of Love* (Grand Rapids, Mich.: Zondervan, 1973) 39.

[55] George Lindbeck, "Barth and Textuality," *Theology Today* 43 (1986) 361.

[56] For an extended discussion of friendship in the New Testament see Alan C. Mitchell, "'Greet the Friends by Name': New Testament Evidence for the Greco-Roman Topos on Friendship," *Greco-Roman Perspectives on Friendship*, ed. John T. Fitzgerald (Atlanta: Scholars Press, 1997) 225–62.

[57] Newman, *Parochial and Plain Sermons,* sermon 5, 258.

[58] Augustine, *The City of God,* trans. Marcus Dods (New York: Random House, 1950) 693.

[59] For discussion of the ordering of love see Stephen J. Pope, *The Evolution of Altruism and the Ordering of Love* (Washington, D.C.: Georgetown University Press, 1994), and his "'Equal Regard' versus 'Special Relations'? Reaffirming the Inclusiveness of Agape," *Journal of Religion* 77 (1997) 353–79. Jean Porter, "De Ordine Caritatis: Charity, Friendship, and Justice in Thomas Aquinas' *Summa Theologiae*," *The Thomist* 53 (1989) 197–239, also discusses *agape* and *philia* in Aquinas.

[60] ST IIa-IIae, q. 26, a. 6, 7, and 8.

[61] Joseph Butler, "Fifteen Sermons," *British Moralists, 1650–1800,* ed. D. D. Raphael (Oxford: Clarendon Press, 1969) 374.

[62] Stephen G. Post, *A Theory of Agape: On the Meaning of Christian Love* (Lewisburg, Pa.: Bucknell University Press, 1990) 104.

[63] Jonathan Edwards, *Charity and Its Fruits* (London: Banner of Truth Press, 1978) 338–9.

[64] Martin Luther King Jr., *A Testament of Hope: The Essential Writings of Martin Luther King, Jr.* (San Francisco: Harper & Row, 1986) 20.

[65] Ibid.

[66] Margaret A. Farley, *Personal Commitments: Beginning, Keeping, Changing* (San Francisco: Harper & Row, 1986) 129.

[67] Robert O. Johann, *The Meaning of Love: An Essay Towards a Metaphysics of Intersubjectivity* (Glen Rock, N.J.: Paulist Press, 1966) 46–7.

[68] See Michael G. Lawler, *Symbol and Sacrament: A Contemporary Sacramental Theology* (Omaha: Creighton University Press, 1995).

[69] Walter M. Abbott, ed., *The Documents of Vatican II* (London: Chapman, 1966) 99.

[70] Aristotle, *Nichomachean Ethics* 8.1.

[71] ST, Ia, q. 20, a. 1 ad 3.

[72] I have treated this matter in detail in Chapter 4.

[73] See Chapter 3.

[74] This section has been greatly enriched by ideas in Robert Nozick, *Love's Bond: The Examined Life* (New York: Simon and Schuster, 1989) 68–86.

[75] See GS 50, *Codex Iuris Canonici* (1983), Canon 1055.1, and Chapter 2 of this book.

[76] FC 16.

[77] See McDonagh, *Gift and Call.*

[78] FC 18.

[79] GS 50.

[80] For detail, see Michael G. Lawler, *Family: American and Christian* (Chicago: Loyola Press, 1998) 3–82.

[81] See Michael G. Lawler and Gail S. Risch, "Covenant Generativity: Toward a Theology of Christian Family," *Horizons* 26 (1999) 7–30.

[82] Augustine, *The City of God,* 693.

[83] ST IIa-IIae, q. 26, a. 6, 7, and 8.

[84] FC 43; see also n. 44.

[85] AA 11.

[86] Cicero, *Friendship,* 18: "What can be more delightful than to have someone to whom you can speak as to yourself?" See also 19: "He who looks on a true friend looks on a kind of image of himself."

[87] Wallerstein and Blakeslee, *The Good Marriage,* 335.

8

Cohabitation and Marriage in
the Catholic Church: A Proposal[1]

Introduction

Emmanuel Ntakarutimana expresses the Central African experience of marrying in the following words:

> Where Western tradition presents marriage as a point in time at which consent is exchanged between the couple in front of witnesses approved by law, followed by consummation, the tradition here recognizes the consummation of a marriage with the birth of the first child. To that point the marriage was only being *progressively realized*.[2]

My four years of field experience in East Africa taught me the same thing. I offer three points of clarification. First, the Western tradition to which Ntakarutimana refers is the tradition of only the past four hundred years; it goes back neither to Jesus nor to the New Testament. Second, even in this Western tradition, indissoluble marriage is not defined by a specific point in time and a specific act that consummates it. Rather, in the received Western tradition, as in the African traditions, becoming validly and indissolubly married is a process which begins with the exchange of consent and ends with subsequent consummation. Third, two ongoing questions arise: What are we to make of the differences between the Catholic, Western tradition of marrying and other cultural traditions, and how long can the Catholic Church continue to insist that the historically recent Western tradition is *the* universal tradition for all?

This essay reflects on these points. It is about marriage, specifically about the process of becoming married in the living Catholic tradition of past and future. As it reflects on the history of marriage in the West, it necessarily uncovers two facts about the phenomenon contemporary society calls cohabitation. First, despite the present hysteria, cohabitation is nothing new in either the Western or the Catholic traditions; second, as practiced both in the past and in the present, Western cohabitation is not unlike the African cohabitation of which Ntakarutimana writes. The essay, then, develops in three cumulative sections. The first section considers the contemporary phenomenon of cohabitation; the second unfolds the Western and Christian historical tradition as it relates to cohabitation and marriage; the third makes preliminary *theological* suggestions about cohabitation and possible pastoral approaches to it. I will develop each section in turn.

Since the second and, especially, the third sections may come as a surprise to many readers unaware of the history of marriage, it is necessary to preface the whole with a brief consideration of the theologian's task in the Church. Catholic theologians in every age are faced with a choice. They can simply repeat the tradition received from the past. In the case of sexuality and marriage, that tradition is clear: "The sexual act must take place exclusively within marriage,"[3] marriage is initiated at a wedding by mutually free consent given publicly in the presence of a priest and two witnesses, and it is consummated by sexual intercourse between the spouses. Within this received marital tradition, cohabitation is immoral because of the premarital sexual acts it embraces. There is, however, another theological possibility. Theologians, as they must, again take account of the received tradition, but this time do not simply repeat it. This time, they take account not only of the tradition, but also of the historical experiences and premises in which that tradition developed and flourished, and they ask what might be different in a contemporary situation where experience and premises have changed. Different experiences, circumstances, and premises, perhaps learned from a close study of the contemporary social, psychological, and theological situation, could certainly lead to different conclusions.

The first approach, repeating the tradition, is easy and safe; but is it pastorally useful in the contemporary situation? Karl Rahner notes that, when one takes account of the historicity of human truth, "in which God's truth too has become incarnate in revelation," then "neither the abandonment of a formula nor its preservation in a petrified form does justice to human understanding."[4] There are two ways to be unfaithful to the historical tradition, Rahner suggests: one is to abandon it, the other is to repeat it endlessly as an unexamined mantra. The second approach is to seek to point the tradition in "new" directions. This approach is more difficult and fraught with risk, for theological history demonstrates how difficult it is to point ecclesiastical magisteria in new directions, especially since they are not in the habit of taking seriously the data of social scientific research. My choice in this essay is respectfully to take the second approach as being more helpful and hopeful in the contemporary, and shrinking, Christian world, where it is now clear that the unnuanced rigidity of the first approach is no longer received by most Catholics as a call to morally responsible behavior.

A word about responsible behavior. The *Catechism of the Catholic Church* teaches that "the Church's social teaching proposes *principles for reflection;* it provides *criteria for judgment;* it gives *guidelines* for action."[5] This trinity of principles for reflection, criteria for judgment, and guidelines for action came into Catholic social teaching via Paul VI's *Octogesima Adveniens* in 1971.[6] It was repeated in the Congregation for the Doctrine of the Faith's important Instruction on Christian Freedom and Liberation in 1986,[7] and underscored again a year later in John Paul II's *Sollicitudo Rei Socialis.*[8] This socio-moral teaching, now an established part of the Catholic moral tradition, introduces a model of relationship-responsibility which increasingly underscores the responsibility of each person. John Paul accentuates this point of view by teaching that, in its social doctrine, the Church seeks "to *guide* people to *respond,* with the support of rational reflection and of the human sciences, to their vocation as *responsible* builders of earthly society."[9] The relationship of the Magisterium and the individual believer which this teaching advances merits close attention. The Church *guides;*[10] responsible persons, drawing on the Church's guidance, their own intellectual abilities, and the findings of the human sciences, respond responsibly.

The notion of responsibility introduces an important dimension of human freedom to the unnuanced notion of response. In social reality, the Magisterium does not pretend to pronounce on every last detail or to impose final decisions; it understands itself as informing and guiding believers, and leaving the final judgment and application to their faithful and responsible conscience.[11] Socio-moral principles are guidelines for reflection, judgment, and action, not categorical moral imperatives based on divine, natural, or ecclesiastical law, and demanding uncritical obedience to God, nature, or Church. John Paul adds what the Catholic moral tradition has always taken for granted. On the one hand, the Church's social teaching is "constant." On the other hand, "it is ever new, because it is subject to the necessary and opportune adaptations suggested by the changes in historical conditions and by the unceasing flow of the events which are the setting of the life of people and society."[12] Principles remain constant. Judgments and actions might well change after reflection on changed historical conditions and the ongoing flow of human events illuminated by rational reflection and the data of the social sciences.

There is, however, a problem. This model of relationship-responsibility seems to apply in the contemporary Catholic moral situation only in *social morality*. A model diametrically antithetical to personal freedom and responsibility applies in *sexual morality*, where there are no principles and guidelines for reflection, judgment, and action, only laws to be universally and unquestioningly obeyed. It is, at least, debatable how this can be. Since social and sexual morality pertain to the same person, it seems illogical that there can be this double and conflicting approach. In fact, because the whole personality is more intimately involved in the sexual domain, should it not "be *more than any other* the place where all is referred to the informed conscience."[13] The choice between the two moral approaches is neither self-evident nor free from risk. But it is a choice that must be made to find the best theological and pastoral approach to the experience of contemporary women and men. Pierre-Olivier Bressoud judges that the choice is clear, and that there is "a manifest link between the notions dear to social morality, namely, person, freedom, relationship, and responsibility, and the notions of individual sexual development and progression toward marriage."[14] I am not convinced that the choice is clear or that the link is manifest to everyone, but in this essay the choice between the two Catholic approaches to morality cannot be avoided.

That both the reader and I might understand from the outset what I am undertaking here, I freely acknowledge that it is not for theologians to formulate the doctrine or moral practice of their Church. That is a task for the entire Church. The theologian's task is embedded within the context of the communion-Church.[15] It is the task of "interpreting the documents of the past and present Magisterium, of putting them in the context of the *whole* of revealed truth, and of finding a better understanding of them by the use of hermeneutics."[16] That is the task I seek to fulfill critically in this essay. What I suggest here, therefore, is to be read as propositions submitted to the critical reflection, judgment, and response of my theological peers. My hope is that reflection will be critically positive, not negative, and certainly not destructive of the communion that is the Church instituted by Christ and constituted by the Spirit of Christ, the Spirit of "righteousness and peace and joy" (Rom 14:17; cf. Eph 4:3).

Cohabitation in the Contemporary West

It is important to define precisely what is meant by the term *cohabitation.* The word derives from the Latin *cohabitare,* to live together. It applies literally to all situations where one person lives with another person: marriage, family, students in a dormitory, roommates in a rooming house. An added specification is necessary to distinguish the meaning of the word in contemporary usage and, therefore, in this essay: cohabitation names the situation of a man and a woman who, though not husband and wife, live together as husband and wife.

Louis Roussel offers a useful typology based on the reason given for cohabitation: "*idealist* cohabitation, where the couple look on marriage as something banal; *anti-conformist* cohabitation, where they seek to express their opposition to society; *prudent* cohabitation, where they live a sort of trial marriage; *committed* cohabitation, where the couple anticipates by several months a marriage for which they are already engaged."[17] I prefer, however, a simpler typology, which highlights the relation of cohabitation and marriage. "Committed cohabitation" I call *prenuptial* cohabitation, because marriage is consciously intended to follow it; all other types I call *non-nuptial* cohabitation, because there is no conscious intention of marriage. It is important for the reader to understand from the outset that everything I say about cohabitation in this chapter is said only of prenuptial cohabitation and cohabitants, that is, those who are already committed to marry each other.

The sharp increase in cohabitation is one of the most fundamental social changes in Western countries today. Over half of all first marriages in the United States are preceded by cohabitation.[18] Studies find a similar trend in Europe,[19] Great Britain,[20] Norway,[21] Sweden,[22] the Netherlands,[23] France,[24] Belgium and Germany,[25] Canada,[26] and Australia.[27] Surveys in France, the Netherlands, Austria, and Great Britain indicate that cohabitation before first marriage reached levels between 40 and 80 percent for recent marriages.[28]

The volume of social scientific research that studies this phenomenon has consistently reported an association between cohabitation and subsequent marital instability.[29] That research, however, does not examine co-habitation or relationship stability apart from numerous other variables. The significance of the association between premarital cohabitation and subsequent marital instability is influenced, and can be attenuated, by a host of other variables: duration of cohabitation, age at marriage, non-marital conception and presence of children, previous marriage, education, religiosity, family background, societal and family attitudes, employment and economics, race/ethnicity, and attitudes about both autonomy and equity within the relationship.[30] When predicting marital stability or in-stability for any particular cohabiting couple, all appropriate factors must be considered to disentangle the effects of cohabitation per se from effects stemming from family background, socioeconomic class, value orienta-tions, and personality characteristics.[31]

To illustrate the nature of the relationship between cohabitation and marital stability, consider two couples. The first couple includes a twenty-three-year-old male from a family that experienced parental di-vorce. He completed high school, is employed but moves from job to job, and cohabited with his first two girlfriends. He and an unemployed twenty-year-old female who also completed high school cohabited for fifteen months prior to marriage, which occurred soon after their first child was born. The second couple includes a twenty-eight-year-old male from an intact family and a twenty-four-year-old female. He com-pleted a master's degree, holds a job that provides economic security, and assists with the youth group at his church. She is a graduate stu-dent, employed part time, and attends her church fairly regularly. This couple cohabited for six months while they were engaged prior to their marriage. In the light of available research data, the first couple is at far greater risk for marital instability than the second couple. In other words, it is not simply the fact that a couple cohabits that puts them at risk for marital instability; other factors may have as much or greater impact on cohabitants' marital outcomes.

The focus on the relation between premarital cohabitation and mari-tal instability or dissolution often obscures the fact that the majority of cohabitants, 81 percent of never married, 61 percent of previously mar-ried,[32] and 75 to 80 percent of all cohabitants,[33] expect to marry their partner and that the relationships of those who plan to marry are not significantly different from marriages.[34] The majority of cohabiting re-lationships are prenuptial, that is, they result in marriage.[35] "Those on their way to the altar look and act like already-married couples in most ways; those with no plans to marry look and act very different."[36]

Cohabitation can be post-marital as well as premarital; the rate of post-marital cohabitation has increased dramatically.[37]

There is already widespread discussion among social scientists about the location of cohabiting relationships in the dating-to-marriage continuum, the nature of commitment between cohabiting partners, and attitudes and values that effect both cohabitational and marital relationships.[38] Research notes that, for some, significant transitions traditionally signaled by marriage, such as conception and childbirth, have already occurred with cohabitation.[39] In fact, cohabitation increasingly involves families with children.[40]

Cohabitation appears to have multiple meanings, to be different from singlehood, and can be understood as either a prelude or an alternative to marriage.[41] Different meanings, particularly across racial, ethnic, and cultural groups, are significant.[42] In the United States, blacks are more likely to remain in cohabiting relationships and whites are more likely to move from cohabitation to marriage.[43] Some groups, such as Puerto Ricans, understand cohabitation as a legitimate alternative to marriage, and others, especially whites, consider it a stage in the process of becoming married. These latter cohabiting couples experience relationship quality similar to that of married couples.[44] In Latin American countries, censuses, surveys, and studies typically recognize all consensual unions, which are often as common as formal marriages, as marital unions;[45] in the Netherlands, cohabitation is viewed by most young adults as a natural element in union formation and a prelude to marriage.[46]

Some of the most recent research, which involves generations who do not consider cohabitation unconventional, suggests a weaker link between premarital cohabitation and marital instability than that found in earlier studies. As the majority pattern becomes cohabitation followed by marriage, the association between cohabitation and marital instability may become weaker.[47] It has been found that as the prevalence of cohabitation rises sharply, the instability of marriages preceded by a cohabitation drops markedly,[48] and that once total length of union is considered, there is no difference in marital stability between those who did and those who did not cohabit prior to their marriage.[49] There is also evidence suggesting that the absence of institutional norms for cohabitation may account for the poorer relationship quality of cohabiting relationships and other differences between marriage and cohabitation.[50] These findings indicate the importance of including cohabitation in research on the marriage process and that ignoring cohabitation misrepresents that process in its contemporary form.

Cohabitation in the Christian Tradition

All theology, perhaps especially the theology of the secular reality of marriage which may or may not become also religious sacrament, must be attentive to social change, especially dramatic social change, and to the wealth of information provided by the social sciences because, as the Christian tradition demonstrates, human experience, which included social change, informs and influences Christian theology.[51] Since theology is and must be rooted in reality, the relationship between the social reality of cohabitation and the theology of marriage must be carefully explored in light of and informed by all available and appropriate sources of wisdom.

Contemporary Christians, especially fundamentalist Christians, both Protestant and Catholic, easily assume that the nuclear family of early-twentieth-century America, the so called "traditional family," is both biblical and natural. It is always a surprise to them to discover that it is neither.[52] There is a similar problem with the contemporary phenomenon of cohabitation. Again, it is easily assumed that it is a new phenomenon; and, again, it is not.

Two imperial Roman definitions have dominated the Western discussion of marriage. The first is found in Justinian's *Digesta* (23.2.1) and is attributed to the third-century jurist Modestinus: "Marriage is a union of a man and a woman, and a communion of the whole of life, a participation in divine and human law." The second is found in Justinian's *Instituta* (1.9.1), and is attributed to Modestinus' contemporary, Ulpianus: "Marriage is a union of a man and a woman, embracing an undivided communion of life." These two "definitions," which are no more than descriptions of marriage as culturally practiced in imperial Rome, controlled every subsequent discussion of marriage in the Western tradition. They agree on the bedrock: marriage is a union and a communion between a man and a woman embracing the whole of life.[53]

Marriage, therefore, in both the Christian theological and the Western legal traditions, is the union of a man and a woman. But how is marriage effected in the eyes of these two traditions which, up to the Reformation, were identical? Already in the sixth century, Justinian's *Digesta* (35.1.15) decreed the Roman tradition: the only thing required for a valid marriage was the mutual consent of both parties. The northern European custom was different: there penetrative sexual intercourse after consent made a valid marriage. This different approach to what made marriage valid provoked a widespread legal debate in Europe.

Both the Roman and the northern opinion had long histories, sound rationale, and brilliant proponents in twelfth-century Europe. The debate was ended in mid-century by Gratian, master of the ancient Catholic University of Bologna, who proposed a compromise solution. Consent *initiates* a marriage or makes it *ratum;* subsequent sexual intercourse completes it or makes it *consummatum.* This settlement continues to be enshrined in the Code of Canon Law: "A valid marriage between baptized persons is said to be merely ratified *[ratum]* if it is not consummated; ratified and consummated *[ratum et consummatum]* if the spouses have in a human manner engaged together in a conjugal act in itself apt for the generation of offspring" (Can 1061).

To be noted and underscored here is the *process* character of valid, indissoluble marriage, *matrimonium ratum et consummatum,* in the Catholic Church, for that process character is central to the argument presented in the next section. The present law requires for valid, indissoluble marriage two distinct acts, the mutual free consent of the couple and their subsequent, penetrative sexual intercourse.[54] How the law was followed in practice is a part of the historical marital tradition of both the Catholic and the Western worlds that has been ignored by those who should know better, and is quite unimaginable by those who assume that the way things are in marrying is the way they always have been.

Gratian's compromise—mutual consent makes a marriage *ratum* and sexual intercourse makes it *ratum et consummatum*—ended the debate between the Romans and the northern Europeans over what effected marriage. Consent could be given in either the future tense *(consensus de futuro)* or the present tense *(consensus de presenti).* When it was given in the future tense, the result was called betrothal, and the process from cause (consent) to effect (betrothal) was known as *sponsalia* or spousals, that is, the couple became spouses. When consent was given in the present tense, the result was called marriage, and the process from cause (consent) to effect (marriage) was known as *nuptialia* or nuptials, that is, the couple became wedded. The first sexual intercourse between the spouses usually followed the betrothal, and this is a fact of both the Western and the Catholic traditions that has been obscured by the now-taken-for-granted sequence of wedding, marriage, sexual intercourse, fertility. It was not, however, until the Council of Trent in the sixteenth century that the Catholic Church prescribed that sequence and decreed that marriage resulted from the nuptials or ceremonial wedding. For over half of Catholic couples in the modern West, the sequence has reverted to the pre-Tridentine sequence: cohabitation, sexual intercourse, fertility, wedding. That sequence is no different from the African sequence described by Ntakarutimana.

The pre-Tridentine sequence has been well documented in sociohistorical sources. Jean Remy describes the situation in France, where sexual relations regularly began with *sponsalia* or betrothal.

> In the sixteenth century, the Churches began to lead a campaign against premarital sex. Previously the engagement or betrothal carried great weight. If the Church frowned on the unblessed marriage she did not forbid it. Very often, above all in the country, the Church marriage took place when the woman was pregnant, sometimes towards the end of her pregnancy.[55]

He also points out that, in a society in which fertility was central to the meaning of marriage, sexual intercourse took place as a test of the required fertility. His statement justifies the pre-Tridentine sequence against the backdrop of its cultural context. It holds equally true for African cultures today.[56]

A host of commentators describe the situation in England and its empire, which for some time included colonies on the eastern seaboard of what became the United States. Lawrence Stone writes:

> Before the tightening up of religious controls over society after the Reformation and the Counter-Reformation in the mid sixteenth century, the formal betrothal ceremony seems to have been at least as important, if not more so, than the wedding. To many, the couple were from that moment "man and wife before God."[57]

The Church recognized this situation, Stone points out, and in the Deanery of Doncaster in 1619 a betrothal was a successful defense in the courts against an accusation of premarital sex. Alan Macfarlane emphasizes that "the engaged lovers before the nuptials were held to be legally husband and wife. It was common for them to begin living together immediately after the betrothal ceremony."[58] "In Anglo-Saxon England," he adds, "the 'wedding' was the occasion when the betrothal or pledging of the couple to each other in words of the present tense took place. This was in effect the legally binding act; it was, combined with consummation, the marriage."[59]

Later, a celebration of the marriage, an occasion for relatives and friends to bring gifts and to feast, was held but, up to the Council of Trent in the Catholic tradition and up to the Hardwicke Act in mid-eighteenth-century England, the central event of the *sponsalia* or betrothal was held separate from the ceremonial event of the *nuptialia* or wedding. After the betrothal, "the couple saw themselves as man and wife, and therefore sexual intercourse was a natural consequence."[60] This meant, of course, as G. R. Quaife points out, that "for the peasant community, there was very little pre-marital sex. Most of the acts seen as such by Church and state were interpreted by the village [the cultural community] as activities within marriage—a marriage begun with the promise and irreversibly confirmed by pregnancy."[61] Parker underscores something central to my argument, namely, that the marital process from betrothal through pregnancy to marriage "was located in a general belief in the ability of public opinion to command obedience to community values."[62] For the peasant community, there was little premarital sex, for acts seen as such by Church and state were seen and enforced by the local community as acts within marriage, made irreversible by pregnancy. In what continued to be the broader northern European tradition, long after Gratian's compromise, pregnancy consummated a marriage.

Neither Church nor state was satisfied with this marital process, but neither had any choice but to recognize the validity of marriages thus effected. Church law, accepted by European states as binding in marital affairs, was clear. Free consent to marry, whether articulated publicly or privately, initiated marriage, and sexual intercourse after consent, with or without subsequent pregnancy, consummated marriage and made it indissoluble. In the eyes of the Church, marriages, however private and secret, which were the result of free consent and subsequent consummation, had to be held as valid marriages and, therefore, when the spouses were baptized, as also valid sacrament. Genuinely secret or clandestine marriages, however, became the scourge of Europe and provoked a change in both canon and civil law.

Clandestine marriages took place for all sorts of reasons: a couple, Romeo and Juliet, for instance, could not marry publicly because their families would not allow it, or class distinction would not allow it, or the fact that one of them was illegitimate would not allow it. Clandestine marriages, because of their very clandestinity or secretiveness, were difficult to verify and frequently ended in clandestine divorce, with charge and countercharge of concubinage, fornication, illegitimacy, and bigamy. That a marriage made valid by mutual free consent, made indissoluble by sexual intercourse, and made sacrament of the union between Christ and his Church would cease to be at someone's unsubstantiated whim was intolerable for the Catholic Church, and in the sixteenth century the Council of Trent moved to preclude forever the possibility of clandestine marriage.

The council's decree *Tametsi* (1563) prescribed the marriage the Church would recognize as valid and sacramental and, when consummated, indissoluble. It would be only that marriage which was publicly celebrated in the presence of a duly appointed priest and two witnesses (DS 1813–6). Only if celebrated in this canonical form, as it came to be called, would a marriage between Catholics be recognized by the Church as valid and sacramental. *Tametsi* transformed the ritual of marriage, namely, the wedding, from a simple contract between families, one not circumscribed by any legal formalities, to a solemn contract, one in which certain legal formalities had to be observed for validity. That canonical change was well within the power of the Church to make; therefore, it is, of course, equally within its power to unmake. In addition to transforming the contractual nature of marriage, *Tametsi* transformed also the *how* and the *when* of marriage. No longer could anyone claim that marriage was effected at betrothal; it could be effected only at a public church ceremony called a wedding. The modern era of marriage had begun. It took another two hundred years, however, for the new marital process to become established in the English-speaking world.

By the middle of the nineteenth century, the marriage custom that had been common practice in England was giving way to competing practices. In the preceding one hundred years, the betrothal, sexual intercourse, fertility, wedding sequence had become a subject of controversy, not around religion or sexuality but around class.

> The ideal of the nuclear family, something that had divided the middle class from the aristocracy in the seventeenth century, now united them in common opposition to their social inferiors. From the mid-eighteenth century onward sexual politics became increasingly bitter as the propertied classes attempted to impose their standards on the rest of society.[63]

Among the upper and aspiring middle classes, betrothal lost its public character and became an internal family affair called *engagement,* a prelude to marriage which was never to be confused with marriage, and which did not confer the rights of marriage, including the right to sexual intercourse. An engaged couple could never be confused with the married couple they would become after their wedding.

This development in the process of marriage, and in the success of the English upper class in imposing its practice on everyone in England, reached its apogee in 1753 when Lord Hardwicke introduced an act to prohibit clandestine marriages. The Hardwicke Act, which became law on May 1, 1754, prescribed that no marriage in England would be valid other than the one performed by an ordained Anglican clergyman, on the premises of the Church of England, after the calling of banns for three successive weeks or the purchase from the local bishop of a license not to call banns. The act exempted the marriages of Jews and Quakers from its provisions, and underscored the seriousness of its intentions by prescribing fourteen years of transportation for any Anglican minister who attempted to conduct any wedding apart from the provisions of the law.

The present process of marriage in the West, specifically the focus on the wedding as the beginning of marriage, has been in effect since only the sixteenth century. The present practice of the English-cum-American civil law has been in effect only since the mid-eighteenth century. In both institutions, the present procedure was enacted, not for some grand theological reason on the one hand or for some grand legal reason on the other. It was enacted to put an end to the scourge of clandestine marriage and the misery it brought to people. Since the process of marriage was otherwise prior to Trent and Hardwicke, it is not unthinkable that it could be otherwise again.

Theological Considerations

Prior to 1564, when the Papal Bull prescribing compliance with the decisions of the Council of Trent became Catholic law, Catholics needed no wedding ceremony to be married. Prior to 1754, the citizens of England and its empire needed no wedding ceremony to be married. That historical reality can never be erased. The process of becoming validly married in the Catholic and Western traditions has not always been as it presently is. That this is so, that Catholic marriage practice was adapted and greatly transformed within historical memory, leads easily to the conclusion that it could adapt and change again. That possible change in Catholic marital practice will be the focus of this section of this chapter. I emphasize from the outset that there is nothing new in the change I will propose; rather, the change is a reversion to something old, something that was part of the Catholic tradition of marriage for centuries before Trent introduced the change that established the present received tradition. A Thomistic principle is in play here: *ab esse ad posse valet illatio* (the conclusion from actual being to possibility is valid). From the actual historical being of the marital sequence betrothal-sexual intercourse-fertility-wedding, the conclusion that it could be so again, albeit in changed circumstances, is logically legitimate. This section will show that it is also theologically legitimate.

The parallel between the pre-modern, pre-Tridentine, pre-Victorian and the modern or post-modern practices is striking. Pre-modern betrothal led to full sexual relations, and pregnancy then led to indissoluble marriage; modern prenuptial cohabitation leads to full sexual relations and then to indissoluble marriage, with or without pregnancy. I underscore here, again, that in this chapter I am focused only on prenuptial cohabitation, cohabitation premised by the intent to marry. Nothing I say refers to non-nuptial cohabitants. "The full sexual experience practiced by betrothed couples [in pre-Tridentine and pre-Victorian times] was . . . *emphatically* premised by the intention to marry."[64] It is only those cohabitants with an emphatic intention to marry who are my concern.

My proposal is straightforward: a return to the processual marital sequence of betrothal (with appropriate ritual to ensure community involvement), sexual intercourse, possible fertility, ceremonial wedding to acknowledge and to mark the consummation of both valid marriage and sacrament. This is not a new proposal. It has been made with different nuances before. The first detailed proposal was made in 1977 by Canadian moral theologian André Guindon; he was followed independently in 1978 by French theologian M. Legrain.[65] Guindon seeks to respond theologically and canonically to the growing prevalence of cohabitation in Canada. He argues that the socioeconomic changes that have taken place over the past two hundred years, the new roles accorded to women, the desire, especially of women, for an adult and satisfying sexuality, the centrality of mutual love in the marital relationship, have transformed the contemporary marital situation. He notes that the human sciences have shown that sexuality is a language to be progressively learned in an ongoing apprenticeship subject to all the laws of human development. Reflecting this social scientific data, he seeks a renewed understanding of consummation, founded not automatically on a first act of sexual intercourse but on the personal, spiritual, and physical union established between the partners. This leads him to propose the consummation of a marriage before its ratification, *matrimonium consummatum et ratum*, rather than the traditional-since-Gratian *matrimonium ratum et consummatum*.

Legrain comes from a different perspective, that of customary African marriage where "even among Christians . . . only those who have followed all the customary tribal requirements, including the performance of the required rituals, are held to be truly married."[66] He, as Guindon, is concerned with the processual character of *matrimonium consummatum et ratum*, particularly with the Roman claim that consummation follows from the first sexual intercourse. That is simply not the case in African custom. Echoing Ntakarutimana, Legrain states what is obvious to all cognizant of the African context: "the marriage of Christians would never be accepted as *ratum et consummatum* until the birth of a child."[67] The birth of a child stamps a union as marital, marks the union in African eyes "with such an intensity that there is truly a real interpersonal union,"[68] the kind of complete conjugal union that truly consummates a marriage.

In Legrain's and African eyes, marriage is not just a wedding, not a moment in time when a couple give publicly witnessed consent, however dear such precision might be to canon lawyers, but a process from betrothal through human, including sexual, intercourse to the consummating birth of a child. Could African customary marital rituals be Christianized? Of course they could, just as imperial Roman and northern European tribal rituals were Christianized to produce the present received tradition. That they have not yet been Christianized is due to the imposition of a Roman canonical form based on the assumption that a compromise twelfth-century European form is *the* unique Christian model for marriage. They could be Christianized by accepting the processual character of African marriages as a human value and adapting, yet once again, legislation, liturgy, and pastoral practice to highlight human, marital, and sacramental value. If what Legrain argues is possible for an African cultural context, and I see no theological reason why it is not, it is also possible for a Western cultural context once again in the full flower of change.

What Guindon and Legrain propose, each in his own way, is an adaptation of Christian, sacramental marriage to diverse cultural realities. They abandon the received Catholic model of becoming married as synonymous with becoming wedded, of marriage taking place at a moment in time, the moment of mutually given public consent, and they seek to replace it with a developmental model, in which marriage takes place in stages.[69] They reject the received, legalistic, reductionist model of Christian marriage[70] as being incapable of responding to the processual nature of interpersonal love, sexuality, and marriage in new, post-modern cultural manifestations. They agree in recognizing a real marriage, *matrimonium ratum,* from the moment of betrothal, and in recognizing a consummated and indissoluble marriage, *matrimonium ratum et consummatum,* when the couple have fully expressed in their marital life the marital values of their culture. Above all, and this is to be underscored for the argument of this section, they agree in condoning sexual intercourse only between couples who have seriously committed themselves to becoming married. For Legrain, those are African Christian couples living out the required customary stages of a marriage; for Guindon, and for me, those are Western Christian couples prenuptially cohabiting with an already-given firm consent to marry.

The most recent and most detailed treatment of the relationship between contemporary cohabitation and marriage is provided by the English theologian Adrian Thatcher, whose concern is "to *preserve the ancient link between betrothal and marriage* while acknowledging that betrothal is not yet marriage and so does not yet preclude the possibility of revoking the multiple intentions which end in marriage."[71] He rehearses the history recounted in this essay, which leads him to the same conclusion I reached earlier: *ab esse ad posse valet illatio.* "Christians who think all pre-ceremonial sex is wrong have wrongly assumed that the ceremonial requirement of a wedding, in fact a requirement of modernity, has always been normative. It has not."[72] History shows that betrothal as entry into marriage, with all the rights of marriage including sexual intimacy, was a pre-modern institution recognized by the Catholic Church and, therefore, also the Western tradition. "Since it is part of the Christian tradition already, conservative orthodoxies can hardly continue to ignore it."[73] The argument that cohabitation presents "'a threat to the institution of marriage and the family' assumes that there are fixed, not changing institutions of marriage and family, and so 'defending' marriage entails defending a peculiar inherited version of it."[74] The version widely received in the Christian marital tradition is, as we saw in Chapter 2, the procreative institution model.

The stumbling block to granting moral legitimacy to any premarital sexual activity in the Catholic tradition, and in all the Christian traditions, is the exclusive connection the traditions see between sexual intercourse and marriage. "The sexual act must always take place exclusively within marriage. Outside of marriage it always constitutes a grave sin and excludes one from sacramental communion." That teaching certainly appears to be a major stumbling block to the claim of this chapter that some pre-ceremonial wedding sexual activity is morally legitimate. There can be no way forward until the traditional and exclusive connection between sexual activity and marriage—which is, in fact, the exclusive connection between sexual activity and procreation—is severed. To get really real about sexuality and sexual activity in the modern world, the exclusive connection between sexual intercourse and procreation has to be abandoned.[75]

At the beginning of this chapter, I suggested that different circumstances and different premises, perhaps learned from a close study of the contemporary social, psychological, and theological situation, would lead to different conclusions. That suggestion is true for sexuality, procreation, and marriage, the connection of which has a long history in the Catholic Church. The earliest Christian theologians learned it from the ancient Stoic philosophers who, basing their explanations of sexuality on their observations of animal behavior, argued that the sexual organs were only for procreation, only to perpetuate the species.[76] This argument, exclusively based on physical structure, organs, and functions, might be a good argument for nonhuman animals whose sexual activity is limited by instinct and fertile periods. Is it a good argument, however, for human animals whose sexuality is not exclusively instinctual, but is under the control of social, psychological, and personal factors, whose fertility is restricted to a few days a month, and whose normal sexual feelings, desires, and activities occur more frequently than, and do not always coincide with, their fertile periods?

Many Catholic and Christian theologians, taught by the insights of the human sciences, believe it is not. They believe that the bodily act of sexual intercourse between humans has a surplus of meaning beyond the physical; they believe it is multivalent in meaning and value. They see it as much more than an animal activity. They see it as a language celebrating personal love, two-in-oneness, and mutuality; a language proclaiming, affirming, and realizing the value of another; a language in which a couple, mutually committed to one another, "make love." They acknowledge that, like any language, the language of sex must be learned with the utmost care, honesty, and ongoing fidelity. It is hardly surprising that with these changed premises, they would come to conclusions quite different from those drawn from a traditional approach.

The Stoic approach to sexual activity and its exclusive connection to marriage canonized marriage in the Western tradition as a *procreative institution,* an institution whose primary end was procreation. Other ends of marriage related to the spouses were acknowledged but they were very much secondary to procreation, and the primary end-secondary end hierarchy dominated the Catholic approach to marriage for centuries. The great Karl Barth once complained that the traditional Christian doctrine of marriage, both Catholic and Protestant, situated marriage in juridical rather than in theological categories.[77] The Roman Catholic Church, as we saw earlier in this book, corrected that imbalance in 1965. The history of marriage in the Catholic tradition has progressed from a model of *procreative institution*, in which procreation is everything, to a model of *interpersonal union*, in which the relationship and love between the spouses is the foundation of the marriage and family. There is no evidence that this theological shift was in any way influenced by the human sciences, but almost forty years later the socio-scientific evidence is overwhelming.

The genuine procreation of children, which intends their education and nurture beyond mere biological generation, which intends human motherhood and fatherhood beyond biological maternity and paternity, depends on the happiness and stability of the relationship between the spouses/parents. Divorce is a result of the breakdown of the relationship between the spouses, and it is now beyond debate that divorce is bad for children.[78] For those parents who do successfully progress beyond maternity and paternity to genuine motherhood and fatherhood, thus successfully nurturing children into functioning adults, in thirty years children are grown up and parents/spouses still have twenty to thirty years to live together. That living together will be successful only if the relationship between the spouses has been a loving and faithful one for the whole of life. If for no other reason than that, it is time for the Church's exclusive preoccupation with procreation and children to yield to present reality; it is time for the Church to preoccupy itself with positive marital relationship.

It is time to return to the claim that the sexual act must always take place exclusively within marriage. It is not a claim that anyone who knows the social-scientific evidence would challenge; inductive experience shows that, for most human beings, all that is expected and desired from a total and mutually self-giving relationship is best delivered in that stable relationship we call marriage.[79] The question arises, however, why is it that the sexual act must always take place exclusively within marriage? I submit that sexual intercourse so radically involves all the potentials of a human person that it is best expressed and safeguarded in a stable and lasting relationship between a man and a woman. That stable and lasting relationship has traditionally been called marriage.

What has happened in the modern age is that those couples whom I have called prenuptial cohabitants are beginning their stable marital, including their sexual, relationship prior to their wedding ceremony. They are committed to one another, though they have not articulated that commitment in public ritual; they fully intend to marry when the psychological and, especially, the economic restrictions modern society puts upon their right to marry are removed. Their prenuptial cohabitation, perhaps even their betrothed or engaged cohabitation, is the first step available to them toward marriage. In the canonico-legal words of the received tradition, their engagement or betrothal *initiates* their marriage; their subsequent ceremonial wedding, before or after the birth of a child, *consummates* their marriage and makes it indissoluble. Since their betrothal, however expressed (and I would prefer that it be expressed in a public ritual), initiates their marriage, their cohabitation is no more premarital than that of a pre-Tridentine and pre-Hardwicke couple. Their cohabitation and intercourse are certainly pre-ceremonial or pre-wedding, though that could be easily remedied by the introduction of a public betrothal ceremony, but they are far from premarital.

A major change in the approach of Catholic ethicists to sexual sin parallels the change in the approach to marriage. Catholic ethicists have agreed for years that decisions of morality or immorality in sexual ethics should be based on *interpersonal relationship* and not simply on *physical acts* like masturbation, kissing, petting, premarital, marital, and extramarital sexual intercourse, both heterosexual and homosexual.[80] Lisa Cahill argues thus: "A truly humane interpretation of procreation, pleasure and intimacy will set their moral implications in the context of enduring personal relationships, not merely individual sexual acts. If human identity and virtue in general are established diachronically, then this will also be true of sexual flourishing."[81] Serious immorality, what is traditionally called mortal sin, is not decided on the basis of an individual act against "nature," that is, the biological, physical, natural processes common to all animals. It is decided on the basis of human goods and human relationship built upon them. Cahill suggests such human goods as "equality, intimacy, and fulfillment as moral criteria."[82] I would add the virtues of love and justice, to make explicit what she clearly intends. Sexuality has three bodily meanings: intimacy of close bodily contact, even bodily interpenetration; pleasure; and reproduction or procreation. All of these meanings are realized and developed over time and in the social institutions which a given society recognizes. Immoral or less than moral behavior is defined not by any sexual act related to these three, but by any less than loving, just, equal, compassionate, and mutually fulfilling act.

In the case of prenuptial cohabitants, a man and a woman who are deeply committed to one another and already betrothed to marry, and whose pre-ceremonial sexual intercourse takes place in this context of personal commitment, the moral argument proceeds along these lines. A man and a woman have a fundamental freedom to marry. Modern society has established socioeconomic structures for marriage which the couple are presently unable to achieve. These circumstances surrounding the intercourse of this couple who are deeply committed to each other, who are in right relationship to both one another and to God, and who fully intend to marry, "may render their premarital intercourse an ontic evil but not a moral evil." That such intercourse is not a moral evil would appear to be true especially, Keane argues, "when the committed couple whose rights are unreasonably prejudiced by society do not experience themselves as genuinely free to take the more ideal route of abstaining from that intercourse that cannot be publicly proclaimed as part of a marriage."[83]

I accept the probative value of this argument. In the proposal I am presenting, however, the mutually committed prenuptial couple are already, if inchoately, married, and their intercourse, therefore, is not premarital but marital, as it was in the pre-Tridentine Catholic Church and pre-Hardwicke England. My proposal envisages a marital process that is initiated by symmetrical, mutual commitment and consent, is lived in mutual love, justice, equality, intimacy, and fulfillment, in a prenuptial cohabitation pointed to a wedding which consummates the process of becoming married in a mutually just, human, and public manner. In such a process, I believe, sexual intercourse meets the legitimate Catholic and social requirement that the sexual act must take place exclusively within a stable marriage.

Concluding Proposal

It is time now to sum up the argument I have been developing, in the schematic presentation of a proposal. I propose that the process of marrying in the Catholic Church revert to the process that held sway prior to the Council of Trent. That process is this:

(A) *Betrothal of the couple or, in the pre-Tridentine language, sponsalia.* The betrothal, for which a ritual highlighting free consent to wed in the future should be developed, would be witnessed and blessed on behalf of the Church community, preferably, though not necessarily, by a parish priest. The betrothal ritual would differ from the present wedding ceremony only in the fact that the consent would be *consensus de futuro,* a consent to marry in the future. Such betrothal, as it did before, would confer on the couple the status of committed spouses with all the rights that the Church grants to spouses, including the right to sexual intercourse.

(B) *Prenuptial cohabitation of the couple.* In this period, the couple would live together as spouses, would have intercourse, including sexual intercourse, with one another in a community-approved, stable environment, and would continue the life-long process of establishing their marital relationship as one of love, justice, equality, intimacy, and mutual fulfillment. This inchoate marriage period would be a perfect time for the Church community to assist the couple in honing their relationship with an ongoing marriage preparation program aimed precisely at their relationship.[84] The social scientific data indicate that relationship is both the core of long-term spousal and parental success and a reality that can be dangerously flawed by both the self-selecting factors which directed the couple to cohabitation in the first place and the experience of cohabitation itself.

(C) *Fertility.* I am fully conscious that this is the part of my proposal which can be expected to cause the most unease among Christians of all denominations. Sexuality and sexual activity have been treated with suspicion in the Catholic Church since the days of the early, Stoic-influenced Christians. That suspicion led to the exclusive focus on procreation which once characterized the Church, and continues to characterize it even now when moral approaches among many of its leading thinkers have changed. I have argued, in the company of other Catholic scholars, that this focus on procreation needs to yield to another focus, namely, the focus on the interpersonal relationship which is at the very root of all spousal and parental success in marriage and family. I stand by what I argued earlier: the moral implications of sexual intercourse, sexual pleasure, and procreation leading to parenthood are best set in the context of interpersonal relationship and not in the context of mere sexual acts. The context of the prenuptial cohabitants with whom I am concerned in this chapter is a context of committed, stable, and intentionally life-long relationship. It is a context which meets the Catholic requirement that sexual intercourse be exclusively within marriage. It is also a context in which the three dimensions of sexual activity I have mentioned—personal and not just bodily intercourse, mutual pleasure, and procreation leading not only to children but also parenthood—might intersect to the benefit of the relationship. Parenthood, particularly co-parenthood, expresses and realizes the union of the spouses as much as intercourse and pleasure. In my proposal, it can be the task of prenuptial cohabitants as much as of married couples in the received tradition.

(D) *Wedding.* There will come a time when the committed prenuptial cohabitants have overcome the socioeconomic restrictions imposed on them by society. There will come a time when their relationship has reached such a plateau of interpersonal communion that they will wish to ceremonialize their loving, just, and symmetrical relationship. That time is the time for their wedding when, with their families, friends, and Christian community, they will renew their consent *de praesenti* and celebrate their union for what it has inchoately become, namely, a symbol or sacrament of the loving union between God and God's people, between Christ and Christ's Church. Their wedding can then be considered the consummation of their marriage, the consummation of a relationship which they have sought to make as humane and as Christian as possible. The process of marrying would then be complete, *matrimonium ratum* would become *matrimonium ratum et consummatum*.

Questions for Reflection

1. How do you understand the claim that marriage is a process? Does that idea resonate in any way with your personal experience?

2. What do you understand by the term *cohabitation*? What do you understand by the terms *prenuptial* and *non-nuptial cohabitants*? Do you see any real difference between the two?

3. How did the Council of Trent change the process of becoming married in the Catholic Church? Do you think it would be a good idea to reintroduce the ritual of betrothal into the marriage process?

4. Do you believe that sexual intercourse has a surplus of meaning beyond its physical meaning? How do you explain this to yourself? Do you believe that sexual intercourse before marriage is always sinful and, therefore, to be avoided?

5. List the positives and the negatives you personally see in the proposal to organize the ritual process of marriage from betrothal, through cohabitation to sexual intercourse to wedding. Evaluate the practicality of this proposal in the present Catholic context.

Notes

¹ This essay is a revised version of one that appeared in *INTAMS Review* 7 (2001) 37–55. It is reprinted here with permission.

² Emmanuel Ntakarutimana, "Being a Child in Central Africa Today," *Concilium* (1996) 15.

³ *Catechism of the Catholic Church* (Mahwah, N.J.: Paulist Press, 1994) 2390.

⁴ Karl Rahner, "Current Problems in Christology," *Theological Investigations,* vol. 1 (London: Darton, Longman and Todd, 1965) 150.

⁵ *Catechism of the Catholic Church,* 2423, my emphasis.

⁶ Paul VI, *Octogesima Adveniens* 4, AAS 63 (1971) 403ff.

⁷ Congregation for the Doctrine of the Faith, *Instruction on Christian Freedom and Liberation* 72, AAS 79 (1987) 586.

⁸ John Paul II, *Sollicitudo Rei Socialis* 41, AAS 80 (1988) 571.

⁹ Ibid., 1.

¹⁰ Ibid., 41.

¹¹ This notion of individual responsibility is analyzed by Jean-Yves Calvez in "Morale sociale et morale sexuelle," *Etudes* 378 (1993) 642–4.

¹² *Sollicitudo Rei Socialis* 3.

¹³ Calvez, "Morale sociale et morale sexuelle," 648.

¹⁴ Pierre-Olivier Bressoud, *Eglise et couple à petits pas: Vers une réévaluation théologique des formes de cohabitation contemporaines* (Fribourg: Editions Universitaires Fribourg Suisse, 1998) 134.

¹⁵ For the notion of Church as communion, see Michael G. Lawler and Thomas J. Shanahan, *Church: A Spirited Communion* (Collegeville: The Liturgical Press, 1995); Jean-Marie R. Tillard, *Church of Churches: The Ecclesiology of Communion* (Collegeville: The Liturgical Press, 1992).

¹⁶ International Theological Commission, *Theses on the Relationship Between the Ecclesiastical Magisterium and Theology* (Washington, D.C.: USCC, 1977) 6, my emphasis.

¹⁷ Louis Roussel, "La cohabitation sans mariage: Des faits aux interpretations," *Dialogue* 92 (1986). See also Louis Roussel, *La famille incertaine* (Paris: Odile Jacob, 1989); and Jean-Claude Kaufmann, *Sociologie du Couple* (Paris: Presses Universitaires de France, 1993), my emphasis.

¹⁸ Larry L. Bumpass, "What's Happening to the Family? Interactions Between Demographic and Institutional Change," *Demography* 27 (1990) 486; Larry L. Bumpass, *The Declining Significance of Marriage: Changing Family Life in the United States* (Madison, Wisc.: Center for Demography and Ecology, 1995) 8; Larry L. Bumpass and Hsien-Hen Lu, *Trends in Cohabitation and Implications for Children's Family Contexts* (Madison, Wisc.: Center for Demography and Ecology, 1998) 7; Larry L. Bumpass and James A. Sweet, "National Estimates of Cohabitation," *Demography* 26 (1989) 619; Larry L. Bumpass, James A. Sweet, and Andrew Cherlin, "The Role of Cohabitation in

Declining Rates of Marriage," *Journal of Marriage and the Family* 53 (1991) 914; Center for Marriage and Family, *Time, Sex, and Money: The First Five Years of Marriage* (Omaha: Creighton University, 2000); David Popenoe and Barbara Dafoe Whitehead, *Should We Live Together? What Young Adults Need to Know about Cohabitation before Marriage* (New Brunswick, N.J.: National Marriage Project, 1999) 6; Linda J. Waite, ed., *The Ties that Bind* (New York: De Gruyter, 2000).

[19] John Haskey, "Patterns of Marriage, Divorce, and Cohabitation in the Different Countries of Europe," *Population Trends* 69 (1992) 27–36; F. Hopflinger, "The Future of Household and Family Structures in Europe," Seminar on present demographic trends and lifestyles in Europe, Council of Europe, Strasbourg, 1991; L. Roussel, *La famille incertaine* (Paris: Editions Odile Jacob, 1989); H. J. Hoffmann-Howotny, "The Future of the Family," *European Population Conference 1987* (IUSSP, 1987) Central Statistical Office of Finland, Helsinki.

[20] John Haskey, "Pre-marital Cohabitation and the Probability of Subsequent Divorce: Analyses Using the New Data from the General Household Survey," *Population Trends* 68 (1992) 10–19.

[21] Oystein Kravdal, "Does Marriage Require a Stronger Economic Underpinning than Informal Cohabitation?" *Population Studies* 53 (1999) 63–80.

[22] Neil G. Bennett, Ann Klimas Blanc, and David E. Bloom, "Commitment and the Modern Union: Assessing the Link Between Premarital Cohabitation and Subsequent Marital Stability," *American Sociological Review* 53 (1988) 127–38; Ann-Zofie E. Duvander, "The Transition from Cohabitation to Marriage: A Longitudinal Study of the Propensity to Marry in Sweden in the Early 1990s," *Journal of Family Issues* 20 (1999) 698–717.

[23] Aart C. Liefbroer, "The Choice Between a Married or Unmarried First Union by Young Adults," *European Journal of Population* 7 (1991) 273–98; Aart C. Liefbroer and Jenny de Jong Gierveld, "The Impact of Rational Considerations and Perceived Opinions on Young Adults' Union Formation Intentions," *Journal of Family Issues* 14 (1993) 213–35.

[24] Henri Leridon, "Cohabitation, Marriage, Separation: An Analysis of Life Histories of French Cohorts from 1968 to 1985," *Population Studies* 44 (1990) 127–44.

[25] R. Lesthaeghe, G. Moors, and L. Halman, "Living Arrangements and Values among Young Adults in the Netherlands, Belgium, France and Germany, 1990," Paper presented at the annual meetings of the Population Association of America, Cincinnati, April 1–3, 1993.

[26] Charles Hobart and Frank Grigel, "Cohabitation Among Canadian Students at the End of the Eighties," *Journal of Comparative Family Studies* 23 (1992) 311–37; T. R. Balakrishnan, K. V. Rao, Evelyne Lapierre-Adamcyk, and Karol J. Krotki, "A Hazard Model Analysis of the Covariates of Marriage Dissolution in Canada," *Demography* 24 (1987) 395–406.

[27] Michael Bracher, Gigi Santow, S. Philip Morgan, and James Trussell, "Marriage Dissolution in Australia: Models and Explanations," *Population Studies* 47 (1993) 403–25.

[28] Haskey, "Patterns of Marriage, Divorce, and Cohabitation," 30.

[29] Bumpass, *The Declining Significance of Marriage;* Larry L. Bumpass, R. Kelly Raley, and James A. Sweet, "The Changing Character of Stepfamilies: Implications of Cohabitation and Nonmarital Childbearing," *Demography* 32 (1995) 425–36; Bumpass and Sweet, "National Estimates of Cohabitation," 615–30; Bumpass, Sweet, and Cherlin, "The Role of Cohabitation," 913–27; Arland Thornton, "Cohabitation and Marriage in the 1980s," *Demography* 25 (1988) 497–508.

[30] See, for example: Jennifer S. Barber and William G. Axinn, "Gender Role Attitudes and Marriage Among Young Women," *The Sociological Quarterly* 29 (1998) 11–31; Ann Berrington and Ian Diamond, "Marital Dissolution Among the 1958 British Birth Cohort: The Role of Cohabitation," *Population Studies* 53 (1999) 19–38; Lenora E. Black and Douglas H. Sprenkle, "Gender Differences in College Students' Attitudes Toward Divorce and Their Willingness to Marry," *Journal of Divorce and Remarriage* 14 (1991) 47–60; Alan Booth and David Johnson, "Premarital Cohabitation and Marital Success," *Journal of Family Issues* 9 (1988) 255–72; Bracher et al., "Marriage Dissolution in Australia," 403–25; Julie Brines and Kara Joyner, "The Ties That Bind: Principles of Cohesion in Cohabitation and Marriage," *American Sociological Review* 64 (1999) 333–55; Bumpass, Sweet, and Cherlin, "The Role of Cohabitation," 913–27; Larry L. Bumpass, James A. Sweet, and Teresa Castro Martin, "Changing Patterns of Remarriage," *Journal of Marriage and the Family* 52 (1990) 747–56; Larry L. Bumpass and James A. Sweet, "Children's Experience in Single-Parent Families: Implications of Cohabitation and Marital Transitions," *Family Planning Perspectives* 21 (1989) 256–60; Center for Marriage and Family, *Ministry to Interchurch Marriages: A National Study* (Omaha: Creighton University, 1999); Albert Chevan, "As Cheaply as One: Cohabitation in the Older Population," *Journal of Marriage and the Family* 58 (1996) 656–67; Marin Clarkberg, "The Price of Parenting: The Role of Economic Well-Being in Young Adults' First Union Experience," *Social Forces* 77 (1999) 945–68; Marin Clarkberg, Ross M. Stolzenberg, and Linda J. Waite, "Attitudes, Values, and Entrance into Cohabitation Versus Marital Unions," *Social Forces* 74 (1995) 609–34; John D. Cunningham and John K. Antill, "Cohabitation and Marriage: Retrospective and Predictive Comparisons," *Journal of Social and Personal Relationships* 11 (1994) 77–93; David R. Hall and John Z. Zhao, "Cohabitation and Divorce in Canada: Testing the Selectivity Hypothesis," *Journal of Marriage and the Family* 57 (1995) 421–7; Rebecca Gronvold Hatch, *Aging and Cohabitation* (New York: Garland Publishing, Inc., 1995); Kathleen Kiernan and Andrew J. Cherlin, "Parental Divorce and Partnership Dissolution in Adulthood: Evidence from a British Cohort Study," *Population Studies* 53 (1999) 39–48; Bijaya Krishnan, "Premarital Cohabitation and Marital Disruption," *Journal of Divorce*

and Remarriage 28 (1998) 157–70; Lee A. Lillard, Michael J. Brien, and Linda Waite, "Premarital Cohabitation and Subsequent Marital Dissolution: A Matter of Self-Selection?" *Demography* 32 (1995) 437–57; Diane N. Lye and Ingrid Waldron, "Attitudes Toward Cohabitation, Family, and Gender Roles: Relationships to Values and Political Ideology," *Sociological Perspectives* 40 (1997) 199–225; Stephen Parker, *Informal Marriage, Cohabitation, and the Law, 1750–1989* (New York: St. Martin's Press, 1990); Zhenchao Qian, "Changes in Assortative Mating: The Impact of Age and Education, 1970–1990," *Demography* 35 (1998) 279–92; Rand W. Ressler and Melissa S. Waters, "The Economics of Cohabitation," *Kyklos* 48 (1995) 577–92; Laura Sanchez, Wendy D. Manning, and Pamela J. Smock, "Sex-Specialized or Collaborative Mate Selection? Union Transitions Among Cohabitors," *Social Science Research* 27 (1998) 280–304; Pamela J. Smock and Wendy D. Manning, "Cohabiting Partner's Economic Circumstances and Marriage," *Demography* 34 (1997) 331–41; Elizabeth Thomson and Ugo Colella, *Cohabitation and Marital Stability: Quality or Commitment* (Madison, Wisc.: Center for Demography and Ecology, 1991); Arland Thornton, William G. Axinn, and Daniel H. Hill, "Reciprocal Effects of Religiosity, Cohabitation, and Marriage," *American Journal of Sociology* 98 (1992) 628–51; Arland Thornton, William G. Axinn, and Jay D. Teachman, "The Influence of School Enrollment and Accumulation on Cohabitation and Marriage in Early Adulthood," *American Sociological Review* 60 (1995) 762–74; Zheng Wu and T. R. Balakrishnan, "Dissolution of Premarital Cohabitation in Canada," *Demography* 32 (1995) 521–32.

[31] Ingrid Moeller and Basil J. Sherlock, "Making It Legal: A Comparison of Previously Cohabiting and Engaged Newlyweds," *Journal of Sociology and Social Welfare* 8 (1981) 97–110.

[32] Bumpass, Sweet, and Cherlin, "The Role of Cohabitation in Declining Rates of Marriage," 922.

[33] Bumpass, "What's Happening to the Family?" 487; James A. Sweet and Larry L. Bumpass, "Young Adults' Views of Marriage, Cohabitation, and Family," *The Changing American Family*, ed. Scott J. South and Stewart E. Tolnay (Boulder: Westview Press, 1992) 145.

[34] Susan L. Brown and Alan Booth, "Cohabitation Versus Marriage: A Comparison of Relationship Quality," *Journal of Marriage and the Family* 58 (1996) 671, 674; Bumpass, "What's Happening to the Family?" 488.

[35] Bumpass and Sweet, "National Estimates of Cohabitation," 615; Center for Marriage and Family, *Time, Sex, and Money*; Robert Schoen, "First Unions and the Stability of First Marriages," *Journal of Marriage and the Family* 54 (1992) 282; Sweet and Bumpass, "Young Adults' Views of Marriage, Cohabitation, and Family," 143; Robert J. Willis and Robert T. Michael, "Innovation in Family Formation: Evidence on Cohabitation in the United States," *The Family, the Market, and the State in Ageing Societies*, ed. J. Ermisch and N. Ogawa (London: Oxford, 1994) 119–45; Michael Murphy, "The Evolution of Cohabitation in Britain, 1960–95," *Population Studies* 54 (2000) 43–56.

[36] Linda J. Waite, "Cohabitation: A Communitarian Perspective," *Marriage in America: A Communitarian Perspective,* ed. Martin King Whyte (Lanham, Md.: Rowman and Littlefield, 2000) 18; see also Brown and Booth, "Cohabitation Versus Marriage," 674; Vivienne Elizabeth, "Cohabitation, Marriage, and the Unruly Consequences of Difference," *Gender and Society* 14 (2000) 87–110.

[37] See, for example: Brian C. Martinson and Lawrence L. Wu, *Remarriage and Nonmarital Cohabitation Among White Women in the United States: Competing Risks and Multiple Dimensions of Time* (Madison, Wisc.: Center for Demography and Ecology, 1998); Arne Mastekaasa, "The Subjective Well-Being of the Previously Married: The Importance of Unmarried Cohabitation and Time Since Widowhood or Divorce," *Social Forces* 73 (1993) 665–92; Howard Wineberg and James McCarthy, "Living Arrangements After Divorce: Cohabitation versus Remarriage," *Journal of Divorce and Remarriage* 29 (1998) 131–46; Hans-Peter Blossfeld, Erik Klijzing, Katharina Pohl, and Gotz Rohwer, "Why Do Cohabiting Couples Marry? An Example of a Causal Event History Approach to Interdependent Systems," *Quality and Quantity* 33 (1999) 229–42; Michael J. Brien, Lee A. Lillard, and Linda J. Waite, "Interrelated Family Building Behaviors: Cohabitation, Marriage, and Non-Marital Conception," *Demography* 36 (1999) 535–51.

[38] See Bumpass, *The Declining Significance of Marriage,* 8–9, 18–19; Clarkberg et al., "Attitudes, Values, and Entrance into Cohabitation," 618–24; Lillard et al., "Premarital Cohabitation and Subsequent Marital Dissolution," 449–55; Monique Nicole and Cynthia Baldwin, "Cohabitation as a Developmental Stage: Implications for Mental Health Counseling," *Journal of Mental Health Counseling* 17 (1995) 386–96; Ronald R. Rindfuss and Audrey Vanden Heuvel, "Cohabitation: A Precursor to Marriage or an Alternate to Being Single?" *Population and Development Review* 16 (1990) 703–26; Sotirios Sarantakos, "Cohabitation Revisited: Paths of Change Among Cohabiting and Non-cohabiting Couples," *Australian Journal of Marriage and Family* 12 (1991) 144–55; Robert Schoen and Dawn Owens, "A Further Look at First Unions and First Marriages," *The Changing American Family,* ed. Scott J. South and Stewart E. Tolnay (Boulder: Westview Press, 1992) 109–17; Thornton, Axinn, and Hill, "Reciprocal Effects of Religiosity, Cohabitation, and Marriage," 647–9; G. E. Wiersma, *Cohabitation, an Alternative to Marriage? A Cross-National Study* (The Hague: Martinus Nijhoff Publishers, 1983).

[39] Larry L. Bumpass and James A. Sweet, *Cohabitation, Marriage, and Union Stability* (Madison, Wisc.: Center for Demography and Ecology, 1995) 1; Larry L. Bumpass and R. Kelly Raley, "Trends in the Duration of Single-Parent Families," Presented at the 1993 annual meetings of the Population Association of America, Cincinnati; Bumpass, "What's Happening to the Family?" 487; James A. Sweet and Larry L. Bumpass, "Differentials in Marital Instability of the Black Population: 1970," *Phylon* 35 (1974) 323–31.

[40] Bumpass, "What's Happening to the Family?" 488–9; Bumpass, "The Declining Significance of Marriage," 10–15; Bumpass and Lu, *Trends in Cohabita-*

tion and Implications for Children's Family Contexts, 8; Bumpass, Raley, and Sweet, "The Changing Character of Stepfamilies: Implications of Cohabitation and Nonmarital Childbearing," *Demography* 32 (1995) 425–36; Larry L. Bumpass and James A. Sweet, "Children's Experience in Single-Parent Families: Implications of Cohabitation and Marital Transitions," *Family Planning Perspectives* 21 (1989) 258; Bumpass, Sweet, and Cherlin, "The Role of Cohabitation in Declining Rates of Marriage," 919; Deborah Roempke Graefe and Daniel T. Lichter, "Life Course Transitions of American Children: Parental Cohabitation, Marriage, and Single Motherhood," *Demography* 36 (1999) 205–17; Wendy D. Manning, "Marriage and Cohabitation Following Premarital Conception," *Journal of Marriage and the Family* 55 (1993) 839–50; Wendy D. Manning and Daniel T. Lichter, "Parental Cohabitation and Children's Economic Well-Being," *Journal of Marriage and the Family* 58 (1996) 998–1010.

[41] Susan L. Brown, "Cohabitation as Marriage Prelude Versus Marriage Alternative: The Significance for Psychological Well-Being," presented at the annual meeting of the American Sociological Association, 1998; Brown and Booth, "Cohabitation Versus Marriage," 668–78; Wendy D. Manning, "Cohabitation, Marriage, and Entry into Motherhood," *Journal of Marriage and the Family* 57 (1995) 191–200; Wendy D. Manning and Nancy S. Landale, "Racial and Ethnic Differences in the Role of Cohabitation in Premarital Childbearing," *Journal of Marriage and the Family* 58 (1996) 63–77.

[42] Nancy S. Landale, "Migration and the Latino Family: The Union Formation Behavior of Puerto Rican Women," *Demography* 31 (1994) 133–57; N. Landale and K. Fennelly, "Informal Unions Among Mainland Puerto Ricans: Cohabitation or an Alternative to Legal Marriage?" *Journal of Marriage and the Family* 54 (1992) 269–80; N. Landale and R. Forste, "Patterns of Entry into Marriage and Cohabitation Among Puerto Rican Women," *Demography* 28 (1991) 587–608; Manning, "Marriage and Cohabitation Following Premarital Conception," 839–50; Manning, "Cohabitation, Marriage, and Entry into Motherhood," 191–200; Manning and Landale, "Racial and Ethnic Differences in the Role of Cohabitation in Premarital Childbearing," 63–77; Wendy D. Manning and Pamela J. Smock, "Why Marry? Race and the Transition to Marriage among Cohabitors," *Demography* 32 (1995) 509–20; R. S. Oropesa, "Normative Beliefs About Marriage and Cohabitation: A Comparison of Non-Latino Whites, Mexican Americans, and Puerto Ricans," *Journal of Marriage and the Family* 58 (1996) 49–62.

[43] Manning and Smock, "Why Marry?" 512–3; Manning and Landale, "Racial and Ethnic Differences," 70.

[44] Brown, "Cohabitation as Marriage Prelude," 2; Brown and Booth, "Cohabitation Versus Marriage," 677; Oropesa, "Normative Beliefs," 54–60.

[45] Susan De Vos, "Comment of Coding Marital Status in Latin America," *Journal of Comparative Family Studies* 30 (1999) 79–93.

[46] Liefbroer and de Jong Gierveld, "The Impact of Rational Considerations," 213–35.

[47] Susan McRae, "Cohabitation: A Trial Run for Marriage?" *Sexual and Marital Therapy* 12 (1997) 259–73; Schoen, "First Unions and the Stability of First Marriages," 281–4.

[48] Schoen, "First Unions and the Stability of First Marriages," 283.

[49] Jay D. Teachman and Karen A. Polanko, "Cohabitation and Marital Stability in the United States," *Social Forces* 69 (1990) 207–20.

[50] Steven L. Nock, "A Comparison of Marriages and Cohabiting Relationships," *Journal of Family Issues* 16 (1995) 53–76.

[51] See GS 44, 58, 59, and esp. 62. John Paul II frequently teaches that the cultural situation is a major source for theological reflection. He explains that "since God's plan for marriage and family touches men and women in the concreteness of their daily existence in specific social and cultural situations, the Church ought to apply herself to understanding the situations within which marriage and family are lived today, in order to fulfill her task of serving" (FC 4). Elsewhere he states baldly that "a faith which does not become culture is a faith not fully accepted, not entirely thought out, not faithfully lived" (*L'Osservatore Romano* [March 8, 1982]).

[52] This is analyzed in detail in Chapter 9.

[53] It is of note that in 1996, under the pressure of the movement to legalize same-sex marriages, the United States Congress passed the Defense of Marriage Act, which repeated the assertions of these Roman definitions that marriage was a union between a *man* and a *woman.*

[54] The addition to the 1983 Code of Canon Law that the consummation of a marriage is achieved only by sexual intercourse *humano modo* (Can 1061), and the lack of definition for intercourse *humano modo,* has made it impossible to say clearly when a marriage is consummated in the law of the Catholic Church. That inability introduces major problems to the entire Catholic theology of marriage, but those problems do not touch the subject under analysis in this essay. For further details, see Chapter 4.

[55] Jean Remy, "The Family: Contemporary Models and Historical Perspective," *The Family in Crisis or Transition,* ed. Andrew Greeley (New York: Seabury Press, 1979) 9.

[56] See Ntakarutimana, "Being a Child in Central Africa Today," 15; M. Legrain, *Mariage chrétien, modèle unique. Questions venues d'Afrique* (Paris: Chalet, 1978).

[57] Lawrence Stone, *The Family, Sex, and Marriage in England: 1500–1800* (London: Weidenfeld and Nicolson, 1979) 626.

[58] Alan Macfarlane, *Marriage and Love in England: Modes of Reproduction 1300–1840* (Oxford: Blackwell, 1987) 291.

[59] Ibid., 309.

[60] G. R. Quaife, *Wanton Wives and Wayward Wenches: Peasants and Illicit Sex in Early Seventeenth-Century England* (London: Croom Helm, 1979) 59.

[61] Ibid., 61.

[62] Stephen Parker, *Informal Marriage, Cohabitation, and the Law, 1750–1989* (New York: St. Martin's Press, 1990) 19.

[63] John R. Gillis, *For Better, for Worse: British Marriages 1600 to the Present* (Oxford: Oxford University Press, 1985) 135.

[64] Adrian Thatcher, *Marriage after Modernity: Christian Marriage in Postmodern Times* (Sheffield: Academic Press, 1999) 119, emphasis in original.

[65] André Guindon, "Case for a 'Consummated' Sexual Bond Before a 'Ratified' Marriage," *Eglise et Théologie* 8 (1977) 137–82; Legrain, *Mariage chrétien.*

[66] Legrain, *Mariage chrétien,* 62.

[67] Ibid., 77.

[68] "Vie de famille et mariage des chretiens en Afrique subsaharienne," *Pro Mundi Vita* (1976) 53.

[69] Jean-Claude Kaufmann coined a perfect phrase to describe this stage theory, *"couple à petits pas,"* couple by small steps. See his *Sociologie du couple* (Paris: Presses Universitaires de France, 1993) 44. The phrase was picked up by Pierre-Olivier Bressoud in his *Eglise et couple à petits pas* (Fribourg: Editions Universitaires Fribourg Suisse, 1998).

[70] See Michael G. Lawler, *Marriage and Sacrament: A Theology of Christian Marriage* (Collegeville: The Liturgical Press, 1993) 67.

[71] Thatcher, *Marriage after Modernity,* 128, emphasis in original.

[72] Ibid., 129, emphasis in original.

[73] Ibid., emphasis in original.

[74] Ibid.

[75] See Christine E. Gudorf, *Body, Sex, and Pleasure: Reconstructing Christian Sexual Ethics* (Cleveland: Pilgrim Press, 1994) 29–50.

[76] See, for instance, Clement of Alexandria, *Stromata (Strom.)* 3.23, PG 8.1086 and 1090; Origen, *Homiliae in Genesim (Hom. Gen.)* 3.6, PG 12.180; Augustine, *De Genesi ad litteram (Gen. litt.)* 9.7.12, PL 34.397; *De bono conjugali (Bon. conj.)* 24.32, PL 40.394; *Bon. conj.,* 9.9, PL 40.380.

[77] Karl Barth, *Church Dogmatics,* 3:4 (Edinburgh: Clark, 1961) 186.

[78] See Judith S. Wallerstein and Sandra Blakeslee, *Second Chances: Men, Women, and Children a Decade after Divorce* (New York: Ticknor and Fields, 1989); Judith S. Wallerstein, "Children of Divorce: Preliminary Report of a Ten-Year Follow-Up of Older Children and Adolescents," *Journal of the American Academy of Child Psychiatry* 24 (1985) 545–53; Judith S. Wallerstein, Julia M. Lewis, and Sandra Blakeslee, *The Unexpected Legacy of Divorce: A 25 Year Landmark Study* (New York: Hyperion, 2000); Sara McLanahan and Gary Sandefur, *Growing Up with a Single Parent* (Cambridge, Mass.: Harvard University Press, 1994) 65–8.

[79] See, for instance, Carl Rogers, *Becoming Partners: Marriage and Its Alternatives* (New York: Delacorte Press, 1972); McLanahan and Sandefur, *Growing Up with a Single Parent.*

[80] Gudorf, *Body, Sex, and Pleasure,* 14–18; Charles E. Curran, "Sexuality and Sin: A Current Appraisal," *Readings in Moral Theology,* vol. 8: *Dialogue About*

Catholic Sexual Teaching, ed. Charles E. Curran and Richard A. McCormick (New York: Paulist Press, 1993) 411–4; Vincent Genovesi, *In Pursuit of Love: Catholic Morality and Human Sexuality* (Wilmington, Del.: Glazier, 1987) 154–5; Philip Keane, *Sexual Morality: A Catholic View* (New York: Paulist Press, 1977) 98; Xavier Lacroix, *Le Corps de Chair: Les dimensions éthique, esthétique, et spirituelle de'l'amour* (Paris: Editions du Cerf, 1992) 346–50.

[81] Lisa Sowle Cahill, *Sex, Gender and Christian Ethics* (New York: Cambridge University Press, 1996) 112.

[82] Ibid., 11.

[83] Keane, *Sexual Morality,* 107.

[84] See Center for Marriage and Family, *Marriage Preparation in the Catholic Church: Getting It Right* (Omaha: Creighton University, 1995); Scott M. Stanley, "Making a Case for Premarital Education," *Family Relations* 50 (2001) 272–80.

9

Toward a Theology of Christian Family[1]

This chapter is an effort toward practical, pastoral, theological correlation, an effort to bring together the American cultural tradition and
the Christian theological tradition. I develop its argument in four cumulative theses: (1) there is a crisis of family in the United States today;
(2) what is said of family in both Old and New biblical Testaments is of
no direct help in that crisis; (3) what makes a family Christian is not the
slavish following of some biblical saying about family but the following
of Jesus confessed as the Christ; (4) the Christian family has an important contribution to make in the contemporary crisis of family in the
United States. I shall develop each of these theses in turn.

Family in the United States

A mounting body of social-scientific research profiles the crisis of
American marriages and families. The profile indicates the greatly elevated
divorce rate with negative impact on the former spouses and their children, the increasingly common social phenomena of single motherhood
and father absence, and the resultant feminization and childrenization of
poverty. Research shows that approximately half of all children under the
age of eighteen will spend at least part of their childhood in a single-parent
family, some 90 percent of those families headed by single mothers.[2] It cor-
relates the widespread separation of fathers from their children to other
societal changes: the declining salience of marriage and parenthood, the

dramatic increase in marital disruption and divorce, and the rise in non-marital childbearing.[3] Research also documents the consequences for children of being raised by only one parent and suggests that the erosion of the cultural norm that mothers *and* fathers live with, support, and nurture their children has serious negative implications for the whole of society.[4]

There is compelling evidence that the marked decline in children's well-being and health in the past thirty years is linked to family disruption and living in mother-headed, fatherless families. The most tangible and immediate consequence is the loss of economic resources: the highest rate of poverty in America is among children, especially the children of marital disruption and nonmarital childbearing.[5] The feminization and childrenization of poverty have converged; families with children are more than six times as likely to be poor if they are headed by a mother alone than if they are headed by two parents.[6] That many fathers neglect their financial responsibility to their children is evidenced by the fact that only 58 percent of divorced, separated, or never-married mothers are awarded paternal child support,[7] and that less than a third of the children owed financial support receive the full amount.[8] The inevitable economic distress associated with family disruption and father absence often translates into vulnerability for single mothers and their children, and is inextricably related to other personal and social problems.[9] All of this is compounded by low educational achievement and consequent chronic underemployment or unemployment in the minority populations.[10]

Inadequate father participation and resulting overburdened mother parenting are linked to other short-term and long-term child and family problems. Research shows that children in single-parent households are more prone to develop serious social and behavioral problems than are children who grow up with both parents. Their socio-emotive skills and their academic achievement are lower, their behavioral problems[11] and delinquency rates higher.[12] Males who experience family disruption in childhood are more likely to drop out of school, leave home, start work, enter relationships, and become fathers earlier. Females who experience family disruption in childhood are more likely to have sexual relations in their teens, to bear children outside marriage, to have a child at an early age outside of marriage.[13] It is particularly troubling that the effects of single motherhood and fatherlessness are neither short-lived nor easily remedied. Though the multiple economic, psychological, and social effects on children of family disruption, single parenthood, and father absence may remain submerged until years later, they can extend into continuing problems across time and generations.[14]

Child development experts argue that paternal contributions are essential for positive child development. Readily available, competent, and nurturing fathers contribute positively to the personalities, cognitive development, and sexual role development of their children; father deprivation is developmentally destructive.[15] In the case of father absence, there is a demonstrated link between the developmental deficits of children and the emotional and parental isolation of mothers.[16] Though the so-called new-style father who is sensitively involved in the care of his children still continues to be more myth than reality,[17] the need for both maternal *and* paternal involvement in child rearing is probably greater than ever before because of the increasing complexity of American culture.[18]

Scholars continue to point out that public policies and laws regulating marriage and family reflect radical structural changes in family, including a shift from so-called traditional parental roles to an emphasis on expressive individualism, radical independence, and autonomy. They find public policy, driven by popular interpretations of economic reality rather than genuinely human aspiration or credible research, to be the primary arena for the showdown between expressive individualism and relational commitment and responsibility.[19] Social theorists criticize public policy as detrimental to children, women, and marriage, pointing out that it often exacerbates rather than eradicates serious family economic and relational problems.[20] They call for policies that recognize family as a small-unit system within the larger social system, policies that promote economic cooperation, respond positively to the needs of the less privileged, including children, and provide the means for nurturing marital and familial systems.[21]

As Americans look forward to a new millennium, family scholars are concerned about the long-term negative effects of expressive individualism on both families and the nation. Their analysis of the situation generates a call for the restoration of a marriage culture in which the roles of wife and husband are complementary and mutual[22] and the parenting of children a cooperative partnership.[23] They argue for political and religious strategies that uphold the value of and reinvigorate the institution of marriage and assert that committed, competent, and generative motherhood and fatherhood, not just biological maternity and paternity, is a critical need that Americans continue to ignore at their peril.

Family in the Bible

Christianity is a "textualized religion."[24] It gives prominence to its canonized writings called the Bible, the very word of God, *Verbum*

Dei.[25] Christianity, along with Judaism and Islam, is and always has been a religion of the Book. It is natural and predictable, therefore, that Christians turn to their Bible to find solutions to their family problems.

Jesus, whom Christians confess as the Christ and the revelation of God, always turned to his Bible, Torah. He appealed to Genesis 2:24 to support his prohibition of divorce and remarriage (Mark 10:6-9); he appealed to Deuteronomy 18:15-22 as testimony to himself and his works (John 5:45-47). Not only did he appeal to Torah, however, he also interpreted every problem in a new way: "I say to you . . ." (Matt 5:22, 28, 32, 34, 39, 44). The writer to the Ephesians[26] appealed to Genesis 2:24 as a basis for his claim that husbands should love their wives and followed Jesus' lead in *interpreting* it anew as referring to the mysterious communion between Christ and his Church (5:25-33). The writer to Timothy interpreted the Genesis story of Adam and Eve in support of his teaching that a woman may not be a teacher of or have authority over men (1 Tim 2:11-14). Those theologians honored as Fathers of the Church continued the practice of citing Scripture *and* interpreting it for their new experience,[27] and theologians of all hues continue the practice into the twentieth century.[28] The rise of historical criticism, however, and its widespread application to reading the biblical text, has made finding contemporary meaning in the Bible problematic. We can make no serious conclusion about family or anything else in the Bible without carefully considering its historical and social context.

Contemporary Christians, particularly fundamentalist Christians, both Catholic and Protestant, too easily assume that the so-called "traditional," nuclear family is both natural and biblical. It is neither, as even the most cursory reading of the Bible demonstrates. The "traditional" family is aggressively and defensively a monogamous institution; for the earliest biblical families, polygamy was the most natural, and therefore most religious, institution in the world. There is no biblical text proscribing polygamy, nor is there any text prescribing monogamy.[29] The American version of the "traditional" family, steeped in Enlightenment individualism, makes a clear division between private family and public social worlds; in the biblical family these two worlds substantially coincide. The "traditional" American family is a small nuclear unit, comprising some 2.63 people; the biblical family was a large, extended unit, comprising up to 100 people and more.

The process which constituted the extended biblical family was incomparably different from the process which constitutes the modern family. In the biblical world, marriage was a family affair; *families* married. "In the first-century Mediterranean world and earlier, marriage symboled the fusion of the honor of two extended families and was undertaken with a view to politic-economic concerns."[30] Elder males drew up a marriage contract, and the father surrendered his daughter to the groom who made her his wife by bringing her into his own household. This process resulted in the disembedding of a woman as daughter from the honor of her father and her embedding as wife in the honor of her husband and his family. It created a special bond between husband and wife, not a legal bond as in the United States but a blood bond, akin to the bond the husband shared with everyone in his extended family. The Torah shorthand for this bond was the common, and commonly misunderstood, phrase "one body" (Gen 2:24).

A biblical wife did not look to her husband for affection and companionship in marriage; she looked to him to be a good provider and an honorable citizen. Love between the spouses was not exclusively romantic love rooted in feeling and passion; it was the love required in the Torah injunction cited by Jesus, "You shall love your neighbor as yourself" (Lev 19:18; Mark 12:31; Matt 19:19). Though feeling is sometimes part of neighbor-love, it is not always part of it and it is never all there is to it. Neighbor-love is more radical than feeling, romantic or otherwise. It is, as we shall see, a love rooted in the will and expressed in active "loyalty, service and obedience."[31] The neighbor-love and, therefore, the spousal love the Bible requires is loyalty/fidelity, service, and obedience or availability to another person.

The differences between marriage and family in the Bible and in the present day are clear. In modern Western societies, marriage is not a family affair in the biblical sense described above. It is a private affair between an individual man and an individual woman who marry primarily for romantic, feeling love. They marry with or without the approval of their respective families, creating between them not a quasi-blood relationship but a legal relationship. When they decide to divorce, therefore, they do not presume to dissolve their marriage themselves, as a biblical man did; they petition the appropriate legal authority to do so. In the divorce proceedings neither is concerned about extended family or honor; they are concerned about money, house, automobiles, and children. So different are both marriage and family in biblical times from their contemporary Western counterparts that Christians need to be very careful about drawing conclusions about one from the other. Before drawing any conclusion from biblical family about American family, the different historical and social contexts need to be carefully considered.

What does the Bible actually tell us about family life? John Rogerson correctly points out that "the families we read about in the Old Testament are almost entirely ruling or leading families."[32] That should not come as a surprise. The history of every nation is the history of its leading families and individuals; the history of the ordinary folks, villagers, farmers, accountants, teachers, is not told by historians. Their story is usually left to the discoveries of later archaeologists.

The Torah story of Israel's leading families is not a pretty story. It is, first, a story of taken-for-granted polygamy. Jacob married Laban's two daughters Leah and Rachel—indeed, Laban tricked him into marrying them both (Genesis 29). Gideon had "seventy sons" and "many wives" (Judg 8:30). Jair the Gileadite had "thirty sons who rode thirty asses" (Judg 10:4), Ibzan of Bethlehem had "thirty sons and thirty daughters" (Judg 12:9), and Abdon the Pirathonite had "forty sons and thirty grandsons, who each rode on his own ass" (Judg 12:14). Though the wives of these Judges are not explicitly mentioned, we can safely assume they were, as for Gideon, many. Seven wives who bore David children are named, and it is noted he also had concubines (1 Chr 3:1-9). Solomon, great king that he was, had "seven hundred wives, who were princesses, and three hundred concubines" (1 Kgs 11:3).

The families we read about in the Old Testament are not families to make anyone proud. The story of Adam's family is a story of jealousy and fratricide; Cain murders his brother Abel (Gen 4:1-5). Isaac's family also suffers from jealousy leading to treachery: Jacob fraudulently steals the birthright of Esau, who plans to "kill my brother Jacob" (Gen 27:41). David's eldest son, Amnon, rapes his half-sister, Tamar, and for his crime is murdered on the orders of his brother, Absalom (2 Samuel 13). Job complains bitterly about his family: "He has put my family far from me . . . . My relatives and my close friends have failed me . . . . My breath is repulsive to my wife . . . . Those whom I have loved have turned against me" (Job 19:13-19). In the depth of his abandonment, however, he gives us insight into Mediterranean and biblical vindication. He professes his belief in his *goel*, his advocate and vindicator, even God himself (19:25-26). This *goel* should be of interest to anyone who wishes to make the biblical family normative for the modern family, for it flourishes in the Torah-legitimated practice of blood revenge. The kinsman of a murdered person became his avenger, his *goel*, and he could exact vengeance on the murderer by killing him in turn (Num 35:9-34). It is in such a *goel*-avenger, God, that Job places his faith.

And what of the New Testament? It is long-traditional among Catholic Christians to speak in glowing romantic terms of the Holy Family,

Joseph, Mary, and Jesus, and to speak of them in the family nuances of contemporary Chicago, Dublin, or Rome. They, of course, never lived in Chicago, Dublin, or Rome, and would be completely disoriented by even the briefest time-warp visit to these modern metropolises. The reality is that there is an almost complete lack of gospel evidence about the family life of Jesus, and anything said about it usually sounds very much like what is regularly said about the culturally taken-for-granted contemporary family. Though we have no evidence about the family life of Jesus and his parents, we do have very disconcerting and, therefore, usually ignored evidence about Jesus' attitude toward the family life of his day.

Mark reports that Jesus had been preaching and healing and that his family, concerned about his conduct which impinged on their honor, came "to restrain" him. When told "Your mother and your brothers are outside asking for you," Jesus responded with a question: "Who is my mother? Who are my brothers?" The American answer is clear: his biological mother and brothers, outside, seeking to restrain his activity for the sake of honor, are his mother and brothers. That, however, is not the answer Jesus gives. His answer is more expansive and other-embracing than the biological answer. Looking around at those who were sitting in the circle about him, he said, "Here are my mother and my brothers. Whoever does the will of God is my brother and sister and mother" (Mark 3:31-33).

The extended biological or blood family was the source of honor and status in first-century Mediterranean society. It was also "the primary economic, religious, educational and social network."[33] To sever connection to that family was to lose connection to everything that was social and, in that corporate culture, personal. Yet Jesus and/or Mark suggest a move away from this family to another surrogate family in which kin is created not by blood but by belief in and loyalty to the God preached by Jesus. The true Holy Family, they suggest, is not Jesus' biological family but the surrogate, fictive-kin family composed of believers loyal to God. This is made clearer in a Lukan parallel in which, in response to a woman who proclaims his mother blessed, Jesus teaches "blessed rather are those who hear the word of God and obey it" (11:27-28). The "blessed" language here is honor language. The woman proclaims the traditional honor due to the biological mother of an honorable son; Jesus responds that for him and his followers true honor derives from fidelity to God and God's word.

Earlier in his gospel, Luke highlighted the issue of breaking with one's biological kin group (9:57-62). He taught that the followers of Jesus would live a deviant lifestyle to the extent that they might live away from their family home (vv. 57-58). He recorded that Jesus rejected a family obligation of the highest order, "let the dead to bury their own dead" (v. 60). He refused to soften the radical break, "no one who puts a hand to the plow and looks back is fit for the kingdom of God" (v. 62). "There can be no doubt about the radical quality of the break that following Jesus requires nor about Luke's understanding of its cost."[34] That a fictive-kin family of brothers and sisters in Christ is to transcend the blood-kin family and that the cost of such a move is high is underscored later in the gospel: "Whoever comes to me and does not hate his father and mother, wife and children, brothers and sisters, yes, even life itself, cannot be my disciple" (Luke 14:26).

Jesus does not demand such a socially suicidal sacrifice without offering some reassurance. Peter asks about the reward: "We have left our homes and followed you." The implication is clear. Look what we have done for you; what will you do for us? Jesus replies that they will receive "very much more in this age, and in the age to come eternal life" (18:28-30). There is little good news here for biological family. There is no suggestion that family, as understood either in first-century Palestine or twentieth-century America, is anywhere close to a divine institution. A forlorn mother in Gerd Theissen's fictional-scholarly account of Jesus' life puts the attitude of parents bluntly.

> He corrupts the young people. It all sounds fine: blessed are you who weep for you will laugh. But what does he actually do? He makes parents weep over lost sons. He promises everything will change. But what actually changes? Families are destroyed because children run away from their parents.[35]

If grace is embedded in the family, and it is, as far as Jesus is concerned it is not embedded in a particular family structure. He clearly does not believe that the structure of Jewish family as his generation knew it is either natural, so that it must be that way always and everywhere, or divinely instituted. Were it so he would never have sought to transcend it.

I do not wish to be misunderstood here. When I say that grace is not embedded in a particular family structure, I am not saying there is no grace in family. There is. For Christians, however, grace is embedded not in a particular family structure, whether it be ancient Israelite or contemporary American, but in the following of Jesus. "Follow me," Jesus invites (Mark 1:17), join my fictive-kin family; and, he promises, "blessed . . . are those who hear the word of God and obey it" (Luke 11:28). In the earliest tradition that following of Jesus is called discipleship and the gathering of disciples is called *ekklesia,* the Church of God (1 Cor 1:2; 10:32; 11:22; 15:9; 2 Cor 1:1; Gal 1:13; Tim 3:5, 15). Again, we need to be careful. This Church, this gathering of disciples, this fictive-kin family is not intended to abolish biological family. It is intended, rather, to embrace and sustain it. Many appear to equate being a Christian with merely being born into this family. That perspective is seriously misconstrued. Being Christian means concretely living a Christian life, and living a Christian life means living a life of service of and care for others (Mark 9:35; 10:45; Matt 23:11-12; John 13:1-16). Living that life of service makes a family Christian, *no matter what its structure might be,* whether it be first-century Mediterranean or twenty-first-century American, whether it be nuclear or single-parent.

I am in full agreement with evangelical theologian Rodney Clapp in what he says about the Bible and the American family. Clapp writes that

> the Bible itself is not a list of abstract, timeless formulas. It simply provides no detailed guidance or techniques, for all times and places, on disciplining children or seeking a mate or determining whether a wife should or should not work outside the home. Rather, the Bible is centrally and first of all the *story* of Israel and Jesus.[36]

What Clapp seeks to offer is a reading of the biblical story with relevance to the Christian family of the twenty-first century. That a family will be a *Christian* family is determined not by its social structure but by its being faithful to the biblical story of God as revealed in Christ. I agree completely. I seek to move toward, therefore, not so much a *biblical* theology of family to be slavishly followed, for I do not believe that is possible diachronically, but a *Christian* theology of family rooted in the Bible as interpreted in Christian history. That theology is rooted in the following of Jesus, that is, in the living of a Christian life.[37]

It remains to uncover what it means in practice to be a family of Christ's disciples, whether that family be biological or surrogate, fictive-kin family. Luke has already given us an important clue: "Blessed are those who hear the word of God and keep it" (11:28). To be a Christian family two things are necessary: hearing the word of God and keeping it, and covenant with the God revealed in Jesus and fidelity to that covenant. The explication of those two things will complete this chapter.

Christian Family

Self-understanding in Torah was rooted in the covenant between the God YHWH and the people Israel. To covenant is to consent and to promise, so that both parties, equal or unequal in other respects, are mutually committed to one another solemnly and radically. It is thus that YHWH and Israel commit themselves to one another in covenant. When the former Egyptian slaves reached Sinai, YHWH instructed Moses what to say to the people:

> You have seen what I did to the Egyptians, and how I bore you on eagles' wings and brought you to myself. Now therefore, if you obey my voice and keep my covenant, you shall be my treasured possession out of all the peoples. . . . You shall be for me a priestly kingdom and a holy nation. . . . The people all answered as one: "Everything that the LORD has spoken we will do" (Exod 19:4-8).

This great covenant, codified in Deuteronomy (7:6; 14:2; 26:18), is neither forgotten nor abandoned by the followers of Jesus (see 1 Pet 2:9-10). It is rather transformed to be rooted in Jesus. Every contemporary Christian, no matter what family structure she or he lives in, is invited to commit to that same covenant.

There are no covenants, as there are no contracts, without stipulations, and the Jewish and Christian covenants with YHWH are no different. There are endless stipulations, but they all spring from the same root, the two commandments on which "hang all the law and the prophets" (Matt 22:40). These commandments are clear in Torah. The first embraces relationship with the covenant God: "You shall love the LORD your God with all your heart, and with all your soul, and with all your might" (Deut 6:4). The second embraces relationship with the covenanted people of God, neighbors, brothers, and sisters in God's extended family. "You shall love your neighbor as yourself" (Lev 19:18). When tested by a "lawyer" about the greatest commandment, Jesus, good Jew that he was, had no hesitation in citing these Torah commandments (Mark 12:28-34; Matt 22:34-40; Luke 10:25-28) and making them stipulations also for those who would covenant in his surrogate ecclesial family. His comment in Luke's version tells all: "Do this, and you will live" (10:28).

There is a caveat here. In contemporary American usage, love almost always means romantic love, a strong *feeling* of affection for another person, frequently a passionate feeling for another of the opposite sex. That is not what neighbor-love means, at least not exclusively. Feeling is often part of neighbor-love, but it is not always part of it and it is never all there is to it. If feeling were essential for love, then the love of neighbors, commanded by Jesus, including those neighbors who are enemies

(Matt 22:39; 5:44), would be impossible, for few of us can *feel* love for our neighbors and even fewer can *feel* love for our enemies. Neighbor-love and enemy-love is more radical than feeling; it is love that *wills* and *does* the good of the other.

The poverty of the English language which has only one word for love causes a problem here. We use the same word to say, for instance, "I love my spouse," "I love my friends," and "I love a good red wine," as if there are no differences between these three loves. But there are enormous differences. The Greeks had three distinct words for those three loves: *agape,* the love of another for the other's good; *philia,* the mutual love of friends; *eros,* the love of another for my good or benefit.[38] A consideration of the relationship between these three words and the conceptual realities they express will clarify the covenant love of God and neighbor.

Though all three words refer to legitimate human love, they each intend something very specific. *Philia*-friendship intends the good of another person, and so does *agape* more unconditionally. As explained in an earlier chapter, I believe *philia* to be the foundational love on which both *eros* and *agape* build. What *eros* builds is essentially something physical called, after Freud, desire. Where *eros* dominates a relationship, equality and mutuality are destroyed and replaced by the desire to possess, to dominate, and to use. That is fine when talking about a red wine or a racing-green sports car, but to seek to possess or to use another human being for my exclusive benefit is, in effect, to abuse her or him. An exclusively erotic approach to the love of another person creates the very situations it seeks to avoid, namely, alienation, isolation, loneliness, emptiness, everything but interpersonal communion. *Agape* intends and actually seeks to achieve the good of the beloved, even while recognizing that the beloved's well-being is the only way to our common well-being and, therefore, to my individual well-being. It is *agape,* willed love translated into actions, not feeling love, that the Bible prescribes when it prescribes covenant-love. Love of God and love of neighbor are essentially willing and actively seeking the good of God and neighbor.

Covenant love is willing, active, and giving love, not just feeling and getting love. In Torah that love is characterized as *hesed,* steadfast, faithful love; in the New Testament, it is characterized as *agape,* the unconditional love of another for the other's sake. I offer only a flavor of the Torah characterization of *hesed,* not to proof-text my claims but to show its ubiquitously taken-for-granted character. YHWH is "a God merciful and gracious, slow to anger, and abounding in steadfast love"

(Exod 34:6; cf. Num 14:18). YHWH is "a jealous God . . . showing stead-fast love to the thousandth generation" (Exod 20:5-6; cf. Deut 5:10; 7:9). So taken for granted is YHWH's *hesed* that it is celebrated in almost every Psalm (5:7; 6:4; 13:5; 17:7; 18:50; 21:7; 25:6-7, 10; 26:3; etc.). The God of the covenant is a God of faithful, steadfast, indissoluble love and, as God is faithful, so are God's people, God's family, called to be a faithful people. The covenant perspective is made clear in the Jewish story of Hosea and Gomer (Hosea 1–3) and is continued in the New Testament where God is characterized as *agape*-love (1 John 4:8) and where the love of neighbor is also *agape.* The verb which prescribes both love of God and love of neighbor is *agape-seis* (Matt 22:37-39), and the same reason adduced by Hosea is repeated by John. "If God has so loved *[egapesen]* us, we ought also to love *[agapan]* one another" (1 John 4:7-12). Love of God and neighbor is not to be confused with fickle feeling-love. It is self-giving love sustained by firm will and intention, unshakeable promise, and steadfast covenant.

Christian Family and the Crisis of Family in the United States

Agape, willing and active love, self-giving love, courageous love, for-giving love, persevering and steadfast love. That is the love the Bible commands for Christians and, therefore, for all Christian families. It is worlds apart from the love into which many Americans "fall" and for which they often marry: involuntary, feeling love; self-getting and self-fulfilling love; self-aggrandizement love; happily-ever-after love (and, if not, then split); unforgiving love; vacillating and temporary love. Al-though the Bible may not, as I have argued, have much to tell us about family *structures,* it has a great deal to tell us about interpersonal *processes* that make it possible for two or four or ten people to live together in family, peace, and communion.

Much has been written over the years about the duties and rights of families, of parents and their children, all of it in a legal mode. For Christians, however, those duties and rights are primarily *theological,* and their theological formulation is clear: "Follow me" (Mark 1:17), that is, model your life after mine. The Second Vatican Council specified three times Christ-like life for parents and families. Parents are to be "the first preachers of the faith to their children,"[39] as long as that preaching is understood as Christian action more than pious Christian talk. The whole Christian family is to provide "active hospitality" and to "promote justice,"[40] again a summons to Christian action operationalized as circumstances dictate. The family is to manifest Christ's presence in the world "by the mutual love of the spouses, by their generous fruitfulness, their solidarity and faithfulness, and by the loving way in which all the members of the family work together."[41] That is, again, about Christian action, for love is always manifested in action.

I suggest that all these concretizations can be instructively subsumed under the one label *Christian fruitfulness.* Fruitfulness is not the bedrock of marriage, for it depends on something more foundational, namely, generativity, the capacity to generate and nurture life, in this section specifically Christian life, beyond one's own. I suggest it is beyond debate that the first Christian life generated in a Christian marriage and family, and the one on which all others depend, is the life of the spouses together, their life of marital love in Christ, their mutual communion, what I have previously called and explained as their two-in-one bodiness. The loving communion between the spouses is a prime end of their marriage, the very reason they decided to get married in the first place, so that they could spend the rest of their lives together as best friends. Communion is also a prime end of their sexual intercourse, for in every loving act of intercourse the communion of the spouses is both signified and realized, a fact enshrined in the common phrase which describes their intimate intercourse as *making love.*[42]

Childless marriages are fruitful marriages if and when they are made fruitful by the two-in-one life of the spouses. The Second Vatican Council taught that though "marriage and conjugal love are by their nature ordained toward the begetting and educating of children," that does not make "the other purposes of marriage of less account."[43] The generation and loving nurture of children can undoubtedly bring spouses together and enhance the life of communion between them, but if there is already a two-in-one communion generated between them, mutual love, mutual care, mutual nurture, mutual enhancement of Christian marital life, their marriage is already generative and fruitful, even if childless.

To be underscored here is the social fact that to be generative of not only children but also functioning adults, and therefore fruitful in marriage and family, requires more than the fleeting act of genital intercourse. It requires also, indeed above all, the loving nurture of the life generated in that intercourse. Beyond facile paternity and maternity, which produce a child, generative fruitfulness requires dedicated motherhood and fatherhood which produce a functioning adult. Though caring for, respecting, and shaping the life of a child is more arduous and time-demanding than its procreation, every Christian parent, summoned to neighbor-love, should understand that long-term nurture is the truly generative dimension of parenthood.

Still more is required for generative fruitfulness. Though the attitude of American parents, rationalizing their every action with the claim they did it "for the kids," is understandable in the light of the value Americans place on the nuclear family, there is also something restrictively selfish about it, something ultimately non-generative, non-fruitful, and non-Christian. After all, if parents leave to their children an unimproved world, what ultimately have they left them? The generative fruitfulness sought by the gospel Christ is a fruitfulness of neighbor-love not only within but also outside the nuclear family. A world of neighbor-love is a world in which neighbors live in mutual love, service, and peace with all in their neighborhoods, their schools, their work places, and their play places. It is a world in which neighbors enliven and nurture neighbors with justice, compassion, and forgiveness, making it possible for children to be not only generated but also warmly nurtured in the love that yields Christian life and adulthood. It is in this context that the now-overused African saying attains to its full truth: it takes a village to raise a child fruitfully.

The caveat mentioned earlier recurs here. Neighbor-love is more substantial and radical than feeling-love; it is *willing* and *doing* love. In Torah, as we have seen, it is *hesed,* steadfast love (Exod 20:6; 34:6; Deut 5:10; 7:9; Num 14:18); in the Gospel it is *agape,* the love of another for the other's sake (Mark 12:30-31; Matt 22:37-39; Luke 10:27). Neighbor-love is willing and doing love, and because it is willed steadfastly it "never ends" (1 Cor 13:8). It is not really Christian marriage that is indissoluble; it is Christian love that is indissoluble and that makes any marriage founded on it equally indissoluble. Neighbor-love is love of another for the other's sake; it "does not insist on its own way" (1 Cor 13:5); it is availability and service. It is love that sums up every commandment (Rom 13:9).

The point here has been put beyond debate by John Wesley. Since the love of God is universal and unrestricted, so also is Christian, neighbor-love universal and unrestricted.[44] Christians are to love, not just their spouses, not just their families, not just their neighbors, but all people. Christian spouses, to be truly *Christian* spouses, must enliven and nurture, not only their own marital communion, not only their own family, but also the human society in which they live and which they will leave to their children and their children's children.[45] They must learn to be fruitful in this third way of Christian living, and not only in the two traditional ways of marital mutuality and children.

Even in the most individualistic of societies, a label readily applicable to the United States, marriage is never just a *private* act between two individuals; it is also a *public* act. Societies, civil and religious, have a stake in marriage, which is why they require for its validity a public celebration before approved witnesses. Marriage is an act by which two individuals, a unique I and a unique Thou, come together to form a coupled-We. It is not, however, an act by which the We so focuses on itself that it excludes all others in the community from which the We emerged. Marriage, rather, is the act in which the We is so constituted in the community that the We becomes open to *all*.[46] Marriage binds a couple to one another, but it binds them specifically to one another *in a wider community;* in Christian marriage that wider community includes the Church, the people who confess the Christ and the God he addressed as Father. If and when the We's love becomes further fruitful in the generation of a child, the resultant family is equally bound to the wider community.

In 1807 the *Churchman's Magazine,* America's first Episcopal journal, argued that "families are the nurseries of societies and states."[47] Almost two hundred years later, John Paul II agrees, insisting correctly that the future of societies, both civil and religious, "passes through the family."[48] I add only the specifically Christian injunction that the family's function is to be not only the nursery for citizens of a society but also the apprenticeship in which they learn the following of Christ and from which they graduate to the service of society.[49]

The definition which has controlled every discussion of marriage in the Western world is that of the third-century jurist Modestinus: "Marriage is a union of a man and a woman and a communion of the whole of life."[50] Marriage is a *union* and a *communion,* a term that links it theologically to Church. "Communion is the very mystery of the Church," John Paul II teaches,[51] echoing the judgment of the secretary of the Second Vatican Council's Theological Commission that the council's vision of church as *koinonia*-communion is its most important teaching.[52] That church communion is manifested sacramentally in the pro phetic symbol[53] or sacrament of Eucharist, which both signifies and effects the communion the church is.[54] That communion is twofold. It is, first, communion with God in Christ through the Spirit and, second, communion with the Church, the fictive-kin family of believers, brothers and sisters in Christ. "The cup of blessing that we bless," Paul argued in the beginning, "is it not a sharing in the blood of Christ? The bread that we break, is it not a sharing in the body of Christ? Because there is one bread, we who are many are one body" (1 Cor 10:16-17). Because believers share food and drink together in memory and in the name of Christ, they are made one in communion.[55] This *koinonia*-communion is exemplified in the earliest Church, which devoted itself to the apostles' teaching and *koinonia* (Acts 2:42) and held everything in common *(panta koina)* (Acts 4:32).

In his treatment of the Lord's Supper, of the Eucharist which derives from it, and of the character of both as memorial meals, Xavier Léon-Dufour underscores an element of the supper that has been obscured by the Catholic emphasis on the transformation of bread and wine. That element is Jesus' washing the feet of his disciples, which Léon-Dufour interprets as integral to the memorial meal. This foot-washing is a prophetic symbolic action that both reveals Jesus' will to be remembered as servant and challenges those who keep memory of him to do the same.[56] John's Jesus underlines the challenge in his final testament: "I have set you an example, that you also should do as I have done to you" (13:15). Jesus, who lived a life of culturally-concretized neighbor-love (Lev 19:18; Mark 12:31), challenged his disciples to do the same.

Contemporary Catholic eucharistic theology has demonstrated beyond doubt that the prophetic symbol of Eucharist is not exclusively about the transformation of bread and wine. It is also about the transformation of human lives. Prophetic symbols do two things: they proclaim the presence and action of God, and they challenge believers to moral action consonant with belief in that presence. The prophetic symbol of baptism proclaims the presence of God as the Creator of new life and demands that the new life be lived as the following of Jesus. The prophetic symbol of Eucharist proclaims the presence of God as the source of communion, peace, and salvation and demands that this communion, peace, and salvation be extended to the entire human community through servant action. Jesus' life brought the compassion of God to those who needed it most. In the meal in which they remember him, his followers remember not only his life of footwashing but also his challenge to them to do the same. When their meal is complete, they are dismissed "to love and serve the Lord and one another." My point in this brief excursus is to suggest that, if that is the case in the larger Church, and it theologically is, then it is the case also in the domestic church called family.

The Second Vatican Council reintroduced to the Catholic theological tradition the designation of family as "domestic church."[57] There continues to be an interpretation in some places that this is a new doctrine introduced to the Catholic tradition, but that interpretation is seriously mistaken. There is abundant evidence in the Pauline letters both of house churches (see 1 Cor 16:19; Rom 16:3-4) and of the fact that the following of Jesus was a guiding principle of those house churches. The household code enjoined upon the Colossians states that principle succinctly: "Whatever you do, in word or in deed, do everything in the name of the Lord Jesus" (Col 3:17-25; cf. Eph 6:1-9). That principle becomes the principle of the domestic church, and two great theologians, one in the East, the other in the West, elaborated this tradition. Augustine declared the family in Christ "a little church," required of it "respect for elders, justice and love,"[58] and begged prayers from the "entire domestic church."[59] John Chrysostom urged spouses to "make your home a church"[60] and to live your family lives "in Christ and in the church."[61] These demands, of course, are no more than the demands made of all Christians. I add here the further theological specification that this family following of Jesus is required for full Christian fruitfulness.[62]

If this *theological* argument sounds strange, it is because the argument has been traditionally couched in *socio-moral* terms. The Catholic moral tradition, following Aristotle, insists that the human animal is a social animal, a premise from which it draws two important conclusions. The first is that no one attains full humanity, or full Christianity, alone; everyone needs friendship and communion with others to reach mature humanity. The second is that beyond the private good of individuals extends the common good of the larger community, and both humans and Christians are required by their essentially social nature, John Paul II teaches, to "situate particular interest within the framework of a coherent vision of the common good."[63] The American Catholic Bishops stress the same common good in different language.

> What you do in your family to create a community of love, to help each other grow, to serve those in need is critical, not only for your own sanctification but for the strength of society and our Church. It is a participation in the work of the Lord, a sharing in the mission of the Church. . . . As Christian families, you not only belong to the Church, but your daily life is a true expression of the Church.[64]

Elsewhere John Paul stresses *interdependence* among the hierarchy of values and teaches that, when interdependence is appreciated, "the correlative as a moral and social . . . 'virtue' is *solidarity*." This solidarity "is not a vague feeling of compassion or shallow distress at the misfortunes of so many people [but] . . . *a firm and persevering determination* to commit oneself to the *common good* . . . to the good of all and of each individual, because we are *all* really responsible for *all*."[65] Following a well-marked magisterial path of recent decades, he later underscores this solidarity as a preferential option or "love of preference for the poor"[66] and proposes as a motto for the time *opus solidaritatis pax,* "peace as the fruit of solidarity."[67] It is not without importance to the present discussion that *peace* and *communion* are regularly linked or even used synonymously.[68] Though this social teaching has in mind primarily the larger community beyond families, it clearly applies also to families, especially to those Christian families who would be domestic churches. What I do in this section is extend it to families in theological terms.

The Church, the fictive-kin family of brothers and sisters in Christ, Pope Paul VI taught, "has an authentic secular dimension, inherent in her inner nature and mission, which is deeply rooted in the mystery of the Word incarnate and realized in different forms through her members."[69] The Christian doctrine of the incarnation of God in Jesus constructs a bridge over the gulf between heaven and earth, between the supernatural and the natural, between the sacred and the secular. The Christian Church, founded and rooted in that Jesus whom it confesses as the Word incarnate (John 1:14), enlivened by his Spirit, and charged with the continuation of his mission, seeks to maintain that bridge. It, therefore, must also be incarnate everywhere in human life. That theological doctrine explains why Pope John Paul II teaches that the lay faithful are marked by a "secular character," and why he insists that this secular character is to be understood in a *theological* and not just a sociological sense.

The world, John Paul means, is both the place and the means in and with which lay Christians fulfill their Christian vocation. God, he explains explicitly and theologically, "has handed over the world to women and men so that they may participate in the work of creation, free creation from the influence of sin and sanctify themselves in marriage or the celibate life, in a family, in a profession and the various activities of society."[70] The reference to Christian spouses and Christian families could not be clearer. They are to sanctify themselves in their marriage and family, of course, but they are to sanctify themselves also by immersion in their community, "in a profession and the various activities of society." They are to live in their community and "permeate and perfect" it "with the spirit of the gospel" (Can 225.2).

The calling of Christians, I have argued, is theologically summed up in the following of Christ, in living a Christ-like life in the world. This is not to be understood as asserting that laity have no role in the sacred, for they have, or that clerics have no role in the secular, for they have. It is merely to state what the Christian churches take for granted, namely, that lay women and men live and work in the world of everyday reality, that they people the professions and the factories, the schools and the hospitals, the offices, the fields, and the homes. It is to state that they are called, as faithful followers of Christ, to incarnate Christ in these everyday places and thereby bring the gospel of neighbor-love, of reconciliation, compassion, forgiveness, justice, and salvation in Christ, directly to that world. I add only that Christian spouses are called to this task to make their Christian marriages truly and effectively generative and fruitful.

John Paul II may have the final word in this extension of the biblical story of Jesus to the Christian message of life and love. He draws attention to a temptation which laity "have not always known how to avoid," the temptation to separate faith from life, to separate "the gospel's acceptance from the actual living of the gospel in various situations in the world."[71] What the Pope implies, and on occasion explicitly says, is clear. To be responsive and faithful to their Christian vocation to follow Christ, Christian families need to reach out in active love to their communities. The fruitfulness, and the Christianness, of their marriages, families, and lives depend on it.

Conclusion

The future of societies, both civil and religious, Pope John Paul II argues correctly, "passes through the family."[72] It is through families that societies develop and perdure, for it is in families that societies' values and traditions are shaped and transmitted to the next generation. If families fail, societies fail, something many commentators fear is now in process in the United States. To establish a first thesis, I documented the data on which this pessimistic conclusion is based. Though I do not believe the data sustains a conclusion of failure, I do believe it shows that families in the United States are in crisis and, consequently, the nation itself is in crisis. That crisis, however, can be misread, especially when it is interpreted against a backdrop of the so-called "traditional" family. Though that "traditional" family was never traditional in the United States and is unlikely to become so in any foreseeable future,[73] the modern family is still in need of serious help to fulfill its most basic function: the generation not only of children but especially of healthy functioning adults.

It is entirely predictable that Christians would turn to their Bible, the very word of God for them, to find remediation for their society's and their families' ills. In a second thesis I argued that this effort is doomed to failure; the cultural and historical distances between biblical and modern families make the diachronic transition impossible. The Bible provides no detailed guidance for all times and places "on disciplining children or seeking a mate or determining whether a wife should or should not work outside the home," or any other family issue.[74] The Old Testament is the story of God and Israel, the New the story of God and Jesus, the Son, the "beloved" (Mark 1:11). In my third thesis, therefore, I advanced not so much a *biblical* theology of family, determined by the following of biblical formulae, but a *Christian* theology of family, determined by the following of Jesus as interpreted in the Christian tradition. That following of Jesus requires the patterning of individual, family, and church life after the life of Jesus as recorded in the Gospels. I summarized and explained that life as a life of neighbor-love (Lev 19:18; Mark 12:28), a life of willing and doing good to and for one's neighbor. My fourth thesis explicates that neighbor-love by uncovering the meanings embedded in the ancient Catholic concept of *domestic church*, following John Paul II in arguing that the moral and social virtue embedded in domestic church is the virtue of *solidarity*,

> not a vague feeling of compassion or shallow distress at the misfortunes of so many people [but] . . . a firm and persevering determination to commit oneself to the *common good* . . . to the good of *all* and of each individual, because we are *all* really responsible for *all*.[75]

This essay began with the claim that it is an effort in practical, pastoral, theological correlation between the cultural situation of marriages and families in the United States and the Christian tradition. It ends with another claim. Many see expressive individualism, against which Alexis de Tocqueville warned so insistently 160 years ago,[76] at the root of every problem faced by marriages and families in the United States.[77] The historical Christian tradition offers as antidote to this exaggerated individualism the understanding that all Christians are responsible for all their brothers and sisters, and the persevering determination to commit themselves not only to the particular good of their own family but also to the common good of all. I offer a theology of family based upon that historical tradition, one that challenges Christians to lives that make explicit their covenant with God and, therefore, with the whole human family.

That theology invites Christians to understand themselves as brothers and sisters in the fictive-kin family promised by Jesus, dedicated to the reversal of the individualistic tide that pulls families and marriages in an isolationist direction and fails to nurture the next generation. It is a theology that is eminently practical for Americans worried about the deterioration of their family and social lives, whether they are single or married, whether they are familied or not. In 1989, when offered alternative definitions of family, only 22 percent of Americans selected a traditional definition based on blood, marriage, or adoption; an overwhelming 74 percent selected "a group of people who love and care for each other."[78] That is a vision of family that resonates with Christians' search for practical responses to Jesus' invitation to neighbor-love and fictive-kin family, or Church, in which all are covenant brothers and sisters in Christ (Mark 3:31-35; Matt 12:46-50; 25:31-46).

Questions for Reflection

1. What is your experience of the crisis family is undergoing in the United States? Do you agree that current public policies are detrimental to relationship, marriage, women, and children?

2. What do you think of the opinion that the Bible provides no detailed guidance on choosing a mate, disciplining children, whether a wife should or should not work outside the home, or any other current family issue? On what basis is such an opinion advanced?

3. What is your evaluation of the judgment that, for Christians, grace is not embedded in any particular family structure but in the following of Jesus? What are the implications of this judgment?

4. Pope John Paul II teaches that the future of societies passes through the family. Do you think this is true? If it is true, what are the implications for both Church and nation in the contemporary United States?

5. Many social commentators see exaggerated individualism at the root of every current problem faced by marriages and families in the United States. What do you think of this judgment? If it is true, what can be done to combat such individualism?

Notes

¹ An earlier version of this essay was published in *Horizons* 26 (1999) 7–30. It is reprinted here with permission.

² Dennis A. Ahlburg and Carol J. DeVita, "New Realities of the American Family," *Population Bulletin* 47 (1992) 2–38; Larry L. Bumpass, "What's Happening to the Family? Interactions Between Demographic and Institutional Change," *Demography* 27 (1990) 483–95; Arlene F. Saluter, "Marital Status and Living Arrangements: March 1994," *Current Population Reports* P.20/484 (Washington, D.C.: Bureau of the Census, 1996) vii–xi; Arthur J. Norton and Louisa F. Miller, "Marriage, Divorce, and Remarriage in the 1990s," *Current Population Reports* C3.186:P.23/180 (Washington, D.C.: Bureau of the Census, 1992) 9–12. See also Larry L. Bumpass and James A. Sweet, "Children's Experience in Single-Parent Families: Implications of Cohabitation and Marital Transitions," *Family Planning Perspectives* 21 (1989) 256–60; David Eggebeen and Peter Uhlenberg, "Changes in the Organization of Men's Lives: 1960–1980," *Family Relations* 34 (1985) 251–7.

³ Bumpass and Sweet, "Children's Experience," 256–7; David Popenoe, *Life Without Father* (New York: Free Press, 1996) 19–51, 192; Irwin Garfinkel and Sara S. McLanahan, *Single Mothers and Their Children: A New American Dilemma* (Washington, D.C.: Urban Institute, 1986) 52–3; Barbara Ehrenreich, *The Hearts of Men: American Dream and the Flight from Commitment* (New York: Anchor, 1993) 119–21; Robert L. Griswold, *Fatherhood in America: A History* (New York: Basic Books, 1993) 230–42; Stephanie Coontz, *The Way We Never Were: American Families and the Nostalgia Trap* (New York: Basic Books, 1992) 185–7; Joseph Veroff, Elizabeth Douvan, and Richard A. Kulka, *The Inner American: A Self-Portrait from 1957–1976* (New York: Basic Books, 1981) 140–241. See also David Blankenhorn, *Fatherlessness in America: Confronting Our Most Urgent Social Problem* (New York: Basic Books, 1995); Sara McLanahan and Gary Sandefur, *Growing Up with a Single Parent: What Hurts, What Helps* (Cambridge, Mass.: Harvard University Press, 1994); Maggie Gallagher, *The Abolition of Marriage: How We Destroy Lasting Love* (Washington, D.C.: Regnery, 1996); Scott J. South and Stewart E. Tolnay, *The Changing American Family* (Boulder: Westview, 1992); Bryce J. Christensen, ed., *The Retreat from Marriage: Causes and Consequences* (Lanham, Md.: University Press of America, 1990).

⁴ Popenoe, *Life Without Father,* 52–78; McLanahan and Sandefur, *Growing Up with a Single Parent,* 135–55. See also Sylvia Hewlett, *When the Bough Breaks* (New York: Basic Books, 1991); Christensen, *The Retreat from Marriage;* Norval Glenn, "The Social and Cultural Meaning of Contemporary Marriage," *The Retreat from Marriage,* ed. Christensen, 33–54.

⁵ Ahlburg and DeVita, "New Realities," 36. See also Karen C. Holden and Pamela J. Smock, "The Economic Costs of Marital Dissolution: Why Do Women Bear a Disproportionate Cost?" *Annual Review of Sociology* 17 (1991) 51–78;

Lenore Weitzman, *The Divorce Revolution: The Unexpected Social and Economic Consequences for Women and Children in America* (New York: Free Press, 1985).

[6] Frank F. Furstenberg and Andrew J. Cherlin, *Divided Families: What Happens to Children When Parents Part* (Cambridge, Mass.: Harvard University Press, 1991) 45. See also McLanahan and Sandefur, *Growing Up with a Single Parent*, 19–26; Linda Barrington and Cecilia A. Conrad, "At What Cost a Room of Her Own? Factors Contributing to the Feminization of Poverty Among Prime-Age Women, 1939–1959," *Journal of Economic History* 54 (1994) 342–57; Emily M. Northrop, "The Feminization of Poverty: The Demographic Factor and the Composition of Economic Growth," *Journal of Economic Issues* 24 (1990) 145–60; Elizabeth Segal, "The Juvenilization of Poverty in the 1980s," *Social Work* 36 (1991) 454–7; Anne Francis-Okongwu, "Looking Up from the Bottom to the Ceiling of the Basement Floor: Female Single-Parent Families Surviving on $22,000 or Less a Year," *Urban Anthropology* 24 (1995) 313–62; Holden and Smock, "The Economic Costs of Marital Dissolution," 51–78.

[7] Ahlburg and DeVita, "New Realities," 29.

[8] McLanahan and Sandefur, *Growing Up with a Single Parent*, 25. See also Judith A. Seltzer, "Consequences of Marital Dissolution for Children," *Annual Review of Sociology* 20 (1994) 235–66; "Relations Between Fathers and Children Who Live Apart: The Father's Role After Separation," *Journal of Marriage and the Family* 53 (1991) 79–101.

[9] Ronald J. Angel and Jacqueline L. Angel, *Painful Inheritance: Health and the New Generation of Fatherless Families* (Madison: University of Wisconsin Press, 1993) 38. See also Deborah A. Dawson, "Family Structure and Children's Health and Well-Being: Data from the 1988 National Health Interview Survey on Child Health," *Journal of Marriage and the Family* 53 (1991) 573–84.

[10] William J. Wilson, *When Work Disappears: The World of the New Urban Poor* (New York: Random House, 1997).

[11] See Dawson, "Family Structure," 579–84; John Guidubaldi, Joseph D. Perry, and Bonnie K. Nastasi, "Growing Up in a Divorced Family: Initial and Long-Term Perspectives on Children's Adjustment," *Applied Social Psychology Annual* 7 (1987) 202–37; Frank Mott, Lori Kowaleski-Jones, and Elizabeth G. Menaghan, "Paternal Absence and Child Behavior: Does a Child's Gender Make a Difference?" *Journal of Marriage and the Family* 59 (1997) 103–18; Blankenhorn, *Fatherlessness in America;* Popenoe, *Life Without Father.*

[12] See Richard E. Johnson, "Family Structure and Delinquency: General Patterns and Gender Differences," *Criminology* 24 (1986) 65–84; Edward L. Wells and Joseph H. Rankin, "Families and Delinquency: A Meta-analysis of the Impact of Broken Homes," *Social Problems* 38 (1991) 71–93.

[13] Kathleen E. Kiernan, "The Impact of Family Disruption in Childhood on Transitions Made in Young Adult Life," *Population Studies* 46 (1992) 232–3; Sara S. McLanahan and Larry Bumpass, "Intergenerational Consequences of Family Disruption," *American Journal of Sociology* 94 (1988) 130–52.

[14] Judith Wallerstein, "The Long-Term Effects of Divorce on Children: A Review," *Journal of the American Academy of Child and Adolescent Psychiatry* 30 (1991) 358–9. See also Judith Wallerstein and Sandra Blakeslee, *Second Chances: Men, Women and Children a Decade after Divorce* (New York: Ticknor and Fields, 1989); Judith Wallerstein, Julia Lewis, and Sandra Blakeslee, *The Unexpected Legacy of Divorce: A 25 Year Landmark Study* (New York: Hyperion, 2000); Paul R. Amato, "Parental Absence During Childhood and Depression in Later Life," *The Sociological Quarterly* 32 (1991) 543–56; Jean Bethke Elshtain, "Family Matters: The Plight of America's Children," *Christian Century* 110 (1993) 710–2; David Finkelhor, Gerald Hotaling, I. A. Lewis, and Christine Smith, "Sexual Abuse in a National Survey of Adult Men and Women: Prevalence, Characteristics, and Risk Factor," *Child Abuse & Neglect* 14 (1990) 19–28; Guidubaldi, "Growing Up in a Divorced Family," 202–37; McLanahan and Bumpass, "Intergenerational Consequences," 130–52; Samuel Osherson, *Finding Our Fathers: The Unfinished Business of Manhood* (New York: Collier Macmillan, 1986); Henry Biller, *Fathers and Families: Paternal Factors in Child Development* (Westport, Conn.: Auburn House, 1993).

[15] Biller, *Fathers and Families,* 52–74; Henry B. Biller, "The Father and Personality Development: Paternal Deprivation and Sex-Role Development," *The Role of the Father in Child Development,* ed. Michael E. Lamb (New York: John Wiley, 1976) 89–156; Norma Radin, "The Role of the Father in Cognitive, Academic, and Intellectual Development," *The Role of the Father,* ed. Lamb, 237–76; Ross D. Parke, *Fathers* (Cambridge, Mass.: Harvard University Press, 1981) 56–77. See also Stanley H. Cath, Alan Gurwitt, and Linda Gunsberg, *Fathers and Their Families* (Hillsdale, N.J.: Analytic Press, 1989); Lee A. Beatty, "Effects of Paternal Absence on Male Adolescents' Peer Relations and Self-Image," *Adolescence* 30 (1995) 873–80.

[16] Marcy Gringlas and Marsha Weinraub, "The More Things Change . . . Single Parenting Revisited," *Journal of Family Issues* 16 (1995) 46.

[17] Dawn Butterworth and Edith Cowan, "Are Fathers Really Necessary to the Family Unit in Early Childhood?" *International Journal of Early Childhood* 26 (1994) 2. See also Frank F. Furstenberg and Christine Winquist Nord, "Parenting Apart: Patterns of Childrearing After Marital Disruption," *Journal of Marriage and the Family* 47 (1985) 893–904.

[18] Popenoe, *Life Without Father,* 188. See also Biller, *Fathers and Families,* 234–5.

[19] Daniel Yankelovich, "How Changes in the Economy Are Reshaping American Values," *Values and Public Policy,* ed. Henry J. Aaron, Thomas E. Mann, and Timothy Taylor (Washington, D.C.: Brookings Institution, 1994) 16–53. See also Andrew Cherlin, *The Changing American Family and Public Policy* (Washington, D.C.: Urban Institute, 1988); Nancy A. Crowell and Ethel M. Leeper, *America's Fathers and Public Policy* (Washington, D.C.: National Academy, 1994); Robert Bellah, Richard Madsen, William M. Sullivan, Ann Swidler, and Steven M. Tipton, *The Good Society* (New York: Vantage Books, 1992) 48.

[20] See Francis-Okongwu, "Looking Up from the Bottom," 313–62; Gallagher, *The Abolition of Marriage;* John E. Rogers, Michael Greene, and Emily Hoffnar, "Does Welfare Cause Increases in Female-Headed Households?" *Applied Economics Letters* 3 (1996) 85–8; Michael Lamb and Abraham Sagi, *Fatherhood and Family Policy* (Hillsdale, N.Y.: Lawrence Erlbaum, 1983).

[21] Cherlin, *The Changing American Family,* 1–29, 219–61. See also Crowell and Leeper, *America's Fathers and Public Policy.*

[22] See Blankenhorn, *Fatherlessness in America;* Gallagher, *The Abolition of Marriage;* South and Tolnay, *The Changing American Family;* Elshtain, "Family Matters," 710–2; Barbara Dafoe Whitehead, "Dan Quayle Was Right," *Atlantic Monthly* 271 (1993) 47–84; Bellah et al., *The Good Society,* 256–61.

[23] See Biller, *Fathers and Families;* Crowell and Leeper, *America's Fathers and Public Policy;* Lamb and Sagi, *Fatherhood and Family Policy;* McLanahan and Sandefur, *Growing Up with a Single Parent;* Elshtain, "Family Matters," 710–2; Don Browning and Ian Evison, "The Family Debate: A Middle Way," *Christian Century* 110 (1993) 712–6.

[24] George Lindbeck, "Barth and Textuality," *Theology Today* 43 (1986) 361.

[25] This is the title of the Second Vatican Council's Dogmatic Constitution on Divine Revelation.

[26] Nothing of the argument in this essay is altered if Paul either wrote or did not write the Letter to the Ephesians or any of the other letters assigned to him.

[27] See Peter Brown, *The Body and Society: Men, Women and Sexual Renunciation in Early Christianity* (London: Faber and Faber, 1990).

[28] See David H. Kelsey, *The Uses of Scripture in Recent Theology* (Philadelphia: Fortress Press, 1975). Though Kelsey's book is an analysis of Protestant uses of Scripture, the very same analysis could be applied to Catholic, including papal, uses.

[29] See Karl Barth, *Church Dogmatics,* vol. 3.4, ed. G. W. Bromiley and T. F. Torrance (Edinburgh: T. & T. Clark, 1961) 199.

[30] Bruce J. Malina, *The New Testament World: Insights from Cultural Anthropology,* rev. ed. (Louisville: Westminster/John Knox Press, 1993) 126. See also Carolyn Osiek and David L. Balch, *Families in the New Testament World* (Louisville: Westminster/John Knox Press, 1997) 36–87; Halvor Moxnes, *Constructing Early Christian Families* (London: Routledge, 1997) 13–102.

[31] William Moran, "The Ancient Near Eastern Background of the Love of God in Deuteronomy," *Catholic Biblical Quarterly* 25 (1963) 82.

[32] John Rogerson, "The Family and Structures of Grace in the Old Testament," *The Family in Theological Perspective,* ed. Stephen C. Barton (Edinburgh: T. & T. Clark, 1996) 25.

[33] Bruce J. Malina and Richard L. Rohrbaugh, *Social Science Commentary on the Synoptic Gospels* (Minneapolis: Fortress Press, 1992) 202.

[34] Ibid., 345.

[35] Gerd Theissen, *The Shadow of the Galilean: The Quest of the Historical Jesus in Narrative Form* (Philadelphia: Fortress Press, 1987) 71.

[36] Rodney Clapp, *Families at the Crossroads: Beyond Traditional and Modern Options* (Downer's Grove, Ill.: InterVarsity Press, 1993) 15, emphasis in original.

[37] Lisa Sowle Cahill makes the same argument in her recent theology of family: *Family: A Christian Social Perspective* (Minneapolis: Fortress Press, 2000).

[38] See C. S. Lewis, *The Four Loves* (New York: Harcourt Brace, 1960).

[39] LG 11.

[40] AA 11.

[41] GS 48.

[42] See Michael G. Lawler, *Marriage and Sacrament: A Theology of Christian Marriage* (Collegeville: The Liturgical Press, 1993).

[43] GS 50.

[44] See John Wesley, "A Plain Account of Genuine Christianity," *John Wesley,* ed. Albert Outler (New York: Oxford University Press, 1964) 184.

[45] GE 3.

[46] See Karl Rahner, "Marriage as a Sacrament," *Theological Investigations* X (New York: Seabury Press, 1977) 207.

[47] Discos Tantalus, "Parental Government: A Privilege to Youth," *Churchman's Magazine* 4 (December 1807) 478–9.

[48] FC 75.

[49] AA 30.

[50] See Justinian, *Digesta* 23.2.1.

[51] CL 18.

[52] Gerard Philips, *L'Eglise et son mystère au IIe Concile du Vatican* (Paris: Desclée, 1966) I.7.59 and II.24.54.159. See also Pier Bori, *Koinonia: L'idea della communione nell' ecclesiologia recente et nel Nuovo Testamento* (Brescia: Paideia, 1972).

[53] See Michael G. Lawler, *Symbol and Sacrament: A Contemporary Sacramental Theology* (Omaha: Creighton University Press, 1995) 5–28.

[54] See Michael G. Lawler and Thomas J. Shanahan, *Church: A Spirited Communion* (Collegeville: The Liturgical Press, 1995).

[55] See David N. Power, *The Eucharistic Mystery: Revitalizing the Tradition* (New York: Crossroad, 1992) 30–2.

[56] Xavier Leon-Dufour, *Sharing the Eucharistic Bread: The Witness of the New Testament,* trans. Matthew O'Connell (New York: Paulist Press, 1987) 82–95.

[57] LG 11.

[58] Augustine, *Epist.* 188.3, PL 33.849.

[59] Augustine, *De bono viduitatis (Vid.)* 29, PL 40.450.

[60] Chrysostom, *Homiliae in Genesim (Hom. Gen.)* 6.2, PG 54.607.

[61] Chrysostom, *In Epistolam ad Ephesios Homilia* XX, 4, PG 11.140.

[62] For a more extended treatment of family as domestic church, see Joann Heaney-Hunter, "Domestic Church: Guiding Beliefs and Daily Practices," *Christian Marriage and Family: Contemporary Theological and Pastoral Perspectives,* ed. Michael G. Lawler and William P. Roberts (Collegeville: The Liturgical Press, 1996) 59–78; William P. Roberts, "The Family as Domestic Church: Con-

temporary Implications," *Christian Marriage and Family,* ed. Lawler and Roberts, 79–90.

[63] John Paul II, *Centesimus Annus* 47, *Catholic Social Thought: The Documentary Heritage,* ed. David J. O'Brien and Thomas A. Shannon (Maryknoll, N.Y.: Orbis Books, 1992) 475.

[64] United States Catholic Conference, *Follow the Way of Love* (Washington, D.C.: USCC, 1993) 8.

[65] John Paul II, *Sollicitudo Rei Socialis* 38, *Catholic Social Thought,* ed. O'Brien and Shannon, 421, all emphases in original.

[66] John Paul II, *Sollicitudo Rei Socialis* 42, *Catholic Social Thought,* ed. O'Brien and Shannon, 425. See also the Letter of the U.S. Catholic Bishops, Economic Justice for All, 90a and 260, *Catholic Social Thought,* ed. O'Brien and Shannon, 600 and 637.

[67] John Paul II, *Sollicitudo Rei Socialis* 39, *Catholic Social Thought,* ed. O'Brien and Shannon, 423.

[68] The conjunction and equivalence of peace and communion is an ancient one. In his many troubles Athanasius proudly claimed that more than five hundred bishops accept him in *koinonia kai agape,* communion and love (*Apologia Contra Arianos,* PG 25.281), and that the bishops of Egypt were united among themselves and with him in *agape kai eirene,* love and peace (*Epistula encyclica [Ep. encycl.],* PG 25.225). It is clear from the contexts that *koinonia, eirene,* and *agape* form a connected cluster signifying what we have called throughout *communion.* The connection continues in the present in the papal practice of addressing encyclical letters to "Patriarchs, Primates, Archbishops . . . at peace and in communion with the Apostolic See."

[69] Paul VI, AAS 64 (1972) 208.

[70] *On the Lay Faithful,* 15.

[71] Ibid., 2.

[72] FC 75.

[73] See Michael G. Lawler, *Family: American and Christian* (Chicago: Loyola Press, 1998) 21–46; Coontz, *The Way We Never Were.*

[74] Clapp, *Families at the Crossroads,* 15.

[75] John Paul II, *Sollicitudo Rei Socialis,* 38, all emphases in original.

[76] Alexis de Tocqueville, *Democracy in America,* ed. J. P. Mayer (New York: Anchor Books, 1969).

[77] See Robert N. Bellah, Richard Madsen, William M. Sullivan, Ann Swidler, and Steven M. Tipton, *Habits of the Heart: Individualism and Commitment in American Life* (New York: Harper & Row, 1985).

[78] *MassMutual American Family Values Study* (Springfield: Massachusetts Mutual Life Insurance Company, 1989) 1. See Lawler, *Family: American and Christian,* 29–33.

Epilogue

This book is a Catholic theological response to the crisis facing marriage in both the Western world and in the Catholic Church. It has, broadly, two major theses. The first is that marriage in the West is in a state of seriously diminished well-being and crisis, which means it is at a time for judgment. The second is that the Catholic tradition, honestly, historically, and critically understood, offers theoretical and practical meanings to shape a strategy for responding to the crisis and improving the well-being, directly of marriages, spouses, and families, and indirectly of society as a whole.

Marriage continues to be a central institution in American society, but it does not play the dominant role it once played. "The proportion of adults who have never been married rose from 15% to 23% between 1972 and 1998. When the divorced, widowed, and separated are added in, three-quarters of adults were married in the early 1970s, but only 56% were by the late 1990s."[1] Three sources are usually suggested for this decreasing salience of marriage: people are delaying marriage to a later age, divorces have increased, and cohabitation has increased as the first form of union formation. As a result of all of these factors, unmarried childbearing and parenthood have increased enormously and so, concomitantly, has the percentage of children growing up in unstable families. Only 5.3 percent of births in 1960 were to unmarried mothers; in 1996, the figure was 32 percent. In 1972, less than 5 percent of children were living in households headed by a single parent; in the mid-1990s, the figure had increased to 20 percent. The negative effects on children, and in the long run on society, are now demonstrated beyond debate.[2]

There is another major factor contributing to the crisis of marriage and family, a central American value run riot. In the 1830s, Alexis de Tocqueville praised the American sense of family, religion, and civic involvement, and underscored the contribution of all three to the American character. He also warned that the American drive toward individualism could ruin family, religion, civic involvement, and the American character.[3] There is enough current evidence about radical individualism in the United States, and its negative impact on relationships, marriages, families, spouses, children, and public civility, to prove him a trustworthy seer.[4] The situation has worsened considerably since a 1976 commentary in the *New Yorker*.

> We are coming to look upon life as a *lone* adventure, a great *personal* odyssey, and there is much in this view that is exhilarating and strengthening, but we seem to be carrying it to such an extreme that if each of us is an Odysseus he is . . . an Odysseus on a journey that has been rendered pointless by becoming limitless.[5]

With so many radically individualistic Odysseuses in America focusing exclusively on their own well-being and happiness to the exclusion of all others, spouses and children included, it is hardly surprising that the well-being of human communities, like marriage, family, church, and nation, is diminished.

The discussions of marriage, sacrament, models of marriage, relationship, bond, friendship, family, and divorce in this book are intended to uncover antidotes to the crisis of marriage and family. I have proposed a normative, and critical, vision of Christian marriage and family, not how Christian marriage and family are or might be but how they *ought* to be. This vision is not derived from the charts and tables of social scientists, though I have been in serious dialogue with those scientists. It is derived from the critically-examined founding documents and on-going tradition of Christianity, which present a vision of men and women, friendship and neighbor-love, marriage and family under the grace of God. That vision, I know, is not normative for all Americans. It is normative only for those Americans who feel called to be, and who in faith call themselves, Christians.

By offering this vision as a strategy for dealing with the marital and familial crises that confront Americans, I have no wish to make the religious claims of Christianity, and still less of Catholicism, normative. To suggest that the beliefs of one religious tradition offer fundamental meanings for individual and communal living is not to exalt those claims over the claims of any other tradition. All the great religious traditions situate marriage and family within a broader, ultimate context. In this book, I directly invite Christians to translate the theological meanings of their religion into practical, bonded, marital and familial living. Indirectly, I invite all religious people to do the same. One thing that social scientific research has demonstrated beyond debate is that shared religion, any shared religion, is good for marriage and family.[6] While I specifically suggest that the Christian tradition has an important message for contemporary Americans, I simultaneously wish to intimate that all religions have a similarly important message.

This returns us to the two dialogues introduced in the Prologue: the internal dialogue between Christians and the external dialogue between Christians and others concerned about marriage and family. In this book I have tried to enter critically into both dialogues. In a genuine dialogue, each partner critiques, tempers, and affects the other, and so it is in the external dialogue. I do not believe it is possible to construct an effective theory of marriage and family only from Christian principles. To take effect in the culture, those principles must be embedded in the culture. John Paul II puts this point bluntly. Synthesis between faith and culture is a requirement not only for culture but also for faith, for "a faith that does not become culture is a faith not fully accepted, not entirely thought out, not faithfully lived."[7] This synthesis between faith and culture must take place in the United States today if the churches wish to maintain any credibility in the continuing debate about marriage and family.

A final thought, diachronically consistent across the centuries, from the Christian tradition: it is not enough for religious people to say they believe. Genuine religious faith is a comprehensive "yes" to God that embraces not only theoretical but also practical belief, that is, belief translated into action. It is not enough, therefore, for Christians to say they believe in the God made known in Jesus; they must also model their life after the life of Jesus. At the beginning of the Christian movement, Matthew's Jesus already proclaimed this connection between belief and action: "Not everyone who says to me 'Lord, Lord' shall enter the kingdom of heaven, but the one who does the will of my Father who is in heaven" (7:21). Cyprian, the third-century bishop of Carthage, put it even more bluntly to his newly-baptized neophytes: "To put on the name of Christ and not continue along the way of Christ, what is that but a lie?"[8] John Wesley, the great English preacher, makes the same point with a different emphasis: since the love of God is universal and unrestricted, so also Christian love is universal and unrestricted.[9] John Paul II, the twentieth-century bishop of Rome, stands firmly in this tradition, though he also gives it his own emphasis. Communion in the Church, he teaches, gives rise to active mission, and "mission is accomplished in communion."[10] This book stands ultimately in this tradition of practical faith. Having critically engaged in the internal dialogue and carefully delimited the Catholic tradition about marriage and family, and having entered into the external dialogue to detail the specifics of the crisis facing marriage and family, it maintains that only when believers translate their beliefs into practice can they hope to have any effect on the current crisis.

Notes

[1] Tom W. Smith, "The Emerging 21st Century American Family," National Opinion Research Center, University of Chicago, www.norc.org/online/emerge.pdf (1998) 1. Statistics which follow in this Epilogue are also drawn from this study.

[2] See Sara McLanahan and Gary Sandefur, *Growing Up with a Single Parent: What Hurts, What Helps* (Cambridge, Mass.: Harvard University Press, 1994).

[3] Alexis de Tocqueville, *Democracy in America,* ed. J. P. Mayer (New York: Anchor Books, 1969).

[4] See Robert N. Bellah et al., *Habits of the Heart: Individualism and Commitment in American Life* (New York: Harper & Row, 1985); Arland Thornton, "Reciprocal Influences of Family and Religion in a Changing World," *The Religion and Family Connection: Social Science Perspectives,* ed. Darwin L. Thomas (Provo, Utah: Religious Studies Center, Brigham Young University, 1988); Robert Wuthnow, *Christianity in the Twenty-First Century* (New York: Oxford University Press, 1993).

[5] "Talk of the Town," *New Yorker* (August 30, 1976) 21–2, my emphasis.

[6] See Tim B. Heaton and Edith L. Pratt, "The Effects of Religious Homogamy on Marital Satisfaction and Stability," *Journal of Family Issues* 11 (1990) 343–59; Arland Thornton, William G. Axinn, and Daniel Hill, "Reciprocal Effects of Religiosity, Cohabitation, and Marriage," *American Journal of Sociology* 98 (1992) 628–51; Linda C. Robinson, "Religious Orientation in Enduring Marriage," *Review of Religious Research* 35 (1994) 207–18.

[7] *L'Osservatore Romano* (March 8, 1982). The Pope repeated this same phrase in his letter to Cardinal Casaroli appointing him president of the Pontifical Council for Culture. See *L'Osservatore Romano* (June 28, 1982).

[8] Cyprian, *De zelo et livore (Zel. liv.)* 12, PL 4.646.

[9] John Wesley, "A Plain Account of Genuine Christianity," *John Wesley,* ed. Albert Outler (New York: Oxford University Press, 1964) 184.

[10] *On the Lay Faithful,* 32.

Index